THE DAWN OF DECISION

Jacques Mordal

translated by Mervyn Savill

NEW ENGLISH LIBRARY/TIMES MIRROR

First published in Great Britain in 1963 by Souvenir Press Limited

Copyright © Jacques Mordal and Presses de la Cité

All rights reserved. No part of this publication
may be reproduced or transmitted, in any form
or by any means, without permission
of the publishers.

First NEL Paperback Edition August 1981

Conditions of sale: This book is sold
subject to the condition that it shall not,
by way of trade or otherwise, be lent,
re-sold, hired out, or otherwise circulated
without the publisher's prior consent in
any form of binding or cover other than
that in which it is published and without a
similar condition including this condition
being imposed on the subsequent
purchaser.

NEL Books are published by
New English Library Limited,
Barnard's Inn, Holborn,
London EC1N 2JR.

Printed and bound in Great Britain by
Cox & Wyman Ltd, Reading

0 450 05004 1

'Jacques Mordal vividly recreates the battle.'
Western Mail

'In terms of pure military history it is probably
the best account of the operation so far published.'
Tribune

'He is notably fair-minded, and his book, though
a serious historical study, is remarkably readable.'
Daily Telegraph

'Holds the reader's attention throughout...
there are also excellent descriptions of how it
all seemed to the French population.'
The Spectator

'Why, M. Mordal rightly asks, was it necessary
to lose 3,250 men and an important amount
of war material in order to relearn lessons
that ought to have been instilled into British
minds by centuries of experience?...
Where was the offensive, lost so humiliatingly
in 1940, to be resumed in Europe?
Why choose Dieppe? Why choose the Canadians?
His answers are full and frank. ... The controversy
about Dieppe is bound to continue for a long,
long time. M. Mordal's book is a most valuable
and constructive contribution to the debate.'
Books of the Month

'The author has become a military historian
par excellence. His latest book reveals his
precision, thoroughness and virtual
absence of any form of partisanship.'
Books and Bookmen

DIEPPE

THE DAWN OF DECISION

Part One

THE ROAD TO DIEPPE

PROLOGUE

THE lieutenant was unhappy. When he had been called up the previous year from the Norman law court where he dispensed justice as quietly as the wrangling spirit of his fellow-citizens allowed, he had tentatively remarked that his legs, covered with varicose veins, would make him a very poor infantry platoon commander. His complaints had been silenced by posting him to a tactical machine-gun company – stable if words have any meaning – with a promise of a transfer to the Military legal corps. Weeks and months had passed. His file was doubtless lying somewhere in Rouen on the desk of some orderly room clerk of the IIIrd Military Region, and, with events as they stood, it would certainly continue to lie there.

But what had he to complain of? Instead of having to drag his painful legs along the Belgian roads or among the sand-dunes of Dunkirk, he was peacefully in Dieppe where, of course, no one would see a German throughout the whole war except possibly a prisoner.

This had perhaps been true a month ago, but it was certainly no longer true that Saturday evening.

For weeks a flood of refugees had poured along the road from Eu. During the first days of June this flood seemed to abate or rather to change its character. It no longer consisted of civilians but of more or less organized soldiers – perhaps rather less than more – most of them without their weapons. The enemy had confiscated these before dismissing them to their own devices because they were too busy to take prisoners. The guns rumbled in the direction of the Bresle. Then suddenly calm was restored and a disturbing silence settled over the countryside.

It was glorious weather. The plain smelt sweetly of newly mown hay. Dotted with scarlet poppies as far as the eye could see, the cornfields were ripening on either side of the main road which runs parallel to the cliff through the Caux country.

It was nightfall when the lieutenant heavily dismounted from his bicycle.

'Seen anything, sir?'

'Not a thing, naturally. We went as far as Belleville and Penly. It gave my poor legs something to do climbing that hill. Oh! I forgot. Rather a dirty business at Berneval. Everyone has pushed off except the owner of the Potinière. It seems he's an Austrian. It stinks of Fifth Column. I must send someone there tomorrow to pick him up if necessary.[1] Has anything happened here?'

The officer cast a swift eye on his road block . . . three derelict wagons borrowed from a neighbouring farmer, and then a more serious glance at the well-posted camouflaged machine-gun emplacements covering the road to Le Tréport, at the point where there was a bend, the only one for 20 kilometres.

'No, nothing's happened, except that the captain sent a message by a cyclist. Here it is. I haven't opened it. It's addressed to you and marked "Confidential".'

It is understandable that the C.O. of the 204th Defence Company should have preferred the message to be opened personally by the officer in charge. It announced that in future he could no longer ensure supplies for the Graincourt post.

'Charming,' the officer muttered to himself. 'In other words, they're withdrawing.'

He was soon disturbed in his gloomy reflections by a distant

[1] The individual in question, a certain Foetzer, was arrested shortly after this by sailors from an observation post. The man in charge called on the curé of Berneval-le-Grand to ask if he would come and administer the last rites to a spy whom they were about to shoot. The Mayor was notified, but he objected that it was not his business since the Potinière lay in the Saint-Martin-en-Campagne commune. This small detail saved the man's life, for while they were discussing his case the Germans arrived. Everyone had to retire and Foetzer managed to make himself scarce.

Subsequently he joined the Todt organization and entrusted his establishment to a man whom we shall see in action at Berneval on the morning of 19th August, 1942.

rumble which gradually grew more distinct. No doubt about it . . . it was the sound of tank tracks.

'Action stations, and remember what I tell you. Don't show yourselves until the last moment.'

They were not called upon to open fire, for it was not the enemy, but the Highland Division withdrawing from the Bresle. The column of tanks, anti-tank guns and self-propelling guns, continued throughout the night.

'Damn it,' said one of the men, 'couldn't they spare us a couple of those guns. It won't be much of a picnic when the Boches really turn up.'

This thought preoccupied the lieutenant. Try as he would, he could not make himself understood. Not until next morning was he able to find an interpreter who took him to see a British colonel.

'I'm here alone to defend the Dieppe road. I've no supplies left and am cut off from the rest of the world. Couldn't you leave me a couple of your anti-tank guns ?'

The colonel agreed and ordered a few other pieces of artillery to be placed on either side of the road block. Not for long, unfortunately, because, towards the end of the afternoon, a motor cyclist reported that advance enemy units had taken up their positions in a small wood a mile away. The Scots left with their guns, and the lieutenant found himself alone with his 40 reservists and even gloomier forebodings. He was still unaware of the strength of the enemy forces advancing towards him – a brigade of motorized marines and a whole infantry division. Fortunately they were in no particular hurry, which gave his captain time to show further sign of life by announcing that a truck was coming to relieve them that evening.

At 2200 hrs, that Sunday, 10th June, 1940, the machine-gunners abandoned their road block, leaving the main road open to the Germans. They had a short rest in Dieppe which enjoyed its last night of liberty. Everyone was evacuated, the luckier soldiers finding a place in some fishing boat, the others setting out by road with orders to make for Fécamp. At Ouville-la-Rivière, on the Saâne, six miles to the west of Dieppe, the lieutenant found a farm where his men could sleep. Again not for long! The Germans could arrive at any minute. At 0700 hrs. on Monday they had to leave. Things went well for about 12 miles as far as Cany when two trucks full of French soldiers that had passed them on the road to the west a few minutes before arrived like a whirlwind. They had made contact with the enemy.

How the hell had they got through? These Boches were everywhere! They were firing in a neighbouring wood and soon the threatening outline of a self-propelling gun could be seen on the top of the crest. This was the signal for everyone to scatter.

The lieutenant left in a Peugeot 302 driven by a sergeant together with a wretched infantryman who was too sick to march any farther. He must retire at all speed along the only road still free – or at least so he hoped, the road that led through the Durdent valley to the sea, at Veulettes.

From here it was possible to reach Fécamp along the coast. Not daring to risk taking the car, he decided to abandon it and, accompanied by his sergeant and the sick soldier, climbed the slope on foot, hoping that at the edge of the cliff he could travel without being spotted the 12-odd miles which separated him from his goal. It was conceivable that the Germans would only bar the main road which ran to this spot about five miles inland. This was a great mistake! Less than two miles away the owner of the charming little château of Auberville-la-Manuel was at that very moment in discussion with German scouts looking for a billet for their general, a certain Erwin Rommel, whose name no one in France had yet heard, but who was later to become a household word.

Hardly had they appeared on the crest than the lieutenant and his comrades were greeted by a hail of machine-gun bullets. The fire was so accurate that a bullet stuck the officer's tin hat. In a flash the three men slid down the slope, their crazy descent arrested only by a compassionate hedge which left them, however, covered with bruises and bumps.

For four hours they remained in this uncomfortable position. Each time they risked showing their noses, the serenade was repeated. For having been too rash, the sergeant was given a burst which left nothing of him except his tin hat; nor did his comrades ever discover the spot where he died. They themselves eventually landed up on the pebbles, black and blue after ten successive falls. Believing themselves to be out of danger, they ventured on to the beach.

Rat-tat-tat! This time they were under direct fire. Posted on the cliff on both sides of the valley, the Germans 'pranged' every moving object they could see on the beach. Things continued like this until nightfall. Then the shooting seemed to let up and, in small groups, a score of men – five Britons, two Customs officers, three naval signallers from Ailly, joined forces with the lieutenant, who decided to skirt the foot of the cliff and try his luck along the pebbles.

But he had forgotten the rising tide, whose waves were lashing the chalk cliff round an escarpment. We've had it this time, he thought.

But he was wrong. A British destroyer was patrolling the coast. The look-out men must have been doing their job well, for they picked up the lieutenant's signals and a launch was lowered.

Was it salvation at last ? Not yet. Hardly had the destroyer got under way than a German gun showed itself on the cliff, and in a flash a salvo of three shells raked the ship. The destroyer replied and started to weave unashamedly to avoid the enemy's fire. But then the aircraft appeared.

Three hits, one in the engines, which killed the chief engineer and five ratings, leaving the vessel rudderless and sinking rapidly. Orders were given to abandon ship.

The lieutenant had already rejoined his group in one of the boats, when the captain changed his mind. He would try and salvage the ship since, although she had appeared to be sinking fast, she was still afloat. All hands to the pumps!

They pumped for 28 hours on end without eating, drinking or sleeping. But their efforts were rewarded on Tuesday evening by the arrival of another British destroyer which took them in tow and delivered them at Southampton by midnight, 11th June, despite further aerial attacks.

And this is how the last defender of Dieppe escaped with the greatest difficulty from the encirclement which was the fate of nearly 50,000 allied troops, who could not be evacuated by sea, because the shore of the Caux country did not allow it.

CHAPTER ONE

AN UNFORTUNATE PRECEDENT

EVERYONE knows in broad outlines the development of the German offensive launched on the 10th May, 1940, on the West front. It is common knowledge that in five days the enemy had consolidated his bridgeheads on the Meuse and that five days later, on the 20th May, he reached the Channel at the mouth of the Somme.

There are various accounts of the battles which took place off the North Sea ports and the conditions under which, at Dunkirk, nearly 350,000 Allied troops were rescued from captivity or destruction by the combined efforts of the British and French navies. On the other hand, little has been said of the operations which developed on the Lower Somme and subsequently in the Caux country culminating on the 12th June at Saint-Valery-en-Caux in the destruction or capture of the whole right wing of the French 10th Army and, three days later, in the fall of Le Havre.

In actual fact, the Germans could just as easily have reached Rouen and cut off Le Havre once they had reached the Somme. They held the river crossing, and their reconnaissance units had advanced in many places far to the south. On the 21st, enemy motor cyclists were reported on the coast as far as the village of Ault and even at Mers. Some it was said had even reached Criel, 12 miles from Dieppe, where they could easily have arrived that day, because there were no troops in that sector apart from a few formations rapidly reformed by the 2nd Military region after the break through at Sedan. At Le Havre itself a kind of panic had descended upon the British base commander, who prematurely evacuated part of his troops to the left bank of the estuary.

But after some hesitation as to what direction he should give to his offensive after reaching the sea, the German commander decided to return north, simply safeguarding his flank on the Somme.

A few days of respite were given to the French High Command to improvise a defensive line on this river from scratch, since all the French and British forces initially deployed on the frontier had advanced into Belgium. When Guderian broke through at Sedan and revealed his intention of advancing towards the sea, General Gamelin followed by General Weygand, who succeeded him on the 20th May, tried to seal up this wound which penetrated more and more deeply into the heart of our territory. On the 15th May General Touchon had taken up his position on the Aisne with the 6th Army. On the 17th, General Georges, C.-in-C. of the North Eastern front called upon General Frère to take command of a new 7th Army – its predecessor had been disbanded after the fighting in Holland – with which on Touchon's left he was to bar the route to Paris. A few days later General Robert Altmayer formed a 10th Army on the left of Frère's army.

The most extraordinary feature, considering the confusion which reigned, is the fact that troops could be found to occupy this Somme front. One day history will have to render justice to the 4th Bureau of the Army General Staff and to the S.N.C.F. for the miracles they accomplished in the course of those tragic days. When one thinks that it needs between 60 and 75 trains to transport a division with all its material! Now, on the 19th May, the 23rd Division of Alpine infantry arrived from the front of the Alps and on the same day was in action at Ham with the fusiliers of the 10th Panzer Division; on its left was the 3rd Light Infantry Division which was in Brittany, preparatory to being sent to Norway. In this way the 24th Army Corps was formed under General Fougères which took up its positions above Péronne.

From Holland General Sciard had been able to rally the basic elements of the 1st Army Corps. He took up his positions below Péronne where, on the 20th May, buses of the T.C.R.P. – it was not yet called the R.A.T.P. – brought him infantrymen from the 19th Infantry Division to Roye. The 7th North African Division arrived at Montdidier and the 4th Infantry Division made for Ailly-sur-Noye. Farther downstream, that is to say from Amiens to the sea, was entrusted to General Grandsart whose 10th Army Corps had been routed at Sedan, now reinforced by the 7th and 5th Colonial Divisions.

All this was very theoretical. It was in fact impossible to find enough troops for the Somme front. It would have needed a magician's wand to deliver them on the 20th May to halt the German armoured divisions, as the Nazis feared, and to re-establish liaison with our encircled armies of the north.

These fears were, alas, unfounded. Flung into the fray as and when they arrived, these units were reminiscent of those bucketfuls of sand thrown by children into the breaches which the sea has opened. They hardly suffice to dam the flood for a moment, before another breach opens a little farther off.

It had been impossible to halt the Germans on the Meuse, nor could they be halted on the Oise. Nothing remained to halt them . . . except the sea.

But there was nothing on the left flank of the Grandsart Corps to cover Upper Normandy and the coastline south of the Somme. The 3rd Light Cavalry Division (General Petiet) was dispatched there; it had been recalled from the east a few days earlier to establish a barrage with the 4th Reserve Armoured Division (Colonel de Gaulle) on the road to Paris where, for the moment, there was as yet no danger. The advanced units of its motorized brigade took up their positions on the river to the east of Longpré-les-Corps-Saints on the afternoon of the 23rd May,[1] and formed up with the advanced guard of the British Armoured Division (General Evans), which had disembarked the previous day at Cherbourg and been carried by rail to Pacy-sur-Eure.

To the west of Longpré there was an impressive void which

[1] These Light Cavalry Divisions, formed during the winter of 1939–40, each consisted of a mounted and a motorized brigade. The former naturally could not follow the record tempo of the latter demanded in their movement. On the 22nd May the 2nd and 3rd Light Cavalry Divisions were still in the region of Varennes-en-Argonne and had to cover more than 230 miles in less than 48 hours. In nearly every case the motorized infantry had to be sent on before the cavalry in trucks.

was to be partially filled on the 25th with the arrival of the motorized dragoons of the 2nd Light Infantry Division at Le Catelet and Pont-Rémy, and subsequently by the massed 2nd and 5th Light Infantry Divisions (Generals Berniquet and Chanoine) between the Bresle and the Somme, opposite the German bridgehead at Abbeville – Saint-Valery-sur-Somme. And finally destined for this sector was the 51st Highland Division (General Fortune), the only division in the whole British Expeditionary Force which had escaped encirclement, because it was in training on the Sarre front. But it did not arrive until the 29th.

In the meantime, the three armoured divisions of the XIXth Panzer Korps (Guderian) had been relieved on the Somme by light divisions of the Wiettersheim Corps which extended over a 60 mile front. An attack in force might have given results, but General Frère had had no time to concentrate his troops at a single point, because, from the 24th onwards, he had been forced to engage them wherever he had any. A few local successes were gained, but nothing decisive. At Corbie and at Bray-sur-Somme the 2nd Reserve Armoured Division won some ground without being able to repulse the enemy on the right bank. Towards Roye the 9th Infantry Division reached the river at Pont-lès-Brie, but could not hold the position. On the other hand at Saint-Christ-Briest, the Alpine troops took 200 prisoners. The colonials of the 7th Colonial Infantry Division were held in check at Amiens. The British of Evans's division were no more fortunate between Longpré and Picquigny. They had to abandon most of their tanks, which were too light and more suitable for patrols and reconnaissance raids than for frontal attacks. On the 26th Picquigny was re-taken, apart from its bridges, one of which, however, was destroyed. The last hopes of re-establishing contact with the northern armies evaporated. The British took to their ships at Dunkirk.

In the meantime, from the 20th May onwards, the Germans did not cease patrolling between the Somme and the Bresle from the sea to the Rouen–Abbeville road. The signal station at Cayeux, defended by a score of sailors, fell on the 23rd after a day's fighting. The outlook post at Ault, captured the same day, was reoccupied on the 29th and held out this time until the 9th June. The number of enemy troops engaged at the start in this sector can be estimated at 1,500. The approach of the Allied forces encouraged them to consolidate more seriously on the bridgehead of Saint-Valery-sur-Somme which, broadly speaking, corresponded with that of Abbeville and extended in depth to nine miles.

This is the reason why G.Hq. had asked the French Admiralty to study the possibility of employing small detachments by sea against the rear of the enemy forces. Captain Lemonnier was sent to Le Havre for this purpose. A few days later he took command of the new naval sector of the Somme, covering the coastline from Saint-Valery-sur-Somme to Veules-les-Roses, with Dieppe as his main port.

Now before the German offensive Dieppe, used by the British as a hospital base, was without anti-aircraft defences in accordance with the Geneva Convention. For the German air force this was an ideal target. The Luftwaffe made its first raid on the 18th May. It was carried out merely by a squadron of magnetic mine-laying aircraft. They dropped 11 in the fairway, two of which exploded. The cargo ship *Pontet-Canet* was bombed and the machine-gun at the entrance to the port was lucky to escape destruction.

On the following day, the 19th, it was more serious. Numerous fires were reported in the town. The German aircraft returned on the 21st, flying low and taking their time to aim with greater precision. The results were disastrous. A train carrying the wounded was blown to pieces beside the hospital-ship *Maid of Kent*, herself sunk in the Paris basin, and from which 400 corpses were eventually recovered. The Greek cargo vessel *Galaxios* met the same fate at the south quay of the Canada basin. A Belgian trawler hit a magnetic mine in the fairway.

On the 25th, a second hospital ship, the *Brighton*, was also sunk in the Canada basin and the Pollet naval yards went up in flames.

Informed by the director of naval transport, who had arrived on the scene, M. Rio, minister of the Merchant Navy, complained bitterly: 'What was the point of having annihilated the submarine war,[1] if the ships and their cargoes were destroyed by aircraft on their arrival in the ports, which would soon be blocked by wrecks ?'

The Army had nothing to offer. All the mobile naval antiaircraft batteries had been placed at its disposal for the operations in Belgium or for the protection of Paris. In short, the British promised two batteries of 40 Bofors, only one of which arrived on the eve of the fall of Dieppe.

As a result the Luftwaffe, without risk, could continue to wreak its havoc on this abandoned town from which the terrified population had fled. On the 25th May there were hardly 200 people in a city which normally sheltered 21,000 souls. The harbour master, the pilots and the customs officers had all left. Blocked by magnetic mines, despite all the efforts of the minesweeping units sent from Le Havre, the cargo vessels were destroyed one after the other in this rat-trap. Nineteen vessels were sunk in less than a week.

In this way Dieppe, whose role could have been vital during the battle of the Somme, was neutralized for lack of a few antiaircraft guns. More serious still, the port could not be used, as was Dunkirk, for rescuing the divisions encircled by Rommel in the Caux country, which between Veules-les-Roses and Saint-Valery-en-Caux were to suffer the tragic end which we shall later relate.

But we must not anticipate.

We have already explained the situation on the Somme on the 26th May. Although all hope of re-establishing contact with the encircled armies of the north had been abandoned, it was still necessary to continue trying to reduce the enemy bridgehead on the left bank of the river, in order to await, in the best possible conditions, the offensive which the Germans would undoubtedly launch at the conclusion of the battle for Dunkirk.

On the lower Somme, that same 26th May, reconnaissance units of the 2nd and 5th Light Cavalry Divisions made contact with the German defences on a perimeter extending to nine

---

[1] It is true that since the beginning of the Norwegian campaign, for which the Germans had recalled nearly all their U-boats, the number of victims had decreased considerably.

miles south of downstream from Pont-Remy. An attack was launched on the 27th by the motorized brigades of the 2nd Light Cavalry Division, each supported by a brigade of the British Armoured Division. It obtained some success on either side of Abbeville where it actually reached the cliffs overlooking the Somme. But the Allies were halted before Moyenneville, and had to retire at nightfall to the line Brutelles–Quesnoy-le-Montant–Béhen–Hocquincourt. The British division suffered heavy losses: 65 tanks destroyed by enemy action and 55 as a result of mechanical defects.

The attack was repeated on the following day. This time it was the 4th Reserve Armoured Division which was in action. Colonel de Gaulle had arrived on the evening of the 27th at Bernapré, the headquarters of the 2nd Light Cavalry Division, to arrange the details. The 5th Colonial Infantry Division (General Séchet) from the neighbouring sector was able to place at his disposal a battalion of the 2nd Colonial Infantry Regiment.

But the posting of the 4th Reserve Armoured Division turned out to be slower and more difficult than had been expected, so that the attack could not get under way until 1700 hrs. of 28th May. It reached Bienfay and Gaumont on either flank of Caubert Hill, which commands the approaches to Abbeville. A number of prisoners and anti-tank weapons were taken. Night fell.

On the morning of the 29th, a further effort allowed the French to reach the river east of Abbeville but not to capture Caubert Hill, where the enemy had been reinforced during the night. To the west Moyenneville was passed and the Somme reached from Petit-Port to Boismont. The arrival of the 51st Highland Division brought some relief to the sector and allowed a last attempt to be made on the 31st May to capture Caubert Hill, which held out once more.

While these different actions were taking place, the front on the lower Somme had finally been organized. The units engaged on the left of the Xth Army Corps, i.e. at the outset, mainly the three Light Cavalry Divisions, were placed under the orders of General Robert Altmayer forming the detachment 'A' Army. On the 29th May this Army detachment became the 10th Army with Hq. at Lyons-la-Forêt and was reinforced by a new corps drawn from the east front, the IXth Army Corps (General Ihler), comprised of the 31st Alpine Infantry Division (Vauthier) and the 40th Infantry Division under the orders of General Durand, with three half-brigades of Chasseurs alpins which had returned from Norway via Scotland after the battle of Namsos.

On the 1st June the lines of the lower Somme were therefore held as follows: From the sea to Abbeville, Fortune's Highlanders and the 31st Alpine Infantry Division; then upstream towards Picquigny, the 2nd Light Cavalry Division, which was to be relieved by the colonials of the 5th Colonial Infantry Division to constitute with the 3rd and 5th what remained of the 1st British Armoured Division, a force called the Petiet group. The Chasseurs alpins of the 40th Infantry Division were assembled in the Bresle sector. A second fighting force, the Audet group, was being formed of the 4th Reserve Armoured Division and two infantry divisions.

On the 31st May General Fortune with his Highlanders and the 31st Alpine Infantry Division resumed the attack on Abbeville between Pont-Remy and Saint-Valery-sur-Somme. He had run up against the same difficulties as de Gaulle's division and his troops emerged very much battered from the encounter. They had hardly been reformed when, on 4th June, a final effort was demanded of them for a new attack carried out on the orders of General Perré with a handful of French tanks, certain units of Evans's division and three regiments of the 31st Alpine Division. There was another setback. The French gained a little ground, but the Highlanders were unable to follow and in a decisive counter-attack the enemy flung back both to their points of departure.

The following day – the 5th June, *Rote Fall*, the Red Plan, was put into execution. Dunkirk had fallen the previous day. One hundred and thirty German divisions attacked to the south, on the Somme and the Aisne.

The front of interest to us was situated in the operational zone of the B army groups (General von Bock), and more particularly of the 4th Army (von Kluge), which the first phase of the campaign had already brought to the Somme. On his left was the 6th Army (von Reichenau), which was to attack Amiens and Péronne, and farther to the east, the 9th (Strauss). Six armoured divisions were operational in this sector. The 7th (Rommel) and the 5th (von Hartlieb) were to force a passage for von Kluge on the lower Somme. The 9th and 10th, 3rd and 4th worked with Reichenau. Four others were massed against the Aisne front. It would be beyond the scope of this book to follow the events which transpired on the whole of this vast front and led, on the 14th June, to the fall of Paris, then, on the 17th at Pontarlier on the Swiss frontier, to the encircle- ment of the last vestiges of the eastern armies defending the Maginot line. We shall concentrate therefore on Upper Normandy.

On the maritime wing of this front, after the abortive attempt of 4th June, the 51st Highland Division held to the west of the Eu–Abbeville railway the villages of Saigneville– Mons–Boubert–Catigny–Tilloy–Pendé and Sallenelles. After abandoning the idea of a landing north of the Somme, the idea of using the 305 mm. naval guns of the old battleships *Paris* and *Courbet* which the navy had declared ready to make 'expendable' for the benefit of the army, was also rejected. General Fortune did not welcome the idea of seeing them in action without aerial observation, which nobody could ensure and without which it was impossible to count on the necessary precision. On the other hand the navy was encouraged to rein- force to a maximum the coastal defences, and they engaged upon this activity with enthusiasm. Two 75s raked the beach at Cayeux, others were brought into position at Ault, Le Tréport and Dieppe. But the danger was not from the sea, and even on the shore the enemy advance would not have proved irresistible, had there not been a repetition of what had hap- pened three weeks earlier on the Meuse – the front was pierced the very first evening on the Somme about 25 miles from the sea by the 7th and 5th Panzers. Rommel had attacked at Condé-Folie, at the junction of two composite Senegalese regiments of the 5th Colonial Infantry Division which had arrived in the line the previous evening. Held in check until about 1600 hrs. at Airaines and Quesnoy-sur-Airaines, he was able to force a passage until late on the 5th. Reaching the sources of the Andelle, where he was temporarily held up by weak units of Evans's division, the 7th Panzers reached Elbeuf on the Seine at about 2000 hrs. on 8th June. Following in his tracks, von Hartlieb's 6th Panzers arrived the following day at Rouen just in time to see the bridges blown up.

In the coastal sector, the 57th Infantry Division and the 11th Brigade of German fusiliers still bore the traces of fatigue from recent fighting. They broke out with comparative ease from the bridgehead of Saint-Valery-en-Caux before the 154th Brigade of the Scottish division, and General Fortune, after sending a dispatch to the commander of the 10th Army asking permission to fall back to the Bresle, undertook this movement of his own initiative, drawing with him as a result the 31st Alpine Division on his right flank.

On the evening of the 5th, the sailors of the Ault post reported that the Highlanders were leaving and that German columns were advancing on Eu, where the Luftwaffe had raised several fires during the night. At Dieppe it was learnt that the British sappers had blown up the bridges at Eu and Le Tréport.

On the orders of the Reserve Petty-officer, Joly, a veteran of the First World War, the 18 ratings of the post defended themselves heroically together with a platoon of 30 Scots until 1800 hrs. Then the latter retired in turn, and Joly learnt that the enemy had already surrounded him, for they were reported in Cise Wood to his rear. He retired to the cliff and, at nightfall, left with his men in some boats he had spotted on the foreshore and rowed across to Le Tréport.

The Bresle, which enters the sea between Mers-les-Bains and Le Tréport, marks the administrative limit between the departments of the Somme and the Seine-Inferieure (today the Seine-Maritime), in other words, between Picardy and Normandy. But the great chalk cliff which runs for 125 kilometres along the shores of the Caux country from Cape Hève, extends in reality as far as the Somme. After the cutting of the Bresle it rises once more to a height of 300 feet at Madone-de-Mers, to fall progressively as far as Ault where it seems to disappear. This is an illusion. In actual fact, its traces continue inland as far as Saint-Valery-sur-Somme. All the lowlands extending beyond it seawards as far as Hourdel Point, were in fact won from the sea by the mass of pebbles whose progress was halted at this spot by the current of the Somme and on which rest the alluvial deposits brought down by the river.

Therefore, from the village of Ault to Le Havre, the Caux country presents itself as a huge plateau, a slice of which has been cut clean by a vertical cliff, broken only by the estuaries of the coastal rivers: Bresle, Yères, Arques, Scie, Saâne, Dun and Durdent. . . . Between these estuaries which vary in breadth, the dry valleys, vestiges of vanished streams, indent the wall of narrow irregularly distributed ravines which constitute the only routes of communication between the inland and the sea shore. Hence the name of 'port' which has been given to them at certain spots – Port de Moustiers, Port de l'Ailly, Port de Mordal, etc. . . . This term must not deceive us. Apart from the estuaries there is no natural port on this shore, which is one of the most inhospitable of the whole French coastline, and as disobliging to anyone coming from the sea as to the landsman trying to gain access to the water by these indentations.

As a result of this geographical feature there is practically no association on this coast between the maritime population and that living on the land. The farms and fields stretch to the very edge of the cliff, but those who own and cultivate them rarely cross the 300 feet which separate them from the water – in a vertical sense.

These particular dispositions will have considerable consequences on the course of the events we are about to relate, just as they will dictate in two years time the setback to Operation *Jubilee*. We shall see, in fact, on the 12th June, 1940, Rommel with a few 105 mm. guns being able to stop the embarkation of General Ihler's forces. Two years later General Haase's troops were able to nail the Anglo-Canadians to the beaches and prevent them from making their way inland. In one sense or another here, more than anything else, it was geography which laid down the conditions of the battle. The break-through of the German armour towards Rouen and the lower Seine cut off Ihler's corps and the Scottish division from the rest of the 10th Army. This isolation was confirmed after the irresistible

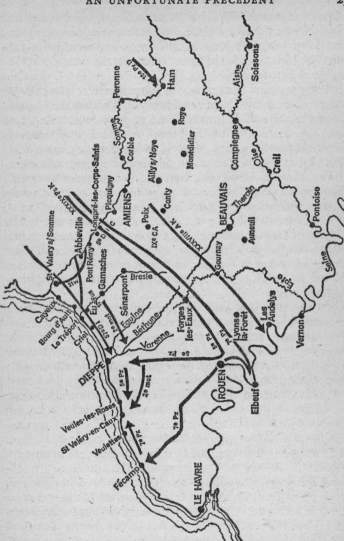

The break-through on the Somme and the fall of Dieppe

advance of the XXXVIIIth German Corps commanded by General von Manstein, which pierced our lines between Poix and Conty on the 7th June to reach the Seine at Andelys on the 9th. The river was crossed by the enemy on the same day in the region of Vernon.

It was in actual fact on the 6th June that Ihler should have tried to fall back to Dieppe and seek his 'Dunkirk' there, had Dieppe not already been in the state we have described. Apart from this fact neither on the French nor the British side had anyone seriously thought of using this port to save the rest of these forces which represented approximately 50,000 men.

Moreover the Allied High Command did not possess at this date the necessary intelligence to order such a radical manoeuvre. Weygand learnt much later 'that the penetration of the armour into the defences of the 10th Army was in reality far deeper than he had thought'. For this reason, on the map of the gigantic battle which had been raging since the 5th from the sea to the Chemin des Dames, the lower Somme front had appeared to him that night no more threatened than that of Péronne or Soissons.

On the spot General Ihler gave up the idea of counter-attacking and thought merely of retiring. On the evening of the 5th he tried to establish a barrage in the region north of Poix with the 3rd Light Cavalry Division and the 22nd Colonial Infantry Regiment. But this precarious front, held by colonials and cavalry, was pierced in turn and the Hq. of the 9th Corps was very nearly captured at La Chapelle-sous-Poix. Ihler lost all contact in the course of this rapid retreat and was out of touch for 24 hours.

When a very anxious Weygand appeared on the evening of 7th June at 10th Army Hq. at Lyons-la-Forêt, General Altmayer reported the situation to him in these terms:

On the Bresle from the sea to Gamaches the 51st Highland Division; then from Gamaches to Senarpont the 31st Alpine Infantry Division; on the Liger from Senarpont to Guilbertmesnil the 40th Infantry Division. Beyond was a breach of eight miles created the previous day by the Germans. Then between Poix and Conty, two machine-gun battalions, and from Conty to Ailly-sur-Noye the 24th Infantry Division still intact.

At the same moment, at 1730 hrs., Rommel had cut the Paris–Dieppe road at Ménerval near Forges-les-Eaux and his reconnaissance battalion was approaching the Andelle at Sigy.

Weygand's first thought was for Rouen. He immediately requested General Evans to arrange with General Duffour, commanding the 3rd Military Region, to defend the approaches to the Norman capital. Then, on his return to Paris, he sent for Captain Auphan, G.S.O.1 of the French naval forces to ask for the co-operation of the navy to prepare a crossing of the lower Seine and the eventual evacuation of Le Havre.

After having given orders on the 7th June at 0115 hrs. to the Auden group to try and close the salient between Hornoy and Poix made in our lines by the advance of Rommel's division; then envisaged a retreat to the Béthune[1] by the units aligned on the Bresle, the French commander, resigned to the loss of the Caux country, gave the formal order at midnight on the same day to retire to the lower Seine. The French and British navies hastily assembled the necessary boats for the evacuation of Le Havre and the crossing of the estuary.

On the 8th General Ihler finally managed to restore contact with his divisional commanders at his new Hq. at Bure-en-Bray on the Béthune. He still counted upon falling back on Rouen in four stages. Events did not give him time. On the 9th the British had blown up the bridges over the Béthune, except that of Bure where the chaos was appalling. The sappers threw a provisional bridge over the river at Mesnières, but the news now spread that Rouen had fallen into the hands of the enemy and the withdrawal had therefore to be carried out in the direction of Yvetot. More than half his soldiers were on foot! Buses were sought for in Le Havre to rescue them.

From this point onwards, Ihler never regained contact with his chief Altmayer who had been forced to retire to Marines, the G.Hq. of the 10th Army. General Fortune alone remained until the end in radio communication with London. Two of his brigades, recalled for the defence of Le Havre, escaped encirclement just in time and were able to be evacuated by sea.

[1] The Béthune which waters the country of Bray receives on its right bank the Eaulne and on its left the Varenne to form some kilometres from the sea the River Arques which enters the port of Dieppe.

The remainder should have found at Dieppe a nearer point of embarkation than Le Havre, but we know in what state that port was at this juncture. Moreover on the 6th the Germans were at Mers less than 19 miles away, and the withdrawal of the 51st Highland Division behind the Béthune, reported to Captain Lemonnier in the evening, left the place wide open. The British admiralty was already preparing three blockade ships which were to be sunk in the Dieppe fairway by Captain Garnoms Williams who, 15 days earlier, had already been in action at Zeebrugge.

The three blockade ships arrived about midnight of the 9th/10th June escorted by the destroyer H.M.S. *Vega*. They were the 1,262 ton *Jacobus* loaded with rails and cement, the 1,525 ton *River Tyne* and the 2,224 ton *Kaupo*. The first two were sunk according to plan in the channel, which the Germans had not managed to clear by the liberation four years later. The third vessel blew up prematurely on a magnetic mine. To replace it, the British demolition crew wanted to scuttle a tug between the jetties, but the French Captain Lemonnier actually carried out the operation between 2200 hrs. and 0100 hrs. At 0200 hrs. the last sailors left Dieppe to rejoin the other units of the defence sector which had retired earlier in the evening. On the 10th the Germans entered the town unopposed. After Rouen a second escape route had been closed.

The tragedy was not to be long delayed.

At the same moment Rommel was busy closing the last two ways of escape; Le Havre and the ferries of the lower Seine, by advancing upstream to Rouen to take the land of Caux obliquely, while his colleague von Hartlieb pushed due north parallel to the Rouen–Dieppe road. The 7th Panzer Division reached the sea at Petites-Dalles about midday on the 10th June, but Rommal lost one day by capturing Fécamp, defended by a handful of soldiers and the crew of a minesweeper which was being repaired in the port.[1] Not until the night of the 11th

[1] The defence of Fécamp was in the hands of Captain Gilles, the town major of Fécamp and Lieutenant Lavenne de Choulot, commanding the auxiliary minesweeper *Patrice II*. They managed to save *Chasseur 44* which was being built in the Normandy yards and was due to be launched on the 9th. It was towed away on the 10th a few hours before the Germans arrived.

did he turn eastward along the shore, crossing the Durdent at Veulettes and reaching the heights dominating Saint-Valery-en-Caux from the west, where Fortune's Highlanders had taken up their positions to bar his passage. Thus, late in the afternoon, it was learnt at Naval Headquarters in Le Havre that almost the entire IXth Army Corps, with which every effort had been made to re-make contact, had called the navy to its rescue at Saint-Valery-en-Caux where it had formed a square. There were 65,000 men there to be evacuated.[1] Scores of boats had already put to sea from Portsmouth, Cherbourg and Le Havre. A French liaison crew, commanded by Lt. Juin, arrived at Saint-Valery on the morning of the 11th in a British ferry boat. Commander Elkins, R.N., prepared to take off the 51st Highland Division.

The operation had been successful at Dunkirk, but at Saint-Valery, with comparable means, it was an almost total failure. Miracles are never repeated. This is because at Dunkirk and off its beaches the flat Flanders coast rises barely a couple of feet above sea level with dunes easy to cross to the rear. There was no difficulty in reaching the water's edge. There are no heights dominating the beaches. As opposed to this the little port of Saint-Valery is flanked by two tall cliffs about 220 feet high. The same applies to Veules-les-Roses where, incidentally, no harbour has existed since 1753, when a monstrous tidal wave obstructed it for ever by undermining the cliff. Furthermore between these two localities some five miles apart, there is no valley and no indentation in the coast.

Debouching, from Conteville-la-Paluel on the cliff below Saint-Valery, Rommel's tanks clashed at first with the Highlanders and, after bitter fighting, pushed them back to the harbour quays. They were stopped as though by a miracle by a road block improvised by about 30 Scots and some French officers. We are now at the 11th June in the middle of the afternoon.

Although Rommel was unable to penetrate to the harbour, he was able to place a 105 field battery on the cliff which kept the beach and the jetties under fire.

As a result of this, Commander Elkins, returning to the beach

[1] This figure was undoubtedly exaggerated.

at about 1500 hrs. after conferring with General Fortune, was astonished to find himself being shot at like a rabbit from the top of these cliffs. He had just time to fall on his belly behind a rock when a voice, which seemed to come from the sky, announced that all that remained was to surrender. On the crest he could see the outlines of a long column of enemy tanks.

*   *   *

Defended to the west by the 51st Highland Division, the Saint-Valery bridgehead was guarded to the east and south by units of the French IXth Corps, which had been able to disengage and fall back on Le Havre or the lower Seine. Ihler had set up his Hq. at Cailleville. The Alpine troops of the 40th Light Division and the 31st Alpine Infantry Division held the line before Saint-Riquier, Pleine-Sève, Ermenouville, Houdetot and Saint-Pierre-le-Viger, facing the 2nd Motorized Brigade of General Crüwel who had just slipped in between the 7th and 5th Panzers. To the east, defending Veules against Hartlieb's armour, Colonel de Reboul commanded a force composed of motorized dragoons and chasseurs alpins with the self-propelling machine-guns of the light cavalry divisions.

In Saint-Valery itself complete chaos reigned. The jam was of such magnitude that there was no room even to set up a battery of 25s. A thousand British and a few hundred French were able to embark during the afternoon before the German gunners took up their positions. This was the end. Everyone who could get away left the Veules beach in extraordinarily difficult conditions. Pinned down at the foot of this chalk wall by the 105 shells which burst all round them, a few men tried to make Veules along the pebbles. Others, arriving directly on the crest, sought for ropes to slip down the cliff face. Those they found were either too short or not strong enough. Many of them broke under the weight, letting fall bunches of human grapes. General Berniquet, commanding the 2nd Light Cavalry Division, received a bullet in the stomach and lay dying for 24 hours.

At 1900 hrs., 11th June, Rommel issued his ultimatum. His messenger was rejected. At 2100 hrs. the bombardment started up again with unheard-of violence. The beach and the port

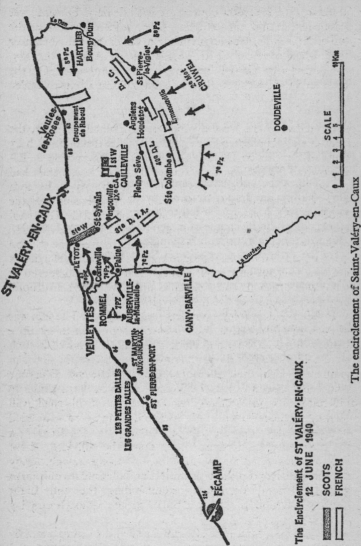

The Encirclement of ST VALÉRY·EN·CAUX
12 JUNE 1940

SCOTS
FRENCH

SCALE
0 1 2 3 4 5   10 Km

The encirclement of Saint-Valéry-en-Caux

were ablaze. Ihler tried to break through in the direction of the Seine. This proved impossible. Fortune announced that he had destroyed his artillery.[1] At 0830 hrs. on the 12th, the command of the IXth Corps gave the order to cease fire.

Nevertheless, the conflict continued in the neighbouring hamlets until the middle of the afternoon, and it was not until 1630 hrs. that two companies of the 13th Battalion of the Chasseurs Alpins, entrenched at Houdetot, finally laid down their arms. During the night a handful of men from the 5th Light Cavalry Division, outflanked on the evening of the 11th at Saint-Colombe, managed in small groups to reach the crossings of the Seine.

At Veules the heroic resistance put up by Reboul's group allowed a few hundred men to be saved. We lost the auxiliary patrol vessel *Cérons*, which fell to Rommel's 105s after an unequal combat, in the course of which he had managed to silence one of the enemy guns with his single 100.

On the 13th, ships were still off Saint-Valery in the hope of rescuing a few men from captivity. The Germans allowed them to approach and suddenly showed their guns and set fire to the Frenchman *Granville* and the British train ferry.

In all, the Franco-British flotillas, which had arrived off Saint-Valery and Veules-les-Roses on the 11th and 12th June, 1940, would have been able to take off 10,000 men. Just a third of this number were actually evacuated.[2]

Le Havre was not defended. The evacuation of the port continued until the early hours of 13th June, under an intense bombardment which caused heavy losses. Admiral Gaudin de Villaine, in command of the sector, put to sea at 0430 hrs. aboard *Chasseur 14*. A few hours later the 5th Panzers entered the town. From Le Havre to Port-Jérome a screen of smoke hid

[1] This testimony figures in the historical account of the 2nd Light Cavalry Division. British historians who deplore the fate of the 51st Division, the only one which managed to extricate itself in the French campaign, insist that General Ihler forced Fortune to capitulate.

[2] 2,130 British and 1,104 French according to Roskill, *The War at Sea*, p. 232. 6,000 British were taken prisoner. The number of French captured amounted to 40,000, if the overall figure of 46,000 given by Rommel is correct, but it seems to be too high.

the sky. All the oil tanks of the lower Seine had been burning for several days.

The disaster of Saint-Valery-en-Caux passed unnoticed in France. Paris fell the following day and the flood of invasion swept the whole country. What were 30 to 40,000 prisoners when their total number was to reach the figure of 1,800,000?

The same did not apply to Great Britain. These 6,000 soldiers of the 51st Highland Division, captured at Saint-Valery in a single coup, were more than the Germans had taken in detail from the B.E.F. throughout the whole campaign. It was the only large unit which was lost in France. The British have never forgotten it.

It is all the more surprising, therefore, that this unfortunate precedent did not deter them from a new adventure on this coast, from which they could never have escaped, even with all the necessary ships at their disposal, and which did not appear *a priori* particularly well chosen to begin operations in the opposite direction.

CHAPTER TWO

THE EMPTY SEA

IN peacetime an incredible number of ships pass through the Channel. Everything sailing to London – the world's leading port – and to the British east coast ports, the Scandinavian countries, the Baltic, the ports of the German Bight, to Hamburg and Rotterdam, Antwerp or Dunkirk, of necessity use the Pas de Calais and the Channel, its natural ante-chamber. A dozen countries, some of which are among the most heavily industrialized in Europe, have to use this exit into the Atlantic unless they wish to circumnavigate Scotland.

At the western landfalls of this main maritime route each day, at Ushant, the Créach Signal Station tallies scores of ships. At Dungeness, at the eastern extremity, the British look-out men record between two and three hundred, and not for one moment during the 24 hours of the day does the sea appear to them empty.[1]

On 1st September, 1939, this traffic suddenly ceased – but only for a few hours. It was merely a question of changing over to a wartime navigational regime, in view of the imminent outbreak of hostilities. The German flag of course had disappeared. The passage remained open to neutrals, provided they identified themselves before entering the straights to the signal stations of Dungeness or Boulogne-Alprech. If the ship had no permit it was inspected at Dunkirk or off the Downs.

In practice, during the first months of the war, there was great activity in the Channel. No U-boat had shown itself in the

[1] In 1960 approximately 24,000 merchant ships passed the English coast and the Varne lightship, without counting those which the fog prevented from being observed. To this number must be added the warships and the innumerable fishing fleets. The importance of this traffic has been stressed by Captain McMullen, R.N. (retired), during discussions of the plan to build a Channel bridge (cf. *Journal of the Merchant Navy*, 28.8.61).

eastern Channel, and all those which had tried to penetrate through the straits had been successfully destroyed. By the third casualty Dönitz had learned his lesson. From the 24th October, 1939 – the date of the destruction of the U.16 – all German U-boats reached their fields of activity via the north of Scotland. In these conditions merchant shipping could continue with relative impunity. The 150 aircraft of General Geissler's[1] Xth air fleet were active above all in the North Sea, to avoid complications with the Dutch and the Belgians, or the A.A. and fighters over French territory. Only two bombing attacks were recorded in the Channel at the expense of the British cargo boat *Domala*, which was set on fire near the Isle of Wight, and on the 20th October at the expense of the *Barn Hill*, which was seriously damaged south of Brighton.

The magnetic mines were to prove more dangerous, but the first offensive, launched on the 20th November, 1939, was directed above all against the fairways of the North Sea where 35 ships were blown up. It came to a temporary halt on the 17th December when the waters from which the 59 Heinkel mine layers took off were icebound.

The Luftwaffe then replaced the seaplane mine layers by land aircraft of the 9th Air Division. The offensive was resumed on the 2nd April, 1940, and 188 mines were dropped off the S.E. coast of England and the Channel ports before the 10th May. But by and large the traffic remained undisturbed.

Things were to change radically from the day the Germans occupied the French coast channel and took possession of all our ports from Dunkirk to Brest. No one in future could sail independently. The British would only risk their convoys along the well observed, defended and mine-swept coastal channels. The rhythm was often disrupted by the Luftwaffe's activities, by the German long-range batteries on Cape Gris Nez, and also by the E-boats.

As for the Germans, they also used the *Rosa* and *Lila* routes skirting the coasts – more than was generally believed, with a

---

[1] The Xth air fleet consisted of Kampfsgruppe 26, equipped with Heinkel 111s, K.G.30 with Junker 88s and K.G.100 equipped with Heinkel 111s. It was engaged particularly in operations at sea or on the British shores.

wealth of precaution and escorts which greatly diminished the return, without the risk being entirely abolished.[1]

Apart from this the sea was empty. Not a ship to be seen. Imagine a motorway, devoid of its impetuous stream of fast cars, and on which were occasionally a few lorries trying to hide themselves by skirting the ditch.

Empty of merchant shipping, yes, but also of big warships. Not of course of that 'naval dust' the mosquitoes of this 'no-man's sea', rapid craft of all types, the British M.T.B.s and the German E-boats, which went out happily every night scouring the enemy waters in search of a justified target for their torpedoes. This is what the British sailors called the *Battle of the Narrow Seas*. It was to continue until the reconquest of the French coastline.

It was started by the Germans. Hardly had the French Pas de Calais ports fallen than the German navy dispatched to Boulogne the 1st and 2nd Flotillas of E-boats, which had won a great success at the expense of the Allied ships engaged in the Dunkirk operations. A few days later the 1st Flotilla was transferred to Cherbourg, where it sank or damaged half a dozen boats off the English coast during the first three weeks of July, without the patrolling British destroyers being able to eliminate them.

These attacks at the outset came within the framework of the preparatory measures ordered by Hitler for an invasion of England, in which the Luftwaffe also played its part by attacking the ports and the fairways of the south coast. Among the first victims were the French sailors, whom the Armistice should in principle have put out of the fighting. In actual fact on 24th July the liner *Meknes*, commanded by Captain Dubroc, left Southampton during the afternoon with 1,180 repatriated sailors and a crew of 104. She was intercepted towards 2300

---

[1] The *Rosa* route was much the same as our wartime coastal route along the coast of the 1st Naval Region. In the Pas de Calais it was doubled by the *Lila* route which ran further to the west from Calais to Ostend.

For example, it must be noted that during the month of January, 1942, the naval forces of west group (whose field of activity extended to the Gulf of Gascony as well as to the Channel) provided escorts for 405 ships representing a total of 294,000 B.R.T.

hrs. by a craft of the 1st E-boat Flotilla 10 miles south of the Isle of Wight. The liner stopped immediately. She was sailing with full lights, decks and rigging normally lit, ports uncovered, the flag lit by two powerful lamps and the marks of her nationality illuminated on the hull. There was no possible doubt. . . .

Nevertheless 10 minutes later a torpedo struck the *Meknes* between Nos. 3 and 4 holds. The vessel broke in two before all the lifeboats could be lowered. 800 sailors and 100 officers were picked up by British destroyers and taken back to Weymouth, but 429 men were lost, half of whose bodies were carried by the current to the coast of France. From the 1st September, i.e. six weeks after this tragedy, corpses were picked up along the whole shore in the Dieppe sector from Saint-Valery-en-Caux to Le Tréport. They totalled 150 by the 20th September and 200 a month later.

On the 23rd July the Germans had notified the French Government that in future they would sink any French ship whose movements had not been reported to them in advance. The French had not yet notified the British Admiralty which, for its part, had not informed us that she was sending the *Meknes* to sea. It had not therefore been possible to warn the German Armistice Commission at Wiesbaden.

But this certainly did not justify the precipitation of the young officer in command of the German E-boat.

Obviously this brilliantly lit ship could only have been a vessel loyal to the French Government. Had it been rallying to the Free French movement it would have sailed with lights dimmed like any other belligerent.

In any case the harm was done and the inhabitants of the Dieppe coast, who buried the unfortunate victims, knew, even if they had ever had any doubts, that the war would continue.

*   *   *

The British Navy had naturally made its disposition to cope with these attacks. From the 3rd July the big convoys of ships leaving the Thames to reach the Atlantic by the Channel were diverted to the east coast and the North of Scotland. The coastal traffic, hitherto free, was grouped into convoys C.W. and C.E., from the mouth of the Thames to the Bristol Channel

and vice versa. 20 to 30 boats, mostly colliers, crawling along at
a few knots within immediate reach of the bombers stationed
on the French coast and E-boats. Let us recall that on the 25th
July out of a merchant convoy of 21 ships – C.W.8 – sailing
west via the Pas de Calais only 11 passed Dungeness, the others
having succumbed to bombs or the torpedoes of the E-boats.
The next convoy, C.W.9 on the 4th August, was equipped with
captive balloons which were later replaced by kites. Next the
size of the convoys was doubled to diminish their vulnerability,
and the number of escort vessels was increased. In the Channel
now could be seen a dozen cargo boats, preceded by minesweepers with an escort of two destroyers, three or four armed
sloops, half a dozen M.L.s and six or eight balloon carriers.
This was the indispensable assurance for delivering each week
the 40,000 tons of coal needed by the south coast ports.

On the 12th August, 1940, the long-range batteries at Cap
Gris Nez went into action for the first time; they were exas-
perating for the morale of the crews sailing at five or six knots
but, if we are to believe Roskill, surprisingly ineffectual. Then
the mines reappeared in great numbers. In 1940 alone they
caused the loss of 309,000 B.R.T. (20 vessels), a large proportion of which was in the Channel. Nearly 700 minesweepers
were engaged in eliminating them.

At this period the German coastal traffic was still insignificant
and the raids carried out by the British flotillas of M.T.B.s or
M.G.B.s often met with nothing except a few auxiliary patrols
or minesweepers.

The R.A.F. naturally played its part in this guerilla warfare.
No. 16 Group in particular was responsible for the Channel
and the North Sea. Nor, of course, did the British delay
sowing their own mines outside the enemy harbour entrances
and on the *Lila* and *Rosa* routes.

The latter became progressively busier. From April to mid-
June, 1941, for example, the Admiralty information service recorded the passage of 29 cargo vessels of more than 1,000 tons
and of 11 destroyers. The R.A.F. re-doubled its efforts, and
towards the end of the year the German traffic by day had
almost entirely ceased. This, however, was due above all to the
fact that the German Navy made its sorties by night. It

managed to use this route for the raider *Komet* which arrived at
Cherbourg on the 26th November and at Hamburg on the 30th,
after severe engagements fought by its escorts between Boulogne and Dunkirk. At the same time the *Thor* was making
preparations to use the same route in reverse, and did so
effectively between the 7th and 16th December, thanks to
carefully calculated runs. Admiral Ruge recalls that in 1942,
5·7 million tons of shipping travelled by sea along the French
coast west of the Pas de Calais.[1]

*   *   *

The opening of the German–Russian campaign resulted in
the withdrawal to the Russian theatre of war of the greater part
of the German air forces stationed on the airfields of northern
France. This gave Great Britain a certain respite and allowed
greater possibilities to the R.A.F. whose raids in the Channel
increased, inflicting heavy losses on the German coastal traffic.
Thus, in October 1941, Captain Weniger, commanding the
2nd Security Division (Sicherungsdivision), was killed off
Dieppe during an attack by Spitfires on the 3rd Minesweeping
Flotilla, together with the officer commanding the flotilla and
several of his skippers. In less than a minute the flotilla lost in
killed and wounded 40 per cent of its personnel.[2] Nevertheless
the Channel remained exposed to the raids of low flying fighter-
bombers, such as the M.E. 109s and the Focke-Wulf 90s.
Furthermore more efficient mines now began to appear –
delayed action, acoustic and ratchet mines.

Nevertheless the Royal Navy, aided by certain groups of
'exiles' – Free French naval forces, Norwegian, Polish and
Dutch sailors – had managed to improve considerably the
conditions of its vital coastal traffic along the south coast of
England.

It was at this juncture that the German Navy succeeded in
bringing off a coup in the Channel which caused an uproar and
which merits our attention here.

In the age of sail the enemies of England whose ports were
situated to the west of the Pas de Calais – at a period, Spain and

[1] Ruge, *The War at Sea*.
[2] Ruge, op. cit.

France – were always greatly handicapped delivering a direct blow to her heart, that is to say in the Thames, because they first needed to sail up this *British Channel*, in others words, the straits in which the wind usually blows from an unfavourable quarter. When it is really fine, it is usually because the wind is blowing from the north-east and, in consequence, against a squadron approaching from the west. When a sou'wester is blowing, i.e. in a favourable direction, it is usually bad weather. In any case, from whichever direction the wind blows, on eight days out of 10 it is in the axis of this narrow sea, and a cross wind for a British squadron leaving the south coast ports to intercept the adversary. Now as everyone knows a cross wind is easier to utilize for a sailing vessel. The British call it a 'soldier's wind', that is to say, a wind in which even a soldier can sail.

This explains why the mouth of the Thames and London were never seriously threatened in the days of sail, except by navies whose bases were situated east of the Pas de Calais. This is the direction from which all the invasions after Julius Caesar came. It is from there that one of the greatest threats that has every menaced the British capital was launched – de Ruyter's foray into the Thames in 1677. As regards those coming from the west, one can count on the fingers of one hand the successful crossings. There was that of the Invincible Armada in 1588, but as everyone knows, it came to grief. The Duke of Medina-Sidonia having no stomach for an attack after crossing the narrows, preferred to flee into the North Sea, where he succumbed to the fury of the elements. In the following century there were Martin Tromp and de Ruyter, who managed on several occasions to block the Channel from end to end, not without having to break off the engagement on the way, and that is all. Tourville in 1690 reached Beachy Head and inflicted a masterly defeat on the Anglo-Dutch forces of Admiral Herbert, but could not pursue his advantage for lack of wind.

Since 1690, therefore, no enemy navy had insulted the British Navy by forging into the Channel and, still less, of forcing a passage from the Pas de Calais from west to east.

The reader will probably say that the age of steam brought great changes. Admittedly, but this did not prevent the German Admiralty, from the start of hostilities, writing off the Channel

route as a possible itinerary for its large surface warships. At a
pinch a raider, a few coasters who, as we have seen, risked the
passage along the coastal fairways under cover of darkness. But
a whole squadron . . . and in broad daylight! It was out of the
question.

But since mid-March of the previous year the battleships
Scharnhorst and *Gneisenau* had languished in Brest where they
had anchored on their return from a 45-day raid in the Atlantic.
Joined on the 1st June by the heavy cruiser *Prinz Eugen*, which
had escaped unscathed from the engagement in which the
Bismarck was sunk, they had been constantly attacked and
seriously damaged by the R.A.F. Each time they were repaired
a bomb or an aerial torpedo immobilized them once more. This
could not go on. Hitler also insisted that his Grand Admiral
should send them back to Germany from where he proposed to
dispatch them to Norway, a theatre of operations on which he
had his own ideas – and by no means foolish ideas if we consider the plans that Churchill was elaborating at the same
moment.[1]

In short, everyone was in agreement that these units should
leave Brest and be brought back to Germany. By what route
was another matter. If they returned via the Denmark Straits
or the Iceland Channel it was obvious that they would not
debouch into the North Sea without having the entire Home
Fleet on their tracks.

Raeder was in a quandary. He was forced to declare at a
conference with the Führer on the 12th November, 1941, that
while waiting for the battleships to be seaworthy, they might
try to pass the *Prinz Eugen* through the Pas de Calais as they
were preparing to do – successfully as we have seen – with the
Komet and the *Thor*.

'But why the *Prinz Eugen*?' asked Hitler. 'Why not all the
ships?'

The admirals began to raise their hands to heaven. Then they
conceived a plan which was undoubtedly one of the best ever to

[1] Did Hitler fear an Allied attack in northern Norway? Churchill
thought very seriously of this. We refer the reader to what he wrote on
Operation *Jupiter*, which was never actually carried out, in Volume IV
of his War Memoirs.

originate from a Hitlerian warlord's brain, and Operation *Cerberus* was fixed for the 12th February, 1942. Not only was Admiral Ciliax, the former captain of the *Scharnhorst*, appointed to Fleet Commander on the death of Admiral Lütjens in the *Bismarck*, to sail his squadron through the Channel and the Pas de Calais, but he was to bring it through in broad daylight. It was tempting Providence, but Providence sometimes has a weakness for people who have bold ideas and put them into practice.

The Channel soon witnessed a feverish but discreet activity. On one side there was Vice-Admiral Ruge commanding the western coastal defences,[1] launching his flotillas of minesweepers along the *Rosa* and *Lila* routes every night. There was General Jeschonnek, G.S.O.I., of the Luftwaffe, trying to assemble as great a number of fighter aircraft as possible on his coastal airfields. It was also necessary to send destroyers and torpedo-boats into the Channel. Some of these would descend as far as Brest, others would hold themselves in readiness to act as escorts on a level with Cherbourg, while the fighter aircraft were to form a permanent air umbrella of 16 machines relieved every half an hour. In the ports of Cherbourg, Le Havre, Fécamp, Dieppe, Calais and Ostend, two minesweepers were to remain on the alert throughout the operation.

One of the first destroyers sent from Germany to Brest, the *Bruno Heinemann*, hit a mine on the 25th January, in the waters off Ruytingen, before even entering the Channel. A week later the Z.29 and the *Friedrich Ihn* were forced to take shelter in Le Havre because of the bad weather. They were able to leave the following day, but the minesweepers of the 4th Flotilla became engaged with the escort of a small British convoy. Actually this was chicken feed. More costly was the loss on the 6th February from the British mines of the coasters *Hermann* and *Schleswig-Holstein*, which went to the bottom with 140 men from the Wehrmacht or the Todt organization. This at least proved one thing – that the enemy did not take long to replace swept mines. However, the disposition of the escort forces was completed. The torpedo-boat Z.25 and the destroyers *Kondor* and *Jaguar* sailed on the 8th from Flushing to

[1] *Befehlshaber der Sicherungsstreitkräfte in Westen* (B.S.W.).

Le Havre, the 2nd Flotilla of E-boats from Brest to Le Havre, and the 3rd from Rotterdam to Dunkirk. On the 9th the destroyers T.15 and T.17 arrived at Dunkirk and the T.11, T.2, T.12 and T.4 at Le Havre. But on the 9th February, three days before the operation, mines had still been found on the *Rosa* route.

The British must therefore have been suspecting something. Obviously and for several reasons. The first being that the overall circumstances which dictate the conditions for carrying out an operation are equally well known to both sides: meteorology, currents, tides, phases of the moon, etc. The Royal Navy by studying these tried to put themselves in the shoes of the enemy and assess the possibilities of an evasion by the squadron from Brest. The result of their deliberations is expressed in an Admiralty note dated 2nd February:

'Although at first sight this passage appears hazardous, they considered that it was, from the enemy's point of view, greatly to be preferred to the long journey by the northern passage to the North Sea, or to attempt to force the Straits of Gibraltar and reach Italian harbours. . . . With remarkable prescience the Admiralty concluded that we might well find the two battle cruisers and the eight-inch cruiser with five large and five small destroyers and . . . 20 fighters constantly overhead . . . proceeding up Channel.'[1]

This was precisely what Admiral Ciliax had arranged.

Every precaution had been taken in England. It was impossible to recall the Home Fleet – actually at its lowest level with regard to material – from its anchorage in Scapa Flow, for the possibility of an intervention by the *Tirpitz* against the Murmansk convoys, not to mention a sortie into the Atlantic at the moment when a large convoy of 26 ships was about to put to sea to transport 45 to 50,000 soldiers to the Middle East, could not be ruled out. At Dover Admiral Ramsay had only six old destroyers and a few M.T.B.s at his disposal. The Admiralty relied largely on the mines laid by the fast minelayers *Manxman* and *Welshman* between Ushant and Boulogne, while Bomber Command dropped 98 magnetic mines off the Frisian Islands.

[1] Quoted by Roskill, op. cit., II, 121. The eight-inch cruiser was the *Prinz Eugen*.

And finally on the R.A.F. Fighter Command had 550 fighters in southern England and Bomber Command 250 bombers. Incidentally none of these were trained for attacking ships at sea, and the specialists in this art were, in the last analysis, the crews of No. 825 Squadron of the Fleet Air Arm, based on Manston Airfield, and equipped with slow, obsolete and . . . unbreakable Swordfish.

A very tight system of reconnaissance patrols over Brest and various sectors of the Channel had been perfected. The submarine *Sealion* risked showing its periscope at the entrance of the Brest Channel where a French naval officer, spying on the German boats, at the peril of his life and that of his comrades – his radio operator, Anquetil, had been arrested and shot – gave the alert. The last message dated the 7th February ran: 'Putting to sea imminent. Stop. Beware in particular the period of the full moon.'

None of this was effective due to a succession of misfortunes – radar apparatus out of action, reliefs of certain patrols not being carried out, and perhaps also the fact that the British did not believe that the ships would leave by night, which would mean passing through the Straits in full daylight. All these factors combined to favour the Germans. Sailing from Brest about 2230 hrs. on the 11th February, shortly after *Sealion* had ended its patrol, and immediately after a raid by the R.A.F. on the port, Ciliax and his three warships were not spotted until after 1030 hrs. on the 12th – in actual fact by aircraft which did not belong to the reconnaissance arm, two Spitfires engaged in a dogfight with German fighters. The scene was somewhere between Dieppe and the bay of the Somme, and the two Spitfires were flying too low over the water to send a radio message and could only report on landing. It was already 1109 hrs. By the time the wheels were put in motion it was 1130 hrs. and eventually Lt.-Commander Esmond's ancient Swordfishes were the first to attack off Calais at 1245 hrs. None of them returned to base.[1]

---

[1] Esmond had brilliantly attacked the *Bismarck* in the previous year. This new attack proved fatal for him. Only five survivors were picked up from his squadron which, despite the sacrifice, did not manage to register a single hit with their torpedoes.

Thus three German capital ships had been able to leave Brest and pass through the Channel from one end to the other before being attacked. Everything attempted against them successively, by the R.A.F., the Harwich destroyers and the M.T.B.s was in vain. But the mines did their job. The *Scharnhorst* hit two and very nearly sank. The *Gneisenau* hit one. This did not prevent them from reaching port, not without great difficulty, and they had to remain in dry dock for many months. The *Gneisenau* was never put into service again. The *Prinz Eugen* alone got through unscathed.

Nevertheless it was a remarkable tactical success for the German Navy and the British press foamed at the mouth. A Court of Inquiry was convened and Churchill was heckled in the House of Commons.

'Vice-Admiral Ciliax,' write *The Times* of the 14th February, 1942, 'has succeeded where the Duke of Medina-Sidonia failed. . . . Nothing more mortifying to the pride of sea-power has happened in home waters since the seventeenth century.'[1]

*   *   *

What perhaps embarrassed the British in this instance was the fact that their chain of radar stations had not yet been entirely organized on the south coast of England. This was not long delayed and the advantages immediately began to be felt. In any case the Royal Navy could not prevent the *Michel* from passing through the Straits of Dover on the 14th March with a strong escort which, supported by the long-range batteries, triumphantly beat off the M.T.B.s and the destroyers deployed against it. On the 13th May the *Stier* passed through in the same conditions, but this time the Germans left some of their feathers behind. The destroyers *Iltis* and *Seeadler* were torpedoed by the swift British M.T.B.s south of Varnes. The British lost M.T.B.22. The *Stier* took refuge in Boulogne and then in turn reached the Atlantic by short night stages.

The loss of these two destroyers seriously affected the German naval staff. It was due to the fact that in the bad visibility conditions reigning, the British had greatly benefited

[1] Quoted by Roskill, op. cit., 215.

from the superiority of their radar equipment, which the German jamming network had been unable to prevent functioning.

In the meantime the sea remained empty. On the French coast alone, during the hours of daylight, small fishing-boats continued to ply their trade within the three-mile limit in which the occupying authorities authorized fishing. Beyond was a complete void, apart from a few raids on both sides by British M.T.B.s and German E-boats.

The latter achieved their greatest success in the summer of 1942. Two flotillas of these fast launches had been transferred to Cherbourg. On the 7th July they appeared in the Bay of Lymes and sunk six ships totalling 12,356 B.R.T. from an English convoy.

A significant detail. The same day the Luftwaffe concentrated on the transport ships assembled off the Isle of Wight, ready for an operation on Dieppe, which was cancelled due to the bad weather.

CHAPTER THREE

PINPRICKS AND BODY BLOWS

ONE outstanding quality of the British is their bulldog tenacity. They have a particularly apposite word to describe everything that is obstinate, self-willed and intractable – stubborn. Expelled from the Dunkirk beaches at the beginning of June 1940, the British reappeared on our coast three weeks later, exactly like some character in a comedy who when chased out of the door returns through the window.

The second phase of the German offensive in France was not yet finished, but the end of the French Army's resistance was already in sight, when the War Office, on the 12th June, 1940, founded its Directorate of Raiding Operations, under the auspices of Lt.-General Sir Alan Bourne of the Royal Marines, and Captain Garnoms Williams, whom we have already seen in action during the Dieppe chaos – a specialist in all forms of demolition.

Ten days later, the new organization launched its first 'show', which passed almost unnoticed. The initial objective was quite ambitious: 200 men to be put ashore on the French coast south of Boulogne, to report on the nature of the defences set up by the Germans, and if possible to bring back prisoners.

It was just a month since the enemy had occupied this coast, since it was on the 22nd May that the German Panzer division, advancing north from the Bay of the Somme, had arrived to invest Boulogne. It is quite possible to set up efficient defences in a month, but on the other hand, the German Army had been fully occupied in reducing the Dunkirk pocket and in pursuing the campaign in France, which now came to a close on this 22nd June, with the signing of the Armistice at Rethondes.

That evening, shortly after nightfall, eight motor-boats – these were all the craft available – most of them manned by fishermen or yachtsmen, assembled in the middle of the Straits to transport to the French coast, not 200 but 115 men – the maximum that could be taken aboard in this rudimentary armada. They were divided into four groups and the operation was directed by Lt.-Commander Milner Gibson and Major Todd. Colonel Clarke, the organizer of the expedition, had insisted upon accompanying them.

The first group landed in the dunes without difficulty, saw nothing, explored a few hundred yards of apparently abandoned terrain and left by the same way it had come. The second fell upon a small seaplane base, which the Germans had recently installed, just at the moment when a seaplane took off a few feet above the boats. The raiding party retired without asking any more questions. The third group, which included the leaders of the expedition, had an encounter with a small party of Germans who had no idea of what was happening. Colonel Clarke left behind a lobe of his ear, snipped off by a bullet. The fourth group however, which had landed on the beach of Merlimont between Berck and Le Touquet, chanced to encounter a couple of German soldiers whom they killed instead of taking prisoner, without even thinking of searching them before retiring. The information gained was very meagre, but at least there had been no losses. It ended in wild farce when, on its return to Folkestone, one of the boats, which no one had expected, was greeted with the greatest suspicion. It was left for a while rocked by the waves outside the nets, where its passengers suffered from seasickness and subsequently intoxication, thanks to the discovery of two jars of rum. Since no one on board was carrying any papers they were all put in jail like common deserters.

Nevertheless from this episode the Commandos were born. They still had to learn their trade.

*   *   *

The foray was repeated three weeks later, not in France this time, but in occupied England. A small part of England had been occupied, to be exact, one of the Channel Islands – Guernsey.

This time the operation was important enough to be given a name – *Ambassador*. The objective this time was more ambitious, since it was a question of occupying an airfield and

putting it out of action. This was to be the job of a small
commando landed from the destroyer H.M.S. *Saladin*, while
another, landed by H.M.S. *Scimitar* on the opposite side of the
island, had to block the roads in order to prevent the Germans
from bringing up reinforcements. Admiral James, C.-in-C.
Portsmouth, who was very short of destroyers, had not concealed the fact that he found it ridiculous to send two of them
to explore the most treacherous waters in the world, particularly now that all the lighthouse beams were extinguished, but
no one asked his advice.

The *Saladin* never found Guernsey and strayed in the direction of Sark and Herm. The party from the *Scimitar* managed
to land, but its exploits were confined to cutting a few telephone wires and to setting up a road blockade. It was about
to withdraw, without having caught sight of a German, when
Lt.-Commander Slater, the officer in command, committed a
faux pas. His revolver went off by mistake, rousing the enemy.
The commandos had to re-embark, abandoning three poor
fellows who did not know how to swim.

Slater himself admitted later that everything would have to
be revised in this business, from the direction in London to the
execution. Churchill was no more gentle: he called it a 'silly
fiasco'.

Nevertheless it was still only the 13th July, 1940, and the
second time within three weeks after Dunkirk that British
armed soldiers had set foot again in occupied territory.

To improve the return from these raids, Churchill, on the
17th July, 1940, decided to appeal to a veteran of the First
World War, Admiral Sir Roger Keyes, whose name remains
for ever associated with the famous blocking of Zeebrugge
in April 1918.

Keyes had left the service long before the outbreak of the
Second World War. He was a Member of Parliament, but this
did not prevent his following operations with the keenest
interest. During the Norwegian campaign he had requested to
be allowed the honour of leading in person – under the orders
of the C.-in-C. Home Fleet, his junior – an attack on Trondhjem fjord. The plan was abandoned. He did not hesitate to
don his admiral's uniform, and to heckle with some violence

the Chamberlain government in the House of Commons. On coming to power Churchill had appointed him Chief of the Military Mission to the King of the Belgians.[1] He seemed the right man to give an impulse to this new service. Everyone knew that at the head of combined operations Admiral Keyes would lack neither imagination nor audacity.

It is obviously beyond the scope of this book to describe all the commando raids which preceded the Dieppe raid. Many of them were mere pinpricks and passed unnoticed. Others were to have great repercussions. On the night of the 27th/28th September, 1940, two small landings were effected in the Bay of the Seine at Courseulles and Saint-Vaast-la-Hougue. The British commandos remained ashore for about 20 minutes and re-embarked after killing three Germans. This would not be worth mentioning except for the fact, by some strange coincidence, that the two landing places approximately mark the limits of the future landing zones of 1944. There were other incursions on the Italian coast, in Libya and on the Channel Islands. There were frequent raids on Norway, notably that of the submarine *Junon* of the Free French Naval Forces, which landed a team of saboteurs far up the fjord with orders to blow up a factory. Moreover, it was in Norway that the first really important raid took place on the Lofoten Islands on the 4th March, 1941, when 500 men from Commandos 3 and 4, aided by a few engineers and some Norwegian exiles under the orders of Brigadier General Haydon, landed at five o'clock in the morning on the islands of Vest and Ost-Vagsö, demolishing everything afloat in the port of Svolvaer, including the *Hamburg*, a German factory ship of 9,780 tons. They re-embarked at 0100 hrs., taking with them 200 German prisoners and about

[1] In the course of this mission, Admiral Keyes happened to be in Zeebrugge on the 25th May when there was once more a question of blocking the port in the face of the German advance. Attempted on the previous night, the raid had failed, partly because the French soldiers of the 270th Infantry Regiment, posted at the mouth of the Leopold Canal, had opened fire on the English launches escorting the blockade ships, because they had not been notified of the operation. Very sportingly the British Admiral insisted on congratulating the battalion responsible for this contempt, for the strict discipline with which it had carried out its firing orders.

300 of the inhabitants who had volunteered to serve with the Free Norwegian Navy. The coup was repeated in December. 16,000 tons of enemy shipping was sent to the bottom.

*   *   *

In the sector with which we are dealing, in other words, the coastline of the Caux country, the most sensational success was the Bruneval raid carried out on the night of the 27th/28th February, 1942. The aim of the operation was to put out of service a recently installed German radar and, if possible, to bring back its main components so that the British experts could examine them.

Let us say a few words about these German radars, which we shall refer to frequently in the course of the Dieppe operation. At the outbreak of war the British were unaware that the Germans had a radar apparatus in service. It was only during the years 1940–41 that aerial reconnaissance photographs, supported by information from agents, allowed the British Command to localize most of the Freya type long distance radars which the enemy had mounted all along the French occupied coast. But it soon appeared that, apart from Freya, the Germans had another apparatus designed to direct their flak batteries and fighters. This apparatus, the Würzburg W.110, was soon adapted for directing night fighters, which constituted a certain menace to our fighter squadrons in their nightly raids.[1]

---

[1] Freya, the Scandinavian goddess of love, gave her name to the first German radar invented long before the war, a certain number of which were already in service at the time of the Munich crisis. Freya gave the distance and the bearings but not the location; it was therefore useful above all for observing naval objectives.

The Würzburg, built a little later by the firm of Telefunken, allowed the altitude of the approaching aircraft to be calculated. It had been difficult to perfect, but the Germans had already mounted it on their coasts at the beginning of the war, and the indications it gave caused heavy losses to the R.A.F. in its first operations over the German Bight in the autumn of 1941.

After considerable experiments, the Luftwaffe developed the pinpointing of night fighters by means of this apparatus, whose operators soon acquired a high degree of precision, leading the fighter aircraft to within 400 yards of their target.

At their first inkling of the existence of the Würzburg, the British quite rightly deduced that it was normally to be found beside a Freya. They carefully examined all their aerial photographs and finally discovered near the Bruneval Freya a suspicious little dot which recurred on several photographs, proving that it was neither a speck of dust nor an accidental stain.

On his own initiative a British airman, Squadron-Leader Tony Hill, flew to reconnoitre the spot and returned delighted with his discovery. It was what he had suspected – a kind of parabolic antenna located 100 yards from the edge of the cliff – 660 feet high at this point – and 1,600 yards south of Cape Antifer, near the valley of Bruneval, which debouches 550 yards farther to the west. Unfortunately, when he tried to develop his photographs, he found to his consternation that the camera had not functioned.

Tony Hill decided to return on the following day. But on arriving at the airfield he learnt that the mission had been entrusted to three of his fellow airmen. Jumping into his machine, he taxied it on to the runway just as the pilots were ready to take off, threatening to shoot them down if he caught sight of them within 20 miles of his objective. He flew to Brunevel and returned this time with perfect photographs.

This took place in December 1941. Operation *Biting* was swiftly staged. It was to be carried out by parachutists. Dropped by Whitley bombers of No. 51 Squadron under Wing Commander Pickard, the skymen found themselves at once on the spot with no difficult problems climbing this formidable cliff. The proximity of the Bruneval gorge would allow them to retire by sea, provided they neutralized the German machine-guns defending the gorge, which could reasonably be attacked from the rear.

The chosen landing area was at Jumel, a few hundred yards inland. It was sometimes used by the Germans as a take-off and landing place for their small Fieseler Storch aircraft. The lighthouse to the north, a large new house adjacent to the radar, and a big farm, Le Presbytère, marked off the sector.

The date had been studied to coincide with the moon and the best tidal conditions. The most favourable nights should have been those of the 24th, 25th and 26th February, but a north-easterly wind sprung up and at the moment chosen for re-embarkation there would have been a big swell running as the tide came in. There was some idea of abandoning the operation and on the 27th, the R.A.F. asked Admiral James if the Whitleys could return to their base. The Admiral was in a quandary. He sent for Lt-Commander Cook, the man in charge of the naval part of the operation. The wind had abated. Would he be content with a tidal timetable less favourable than on the previous day? Cook decided to try and the small flotilla put to sea – two destroyers and two M.G.B.s escorting one L.C.I. (landing craft infantry).

At 2200 hrs. the 70 men, selected from the units which were eventually to form the first British Airborne Division, took their places in the Whitleys under the orders of Major Frost. The key man in the raid was a certain Flight-Sergeant Cox, a radar specialist whose job would be to check the apparatus for the component parts most interesting to capture. He had never jumped before and was airborne for the first time.

Apart from a few minor details the operation took place exactly as it had been planned. From Portsmouth, as can be imagined, Admiral James followed in great excitement the signals from the aircraft announcing between 0200 hrs. and 0300 hrs. the successive drops, all of which, except two, landed in the target area. The surprise element was 100 per cent successful. The Würzburg had signalled the crossing of the Whitleys, but subsequently the radar men lost interest, and by the time they returned the parachutists were already upon them. Cox was able to capture everything of interest, after which the radar was blown up. In the meantime the two groups which had been dropped too far to the south, on the far side of the Bruneval valley, guided by the Antifer lighthouse, attacked the enemy machine-gun posts and reduced them to silence. The group re-embarked almost at full complement, leaving behind only one dead and six missing but bringing back two prisoners.[1]

[1] According to the German reports, the losses were as follows: British, one dead, four prisoners; Germans, two dead, three wounded, four missing.

Three days later the W.110 did not report the raid directed against the Renault factories at Billancourt. Better still, the British now had in their hands all the elements necessary to organize the jamming of the German radar. They could also congratulate themselves on the success which had only been made possible on this inhospitable coast by a happy transport combination – the troops being airborne on the outward journey and seaborne on the return.

The Germans were far from pleased. They accused the 332nd Infantry Division, responsible for this sector, of lack of vigilance and the Navy was only too glad to put on record that defence was the job of the Army, and that as far as they were concerned the alarm had been given with the least possible delay. Where would the enemy strike next? Would he take it into his head to kidnap Admiral Dönitz, the submarine commander, in his headquarters at Kernevel near Lorient? Would he sabotage one of the new submarine bases? The Admiral commanding the Kreigsmarine in France was ordered to redouble his vigilance. Hitler issued a directive – directive No. 40 – enjoining the army commander to give similar orders to all the representatives of the three services.

*   *   *

The enemy was quite right to be suspicious, for the combined operations team was preparing a new coup, which was going to create an infinitely greater stir throughout the world than the Bruneval raid, which had passed almost unnoticed.

On the 27th October, 1941, Admiral Keyes had been replaced at the head of combined operations by a cousin of King George V, Captain Lord Louis Mountbatten, who had recently taken over command of the aircraft carrier H.M.S. *Illustrious*, undergoing repairs in the U.S.A., after surviving the sinking of his destroyer H.M.S. *Kelly* during the operations in Crete.

To stress the importance attached to combined operations and the close collaboration expected from the three services, the new chief – although he was only 43 – received simultaneously some weeks later the rank of temporary Vice-Admiral, honorary Lieutenant General (Divisional Commander) of the ground forces and honorary Air Marshal of the R.A.F.

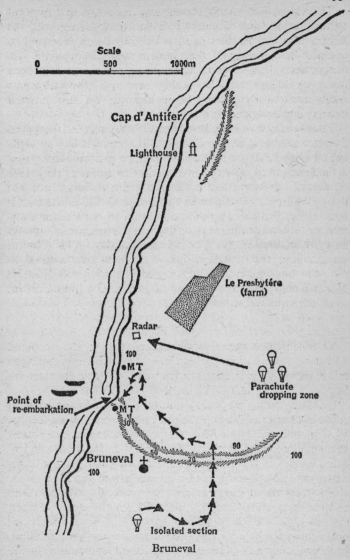

Scale

0   500   1000m

Cap d' Antifer

Lighthouse

Le Presbytère
(farm)

Radar

100

•MT

Point of
re-embarkation

•MT

30

Parachute
dropping zone

Bruneval

100

50

90

100

Isolated section

Bruneval

A British author, whom I must take seriously, since he is a general, insists that Mountbatten was consumed with a desire to wear the three uniforms in turn.[1] But this is a royal prerogative, and would have been tantamount to *lèse-majesté*. The fact remains that his service activities did not slow down – very much to the contrary. A veritable retort in which the most audacious plans were brewed, Combined Operations Headquarters, actively pursued the training of personnel from the three services, in using new weapons designed by its ingenuity. It was responsible for most of the landing-craft and equipment which permitted the invasion of Europe in 1944, and which although built in America, was nearly all the fruit of British genius and of Admiral Mountbatten in particular, because he was quick to enthuse upon an original idea and to champion it vigorously. With so much vigour, in effect, that if we are to believe General Hollis, at that time secretary of the Committee of British Chiefs of Staff, he brought one day into the board-room a lump of ice and a block of frozen cement to show the possibilities afforded by these incongruous materials for shipbuilding. Suddenly jumping to his feet, he pulled out his revolver and fired three bullets at each of them. The bullets scattered in all directions and a terrified orderly raised the alarm in the next office. 'Quick, come quickly, the chiefs of staff are firing at each other!'[2]

[1] Brigadier-General Ferguson, *The Watery Maze*, p. 125.
[2] Lt.-General Sir Leslie Hollis, in the *Journal of the Royal United Services Institution*, 1950, p. 558.
According to another account, the bullets as they ricocheted nearly killed the American Admiral King and Air Marshal Portal.
This crazy story – and the word is justified because its originator spent several periods in a lunatic asylum before committing suicide – was taken sufficiently seriously for a credit of 150,000 dollars to be put at his disposal. Mountbatten, always on the look-out for creative ideas, had sponsored at C.O.Hq. a certain Geoffrey Pyke, who had designed the plans for a two million-ton aircraft carrier, 1,800 ft. long, with a 300 ft. beam and a hull consisting of a 40 ft. thick 'pycrete' caisson, a compound of ice and wood shavings, which was proof against the largest bombs or torpedoes. The idea was born from observing the difficulties encountered by the polar patrols in destroying icebergs with explosives. The addition of sawdust increased even further the resistance of the ice. Under the influence of Mountbatten, Churchill,

Under Keyes, a sailor of the old school, the elaboration of Combined Operations had been conducted in a rather empirical fashion, by personal contacts and due regard for 'the old school tie'. Under Mountbatten things were conducted more methodically.

It was under his direction that the second raid on the Lofotens and the Bruneval affair were staged. The raid on Saint-Nazaire, which took place a month later, on the 27th March, 1942, was far more adventurous in character and employed relatively important means. It was no longer a pinprick, it was a body blow.

The operational plan was very reminiscent of those at Zeebrugge and Ostend under Sir Roger Keyes in the spring of 1918. With the difference that the distance was infinitely greater, for instead of about 100 miles, the raiders had to cover more than 400 from its bases, Falmouth and Plymouth, skirting the coast of Brittany, before reaching the mouth of the Loire. The plan was to immobilize the great lock built for the *Normandie* by demolishing the seaward door and also the pumping station.[1] To ensure its destruction it was planned to

[1] For some reason the British Admiralty believed that the Saint-Nazaire dock was the only one on the French coast capable of housing the *Tirpitz*, should it return from an Atlantic raid with damage received in battle. In actual fact, access to it was not so simple, and one is entitled to wonder whether the Kreigsmarine would have risked a capital ship of the importance of the *Tirpitz* [35,000 tons in theory but actually more than 45,000] in the Loire channel, particularly when burdened by the waterways which could considerably increase its draught.

On the other hand the Admiralty might have deduced from the escape of the German battleships from Brest – an escape that still rankled – that the R.A.F. bombing had rendered this port untenable for large surface ships. In these conditions Saint-Nazaire, much farther away from the R.A.F. bases, remained the only possible shelter for a ship the size of the *Tirpitz* which had just turned up in Norway, and which could be expected any day to try to break through into the Atlantic.

and later Roosevelt, let themselves be persuaded. It was decided that a 1000 ton model should be built in Canada, but the British and American Admiralties intervened, and Operation Habakuk received its death blow, when its most ardent champion Admiral Mountbatten left Combined Operations Headquarters for the Far Eastern sector in August 1943.

launch against its gate the obsolete destroyer H.M.S. *Campbeltown*, stuffed with explosives, exactly as the ancient cruiser H.M.S. *Vindictive* had berthed alongside the Zeebrugge mole on the 22nd April, 1918, in heroic circumstances which have become legendary, returning 15 days later filled with cement to founder across the entrance to the port of Ostend.

It would take too much space to enter into details of this operation about which a great deal has already been written. It served its purpose at the cost of very heavy losses. On the German side, the rather minor initial losses were considerably increased by the delayed explosion of the *Campbeltown* which had been equipped with delayed action fuses. The destroyer blew up at 1145 hrs. on the 28th, several hours after the raid, when numerous Germans were aboard in search of any secret documents the British might have left behind.[1] Unfortunately a great number of French workers, who were employed nearby, were also victims of this explosion.

On the other hand, what interests us most is to discover in what conditions surprise played such a favourable role for the British at Saint-Nazaire, in conditions infinitely more tricky than at Bruneval, and to follow the reactions of the German High Command to avoid any repetitions.

Undoubtedly the surprise attack on Saint-Nazaire caused a certain confusion at all levels of command, even at the Führer's Great Headquarters. A tardy confusion like the delayed action

[1] These were only too numerous, for the British had not learned the art of preserving their secrets as they were to do later. They literally scattered behind them in their retreats the most important documents. Thus in Norway during their retreat from the Gudsbrandal in April 1940, they abandoned all the War Office operational plans, none of which had yet been carried out, so that one might wonder why the expeditionary force had ever been carrying them. This delighted the heart of the German Minister of Propaganda who proceeded to publish a very edifying white paper. At Saint-Nazaire they left behind in the *Campbeltown* all the operational plans, which is even more surprising, since they knew well in advance that the ship was to be sacrificed. The Germans had time to salvage them before the explosion, and at the same time made the uncomfortable discovery that the enemy was in possession of the reconnaissance signals of the German Navy, from the 26th February to the 3rd March. The same stupidity was to occur at Dieppe.

fuses of the *Campbeltown*, for the first reports of the raid did not
arrive until several hours after the British naval force were on
the way back to their bases. The presence of an enemy force
60 miles south-west of Saint-Nazaire was learned at Naval
Headquarters via the radio-telegraphic interception centre,
slightly before 0800 hrs. No one in high places imagined that
this was the assault force on the way home. It was understood
a little later on receipt of the first reports received by
Admiral Lindau, in command of the Atlantic coast, whose
headquarters were at Royan. The more or less mutilated news
sent to the Führer apparently revived in his mind great anxiety
for the safety of Dönitz's headquarters, and he ordered its
immediate transfer far inland. The measure was in any case
being carried out in compliance with directive No. 40, which we
have already mentioned. As a result of this, the commander-in-
chief of submarines promptly left Lorient with his staff and
made his headquarters in Paris, on the boulevard Maunoury,
at the entrance to the Bois de Boulogne.

The reason that the British had profited by total surprise,
was partly because the chain of German coastal radar stations
was still very incomplete, and, in particular, because the short-
age of apparatus on the west front did not allow the regular
picking up of aerial patrols at sea.

But notwithstanding these deficiencies, a fortuitous circumstance should have raised the alarm 15 to 18 hours before the
attack. On 27th March, between 0600 and 0700 hrs., a German
submarine had reported the presence of three destroyers accompanying 10 launches sailing on a westerly course in the
quadrant BF5468. As a result of negligence on the part of the
duty officer – he was subsequently severely reprimanded – this
information was not passed on to Admiral Lindau, to whom it
was of vital interest, until after the start of the attack. Why?
Because the square BF5468 covered the entrance to the Gulf
of Gascony, in other words, precisely in his zone of responsibility, and the presence of these three destroyers and 10
M.T.B.s could not fail to have given him cause for reflection.
It was obviously not a question of a normal convoy. The fact
that it was sailing west proved nothing. No one in wartime
could expect a naval force always to sail a direct course. Was it

simply a convoy escorting forces to Gibraltar ? But such small
craft were not sent on such a long journey, without particular
precautions. In any case, there was a sufficient doubt to alert
the Luftwaffe and to ask for an immediate air reconnaissance.

It was of course the small force en route for Saint-Nazaire
that the submarine had observed. It had merely counted in-
correctly for there were 21 ships and not 13. The submarine
had also been spotted and attacked. No mention of this was
made in its warning message. At 0700 hrs. H.M.S. *Campbeltown*, H.M.S. *Atherstone* and H.M.S. *Tynedale* were steaming
with their M.G.B.s and M.L.s 100 miles south-west of Ushant.
The small craft sported the White Ensign and the three
destroyers were flying the Nazi flag. On seeing the submarine
surface, the *Tynedale* set her course for it, and at a range of
4,000 yards rapidly exchanged the enemy colours for her
national flag – this is the tradition – before opening fire. The
submarine submerged immediately. The *Tynedale* dropped
depth charges. The submarine surfaced to be once more
'plastered' by all the guns of the British destroyer. Twenty
seconds later it disappeared for good and the British were so
convinced that they had sunk it, that Admiral Forbes, the
C.-in-C. Plymouth, in his report attributed to this victory the
fact that the expedition had not been reported, and had thus
preserved the advantage of surprise. We already know what to
think of this.

Besides it is of no importance. The essential is that the surprise element existed and that the operation was successful.
Its hero, Commander Ryder, was awarded the Victoria Cross.
For the Royal Navy, as for the whole of Great Britain, it was a
ray of sunshine in a series of catastrophies which had befallen
the Allies in all the other operational theatres of war. C.O. Hq.
was exultant, and it was in this euphoric atmosphere that the
name of Dieppe was soon to be cast on to the conference table.

But in the German camp there was great despondency and
the Saint-Nazaire raid was to cause a veritable crisis between
the Kriegsmarine and the Wehrmacht. Unfortunately there
was no one competent and expert enough to inform the
Führer in a suitable manner. There were plenty of back-biters
at G.Hq. to run down the Navy, and Hitler was given a few

crumbs. He ordered an inquiry, which Marshal Keitel, chief of the general staff, entrusted to Marshal von Rundstedt, C.-in-C. West, over the head of Raeder, and in terms which put the Grand Admiral into a furious rage. Hence the bitter telegram he sent to Keitel on the 1st April.

Marshal von Rundstedt, a man with a certain sense of etiquette, was quick to proclaim that the Navy had done its duty, and was careful to send Raeder a copy of his report. In the meantime, Keitel replied with great lack of deference, that he had only carried out the Führer's orders, and that if there were any grievances, it was to the Führer that the complaints should be made.

The atmosphere was even more tense because at Saint-Nazaire a part of the population had sided heavily with the commandos, who had been unable to re-embark, and had hidden them in the port. The Army declared a state of siege. There were 80 arrests and several scores of executions, after a summary trial. Calm was not restored until the 31st March.

A veritable procession of V.I.P.s resulted. Keitel had sent his Adjutant General Jodl to the scene, Raeder intended to go in person to find out exactly what had happened. He sent as his deputy Captain Schubert, whose conclusion was that everyone had done their duty. There was, however, one tiresome detail. Captain Kellerman, naval commander at Saint-Nazaire, had been absent on the day of the raid, and his adjutant, a young reserve lieutenant, had not shown himself energetic enough to insist on the towing of the *Campbeltown* from the dock which might possibly have saved the lock gate.

Hitler, however, declared himself dissatisfied with both Rundstedt's first report and with that of the Admiral Frankreich (Naval C.-in-C. for France), which had reached his headquarters. He demanded additional information from Raeder who delivered it on the 16th April. There was definitely something amiss: a naval force dispatched against Saint-Nazaire had been able to remain for 35 hours at sea, to round the occupied coast of Brittany and to approach without being detected.

There was an acrimonious discussion. The Führer examined point by point all the elements of the attack, demanding explanations of the exchange of reconnaissance signals which he criticized, of the long delay which elapsed before the alarm was given, the absence of air reconnaissance, the utilization of searchlights and flares, and the dangers which could threaten other sensitive points in the future, etc. He spared no details.

The crisis of Saint-Nazaire must have left the German High Command in a state of constant anxiety. In the course of the ensuing weeks it caused several security measures to be taken of which we shall tell later.

CHAPTER FOUR

THE LOWEST EBB

THE war had lasted for two and a half years. The military power of the Axis seemed at its zenith in all theatres of war. Germany imposed its will upon Europe. From the Gulf of Finland to the Bidassoa, from the North Cape to the banks of the Vardar, the Wehrmacht had its garrisons. The summer campaign was to take it as far as the peaks of the Caucasus and the banks of the Volga. In Africa, Rommel was preparing to conquer Egypt; in the Atlantic, Dönitz's U-boat commanders had attained – if not exceeded – the result which had allowed their forefathers of 1917 to bring the Entente to the brink of ruin. Over the whole Pacific and as far as the Indian Ocean, the standard of the Rising Sun flew victoriously. The Allies had never appeared to be so near the abyss.

And yet six months earlier, during the last weeks of autumn, 1941, things had not looked so bad. On the eve of the Japanese attack on Pearl Harbour, the German armies actually suffered their first setbacks. During the night of the 5th/6th December, the 3rd and 4th Panzer Armies, having arrived at within 35 miles of the Kremlin, had to break off their attack. On the 6th Marshal Zhukov launched his counter-offensive and the German retreat in Russia began.

At the same moment the counter-offensive launched by General Auchinleck in Libya on the 18th November was developing favourably. On the 5th December, after a grim tank battle, Rommel had to give the order to retreat for the first time since he had been in command of the Afrika Korps. On the 8th December the 8th Army relieved Tobruk, which had been encircled for 240 days.

The very same day, the war in the Pacific started, and the serious reverses suffered by the Allies in the Far East cancelled out the successes which were only temporary. In Russia the Wehrmacht hung on desperately, and without too much difficulty repelled the double offensive of the Russians and of 'General Winter'. In Africa, Rommel, after retreating to El Agheila in the Gulf of the Grand Syrte, suddenly went over to the attack on 18th January, taking advantage of the fact that the Italian Navy had managed to bring him some reinforcements, and that the British had been forced to rob Wavell of part of his forces to send them with all speed to the Far East, where the Japanese onslaught had assumed alarming proportions. Thus the first months of 1942 were extremely anxious ones on all fronts, until the situation began to re-establish itself, when everything might have been considered as lost.

This crisis, of course, did not materialize in a single day, nor did it mature at the same date in all theatres of war. There was no 'turning point in the war' to use that much abused expression; there were in fact half a dozen, 'staggered' in time and space.

At Combined Operations Hq. no account was taken in principle of 'grand strategy'. We shall see elsewhere in action the men who were busy giving the war the direction which seemed to them most favourable. What was demanded of C.O. Hq. was to have ideas and to try and put them into execution. After which it was up to the Supreme Command to choose one out of the bag, and to launch it at what they considered to be the most favourable moment. In the meantime the war went on, and the majority of these plans were shelved before they had even been studied in detail. We shall quote a few which competed with the Dieppe operation, and whose objectives in retrospect give some cause for reflection! What I have endeavoured, above all, is to try and describe as precisely as possible the circumstances in which Operation *Jubilee* was launched – in other words to retrace briefly the general evolution of the battle on all fronts, from the day when the name of Dieppe was broached at C.O. Hq. until the day when Captain John Hughes-Hallett set sail with the small armada, which was to carry the Canadian soldiers and the British commandos to that bloody adventure. In other words, between 3rd April and the 18th August, 1942.

*   *   *

Operations had come to a standstill in Africa at the beginning
of April. Rommel, after pushing the 8th Army back to the
Ain-Gazala-Bir-Hakeim line, had stopped for a breather and
was now squabbling with his superiors, to obtain a few more
divisions with which he proposed in the summer to solve the
question of Egypt and the Suez Canal. In the Mediterranean,
Malta was reeling beneath the blows of the XIth Air Corps
which, since January, had subjected the island to non-stop
bombing. Despite great efforts and considerable sacrifices, the
Royal Navy had not succeeded in supplying the island effectively. Nearly everything which left either from Alexandria or
Gibraltar was sunk within sight of the port or forced to put
about. Of the 26,000 tons of precious supplies which left
Alexandria on the 20th March in four cargo ships, only 5,000
were unloaded on the island. The fruit was ripe to be plucked.
Had Hitler decided to launch the famous operation Hercules
planned for the conquest of Malta, one wonders how the
garrison would have defended itself. . . .

On the eastern front the Russian winter offensive had come
to a halt in mid-February. The Germans had retreated nearly
100 miles, but they had retired in good order, and their lines
had not been broken. For once Hitler had been correct in
giving orders to hold fast, fearing that an officially accepted
withdrawal would have turned into a rout, as had happened
once before to Napoleon's Grande Armée. The time was spent
in re-forming and equipping for the summer offensive. In the
Crimea, General von Manstein was preparing to launch a third
assault on Sebastopol – the Russian Tobruk – which, besieged
since the 20th October, 1941, had already victoriously repelled
two extremely powerful attacks in November and December.
But for the moment calm reigned on the front.

The disaster was in the Pacific and in the Indian Ocean.

Since Pearl Harbor, at lightning speed, the Japanese had
conquered in succession, the Gilbert Islands on 9th December,
occupying Thailand on the same day, Guam on the 10th, Wake
Island on the 23rd, and Hong Kong on the 25th. By the 2nd
January they controlled all the Philippine Islands, except the
few besieged forces which held out in Corregidor. On the 11th,
they started their conquest of the Dutch East Indies which was

completed by the 9th March. On the 22nd January they landed
in New Ireland, on the 23rd in New Brittany and the Solomon
Islands. On the 15th February 80,000 British laid down their
arms in Singapore. On the 8th March the Japanese occupied
Rangoon in Burma and landed in New Guinea; and the 9th
Java surrendered. On the 1st April came the fall of Bataan, the
last American stronghold in the Philippines and also the end of
all resistance in Burma.

Three days later the Japanese navy turned up even farther
afield, bombarding Colombo on the 4th April, and Trincomalee
on the 8th. . . .

Where would this invincible adversary stop? Would he
pursue his advance to the west, conquer India – the frontier
was actually crossed on the 15th May – join hands with the
Axis forces attacking from Libya in the direction of Suez and
the Middle East, from the Russian front to the Caucasus and
Persia?

In actual fact the Japanese advance had spent itself, but no
one was to know this for certain until some weeks later after the
battle of the Coral Sea, which took place between the 4th and
the 8th May, 1942, and in the course of which the American
navy definitely halted the Japanese advance towards Australia;
and then after the battle of Midway (4th to 6th June, 1942),
which decisively put a stop to Japanese expansion eastwards
and to some extent marks the spread of the war in the Pacific.

Grievously damaged by Pearl Harbor, the United States
navy made every effort to restore its fighting strength. The
entire skill of its engineers, the activity of its yards and its
immense industrial potential, were all diverted to this extraordinary effort. But despite the economic potential of a country
like the United States, we are no longer in an age when the
shipwrights of Rochefort could congratulate themselves on
building a vessel in one day. In the course of the six months
which elapsed between Pearl Harbor and Midway, the list of
losses increased, and it was with its remains that the Pacific
fleet won the decisive battle. For this great courage and skill
were needed but also a great deal of luck – luck which could
not have been foreseen a few weeks earlier.

Now the Americans could take a breather and wait until their new ships came into service, which was to allow them, after three years of effort, to reclimb the slope and progressively to invest the Japanese fortress. They had already delivered the first blows by bombing Tokyo on the 18th April – a very modest raid which most of the inhabitants did not really notice, but whose symbolical value and the sporting character of the exploit cannot be denied. Two months after Midway they would be able to undertake the first step towards reconquest by landing General Vandegriff's 1st Division of Marines on the Japanese occupied island of Guadalcanal. This operation took place on the 7th August, 1942, precisely 12 days before the Dieppe raid, giving the signal for a bloody campaign which was to last for six months. It was, however, the first American offensive in the Pacific war and it ended in ultimate victory.

* * *

But the Pacific war was only one panel of the diptych. The Americans and British had agreed that Germany was the more dangerous enemy against which the maximum effort had to be brought to bear. Hitler first! Let's settle with Hitler first! It would be a lengthy struggle.

For just as things appeared to be prospering in the Pacific they blew up in Africa where, on the 27th May, Rommel suddenly went over to the attack on the line Ain-el-Gazala – Bir-Hakeim. The unexpected resistance put up by the garrison of Bir-Hakeim, held by the 1st Free French Brigade (General Koenig) put him in a difficult position for some days, but he finally reduced the garrison on the 11th June. On the 14th the British evacuated their positions at Gazala and Tobruk surrendered on the 21st.

Since the siege of the preceding year, Tobruk had become a symbol of British tenacity. By holding out it had wrecked, at the gateway to Egypt, all Rommel's efforts in 1941. It was thanks to Tobruk that the 8th Army had been able in November to stage an offensive which nearly proved decisive. Its fall caused general consternation in the Allied camp.

Churchill learnt the news in Roosevelt's private office at the White House. Five days later he had to face an infuriated House of Commons in London, which had been called upon to pass a vote of censure. The same day, 26th June, 1942, he summoned Mountbatten, to ask him whether he was in a position to guarantee the success of the operation planned on Dieppe.

'Good heavens, no!' replied Mountbatten.

But we must not anticipate.

Without lingering at Tobruk, Rommel pursued his advance in the direction of the Egyptian frontier, which was crossed on the 24th. Mussolini made preparations to visit Libya in order to enter Cairo on a fine white charger. He actually landed with a large retinue on the 29th on the airfield of Giovanni Berta. Alexandria was in a state of panic. Admiral Harwood ordered the fleet to sail into the Red Sea. Women and children were taken aboard the warships. In Cairo heavy volumes of smoke wreathed the Embassy and the British G.Hq. The American liaison officer left in the night for Khartoum. Everyone believed that Suez would fall. What would happen then? Any developments would be possible.

The New Zealanders, under General Freyberg – a magnificent soldier who had won the V.C. in the First World War – saved the situation by standing firm at El Alamein on the 3rd July, 45 miles from Alexandria. But how long would they be able to hold out? No one could say. The British were forced to send reinforcements via the Cape. The American army bled itself white to send 400 Sherman tanks, whose 400-h.p. engines, injudicially loaded on the same cargo boat, were sent to the bottom by a well-aimed torpedo from the U.161. By scraping the bottom of the American war chest, 400 more were found to replace them; these arrived safe and sound. But in the meantime the anxiety had not been dispelled. A few unfortunate generals were axed. Auchinleck was replaced by General Alexander, C.-in-C. Middle East; Montgomery took over the 8th Army from General Ritchie.

But we are still a long way from describing the true picture of the disastrous situation that faced the Allies in the month of July 1942.

In Russia, as we have already mentioned, the Wehrmacht had suffered a grave setback before Moscow. It had managed to re-form by about the 15th January, and from that date the front had been comparatively calm. The summer offensive was being prepared. It was scheduled for June, but on the 12th May the Russians took the initiative by launching a large scale offensive led by General Timochenko on the Donetz front, north and south of Kharkov. There was some bitter fighting but the Germans won in the long run and managed to encircle three Soviet armies, which left 240,000 prisoners on the battlefield. The German offensive began at the end of the first fortnight of July with prospects which, according to Liddell Hart, had never appeared so brilliant.[1]

The main objective, Stalingrad, could have been taken in a fortnight, practically without a battle, by the 4th Panzer Army . . . when Hitler, who had dominated the situation so masterly during the winter after the setback before Moscow, committed the monumental error of being diverted from his goal, by dispatching to the oilfields of the Caucasus the divisions of General von Kleist who had no need of oil, and whose objectives, strategically speaking, were far less interesting.

But this is immaterial. What matters is, that it is the end of July 1942, at the moment when we are to witness the Dieppe raid planned for the first weeks in July, then abandoned on account of the weather, emerge from its file, this time for good. In Russia the situation was really catastrophic.

Sebastopol had fallen on the 3rd July. Supported by 2,000 aircraft, the armies of Weichs went over to the attack on the Don with Stalingrad as the objective. The Red Army retreated. By the end of July the Wehrmacht occupied most of the Don and Donetz basins. Rostov on the Don fell on the 27th. Germany now controlled 48 million Russians, plus half the mining resources of the U.S.S.R., and was preparing to add the oilfields of the Caucasus to this booty.

'*Der Russe ist tod.*' The Russian is dead, Hitler continued to proclaim. Who would have dared to contradict him? Both in America and Great Britain the military leaders were in agreement that it would be very lucky if Russia managed to stay in the war until the end of 1942. In London there were two schools of thought: either she would be defeated in October, or she

[1] B. H. Liddell Hart, *The Other Side of the Hill*. Cassell, 1951, p. 306.

would hold out until 1943, considerably weakened in men and material.[1]

*   *   *

It should be mentioned that at this period the Western Allies, which to the best of their capability were trying to deliver war supplies by the dangerous Murmansk route, informed Russia that she could no longer count on this co-operation, for which the Red Army had such an urgent need.

The first six months of 1942 had taken a terrible toll of the Allied merchant navies. Under the combined action of U-boats, aircraft, mines and surface raiders, the monthly figure of losses had continued to rise, until at the end of June the catastrophic figure of 834,196 tons from 173 ships had been reached. The total losses for the six months – 4,147,400 tons (989 ships) spoke eloquently enough for the gravity of the situation. According to the statistics of March 1942, the British and Americans lacked more than half the necessary escort forces to defend themselves effectively and everything that could be done to increase the number of escort vessels was obviously at the expense of the landing-craft. These were under construction for the purpose of the cross-Channel landing, which it was hoped to carry out in 1943.[2] It was a vicious circle. For lack of escorts there was a prospect of losing the battle of the Atlantic and in consequence the war against Germany. For lack of landing-craft the European fortress could never be invaded and in consequence liberated.

It was in this dramatic situation that the Allied navies, uncertain as to whether they could ensure the very survival of the British Isles by bringing in American troops and material, had in addition to try and supply the Red Army via Murmansk.

The first convoys had got through, but at the beginning of April, P.Q.13 lost five cargo ships out of 19 to Luftwaffe attacks. Only eight ships out of 23 from P.Q.14 arrived. Another 10 were lost in the two following convoys. But the greatest disaster

[1] Colonel Harrison, *Cross Channel Attack*, p. 24. Office of the Chief of Military History, Washington, 1941.

[2] Cf. Roskill, op. cit., p. 92. The picture given by the author reveals that the Anglo-Americans possessed 505 escort vessels when they needed 1,315.

befell convoy P.Q.17 in July when 23 ships out of 35 were sunk. This was the end. The British Admiralty announced that it could not continue these operations until the long Arctic nights had returned, to extend its protective darkness over these unfortunate ships, which the German pilots and submarine commanders, like a pack of hungry wolves, disputed the right to kill.

We shall see Stalin's view, by studying successively the two main problems which in the spring of 1942 faced the Anglo-Saxon Allies: to maintain Russia in the war at all costs, to avoid the possibility of an entente with Germany, and to determine at what point and with what weapons a foothold in Europe was to be obtained.

CHAPTER FIVE

A DEMANDING ALLY

NEITHER in England nor in France had Russia been in good odour at the beginning of the Second World War. The two Allied governments still smarted under the humiliation of their abortive military treaty, swept away by the signing of the Russo-German Pact of 23rd August, 1939, which had left Hitler free to attack Poland. Then the Russo-Finnish war had roused world opinion against the U.S.S.R. and the highly equivocal attitude of the Communist Party, manifestly directed by Moscow, had scandalized opinion. Even with France out of the game and Great Britain on her own, trying in vain to find the continental ally she had always managed to engage in past wars, it would certainly have surprised the man in the street in England, had he been told that a year later the U.S.S.R. would be associated with the United States and Great Britain in what Churchill in his War Memoirs terms the 'Great Alliance'.

It needed six whole months to change public opinion in Britain. Doubtless, thanks to his profound realism, the average Englishman was fully aware that the Russo-German war constituted an unhoped-for diversion, but many people at the time, such as Lt.-Colonel Moore-Brabazon, Minister of Air-craft Production, considered that the ideal would be to see the German and Russian armies destroying each other, while England conserved her strength to come out as the winner.

These were views he was entitled to hold, but he had no right to express them publicly, as a member of the Government, whom circumstances had made the ally of the Soviet Government.

Doubtless Moore-Brabazon had not considered the matter carefully enough before he spoke. Nevertheless his remarks were recorded by certain American and British newspapers. They caused a fine scandal.[1]

[1] Cf. William Hardy McNeill, *America, Britain and Russia*, Survey of International Affairs, 1939–46. O.U.P., 1953, p. 51.

To sum up, during the first stage of the Russo-German war – and even after Stalingrad – the nightmare of the British Government was to see Stalin come to an agreement with Hitler, either out of self interest or simply because it was a matter of necessity. This seemed particularly plausible in view of the turn of events which had occurred in the summer operations of 1941.

Correspondingly in Russia there would always be the suspicion that the Allies would try to make her bear the whole brunt of the war, a suspicion which was not without foundation, chiefly at the outset, for apart from the Battle of the Atlantic, in the summer of 1941, when the German hordes swept across Russia, the British only had troops engaged in Libya where, let us mention in passing, she relied far more on soldiers from the Dominions than on the men of the British Isles.

It was in this mutual spirit that the pact of 12th July, 1941, was signed, according to which the new Allies would mutually engage not to conclude an armistice or a separate peace unless by common agreement. And while Britain was wondering how she could best bring aid to Russia to prevent her collapse, Stalin began to ask the question which was to poison the relationship between Russia and the West for nearly three years: 'Where d when are you going to open a Second Front in Europe?'[1]

After all, he was not the only one to mention the subject. The headlines of the *Sunday Express* of 6th July, 1941, asked: Where's that Second Front? And the whole Labour Party Press took up the chorus, nearly a fortnight before the question was officially asked by the head of the Soviet Government (18th July, 1941).

Something had to be done. But what? Send troops to fight in Russia? Some thought was given to this, of course, but it appeared impossible before redeeming the mortgage which the Afrika Korps had laid on the Middle East. Send material then? Yes, of course. But we were not particularly rich and how could it be delivered?

[1] Like the landings in North Africa, the invasion of Italy was in Stalin's opinion, nothing more than a diversion. In actual fact he never admitted the existence of a second front, until the landing in Normandy.

America, which was not yet in the war, made a gesture. On the 21st July, President Roosevelt decreed that war material could be sent to the U.S.S.R. on condition that it was paid for in cash. Moreover, America had not very much to deliver. Her rearmament programme had not really got under way, and at the outset it was from Great Britain's meagre reserve stocks that equipment was dispatched to the Red Army.

As for opening a Second Front, no one as yet dreamed of it. The idea was so remote that, in August 1941, at the time of the Atlantic Conference, the British chiefs of staff produced a memorandum which read: 'It is possible that the methods described herewith (bombing, blockade and subversive activities among the conquered European populations) may in themselves force Germany to sue for peace.' In any case the best British strategists considered that it was out of the question to envisage a landing for three years and, if the air offensive proved ineffective, this landing would be pointless.[1]

Stalin did not see things in this light. He had taken it amiss that the famous 'Atlantic Charter' made no mention of the U.S.S.R. Furthermore, the poverty of British aid at the moment of the German Advance on Moscow, provoked a very blunt correspondence between the two heads of state. It can be maintained that in the autumn of 1941 the relationship between the two Allies was at its coldest, when Churchill, aware of the need for producing some concrete testimony, authorized his Minister for Foreign Affairs, Anthony Eden, on the 5th December to promise six R.A.F. squadrons for the Eastern Front, resigned himself the following day to declare war on Finland, which Stalin had been advocating for months, and dispatched Eden on the 7th to Moscow to study on the spot the possibilities of an intervention by British land forces in the Caucasus and on the southern sector of the Russo-German front.

Nothing materialized – except the declaration of war on Finland, which was purely a formality, for on the 7th December the Japanese offensives began from Pearl Harbour to Malaya.

The temperature of the alliance rose a trifle, because the successful defence of Moscow, followed by the Red Army's

[1] McNeill, op. cit., p. 36.

winter counter-offensive, made Russia's needs less pressing.
Besides, America had just entered the war. The U.S.S.R. was
now to benefit by Lease-Lend with repayment five years after
the conclusion of hostilities. The weighty Anglo-Russian
tête-à-tête became a meeting of three – which was less strenu-
ous. Nevertheless, there were plenty of subjects for friction.
The U.S.S.R. refused to declare war on Japan, with whom she
had signed a neutrality pact on 13th April, 1941. She showed
herself adamant on the question of the Polish frontiers, at a
period when Great Britain had not forgotten that she had
entered the war to defend the integrity of Polish territory.[1]

In addition to this Stalin was at pains to let it be understood
that he had not entirely abandoned all idea of a compromise
with Germany. 'The Red Army,' he declared on 23rd February,
1942, 'has no intention of exterminating the German nation
and of destroying the German state.'

A word to the wise! This held good for London as much as
for Berlin. To Hitler, or failing him, to the German people, the
question arose as to whether they were interested in a separate
peace. To the Anglo-Saxons the substance of the declaration
was: 'If you won't play ball with me, I've always one solution,
to come to terms with Hitler.'

Although there was no echo in Berlin, this speech was
perfectly well understood in London and Washington, where
it contributed greatly in promoting the ardour of the planners.
In any case the coincidence is striking, when one studies the
developments of the Allied strategic plans of 1942, which I
propose to summarize in the following chapter. There were also
the repercussions on public opinion; a rare occurrence was
seen – a pro-Communist manifestation on 29th March, 1942,
in Trafalgar Square under the slogan: 'Victory in 1942',
demanding an immediate opening of the Second Front at all
costs. This march received the general approval of the public.

*　　　*　　　*

It was at the precise moment when Stalin uttered his scarcely
veiled threat, that the German aircraft massed on the airfields

[1] This discussion delayed the signing of the Treaty of Alliance
between the U.S.S.R. and Britain until 26th May, 1942.

of the North Cape and the submarines from their northern Norwegian bases, began seriously to harass the Murmansk convoys, while the material piled up for Russia clearly exceeded the capacity of the transports. The arrival of the *Tirpitz* at Trondhjem necessitated a considerable reinforcement of escorts and Churchill was very anxious as to Russian reactions, should he be obliged for one reason or another to interrupt these convoys. Roosevelt on the 3rd May had suggested that the Russians should reduce their demands to a minimum, but three days later a telegram from Stalin reminded the British Premier that 90 ships loaded with very important war materials for Soviet Russia were in Iceland waiting for a British escort.

A few days later, on the 20th May, Mr. Molotov, the Soviet Minister for Foreign Affairs, arrived in London to settle various questions, but above all to find out the date planned for the opening of a Second Front, and the methods the British Government intended to use to force the Germans to withdraw part of their forces from the U.S.S.R.[1] The conversations led to the signing of a formal treaty on the 26th May. It was no more than a favourable gesture. The Russians certainly did not care if circumstances should lead them to seek a compromise with the Germans. Churchill was so well aware of this that he telegraphed to Stalin to congratulate him on this welcome treaty. He did not fail to inform him of the progress of the convoy P.Q.16 which was on the way to Murmansk, and which at the moment was being attacked by the Luftwaffe, with the result that six ships out of the 34 never arrived.

With regard to the Second Front, the British Premier had to use all his eloquence and powers of persuasion to explain to Molotov that there could be no question of one being opened that year. The building of the landing-craft was not sufficiently advanced and, with the stocks at their disposal, they could not possibly in 1942 undertake an action capable of forcing the enemy to withdraw an important part of his land forces from the eastern front.

But this was not the point of view held by the American chiefs of staff with whom the Russian minister was to confer in

[1] Churchill, *War Memoirs*, Vol. IV, p. 350.

Washington a few days later. In the course of a conversation which Molotov had with President Roosevelt, his adviser Harry Hopkins, General Marshall, the chief of the Army General Staff, and General King, C.-in-C. U.S. Navy, the Foreign Minister did not hide his fears that the Red Army would be unable to withstand the German summer offensive unless Great Britain and the United States opened a Second Front, which would force the enemy to withdraw 40 divisions from the East. Were they disposed to do this ? Here he was asking a question to which he had been unable to obtain a categorical reply in London.

Roosevelt was formal. After taking advice from General Marshall, 'the President authorized Mr. Molotov to advise Mr. Stalin that we intend to open a Second Front this year.'

This promise was published in a communiqué from the White House dated 11th June, which stated that complete agreement had been reached on the most urgent need to open a Second Front in Europe. It was a very imprudent communiqué to which the British Government only agreed to subscribe with certain reservations and which was to arouse interminable discussions, often of the most acrimonious nature.

In the circumstances, the Americans had incontestably shown themselves far more disposed to issue a pledge than their British Allies. They had reinforced this promise by a tangible proof of their goodwill. By a decision taken on the 11th June, Roosevelt cancelled the clause obliging Russia to repay the lease-lend consignments five years after the war. From this point of view the Russians now found themselves treated as generously as the British.

There is no doubt that this American complacency enabled Stalin to take a tougher stand against Churchill. And then, after a few weeks, came blow after blow in quick succession – the fall of Tobruk on the 21st June, the fall of Sebastopol on the 23rd July, followed by the disaster of P.Q.17 to which we have already referred. The Admiralty chiefs declared that they would have to postpone the Murmansk convoys until the return of the long polar nights. Churchill asked them, in spite of this, to send P.Q.18, with a formidable escort. The two battleships, H.M.S. *Nelson* and H.M.S. *Rodney*, four combat aircraft carriers, five escort carriers, and a permanent air umbrella of 150 fighter aircraft. . . .

The Admiralty refused to be convinced and, on 17th July, Churchill was forced to send Stalin a long telegram in which he tried to explain the impossible conditions under which the convoys sailed, and the imperative necessity which had forced him to cancel the sailing of P.Q.18.

Stalin replied curtly on the 23rd, that he was forced to point out that, *firstly*, the British Government refused to send war material by the northern route and, *secondly*, despite the communiqué concerning the need for opening a Second Front in 1942, it was postponing its realization until 1943.[1]

This was completely unjust. In particular, by agreeing to subscribe to the communiqué of 11th June, Churchill had expressly said in a memorandum that he could make no promises in this respect. He decided not to reply, but three weeks later on 12th August, he was in Moscow with a rather cantankerous Stalin to whom once more it had to be explained in a *tête-à-tête*, why it was impossible to open a Second Front in France that year. It was a disagreeable discussion. After an oppressive silence, Stalin declared that: 'If we could not carry out a landing in France this year, he was not qualified to demand it with insistence, but that he was obliged to tell me that he did not subscribe to my arguments.'[2]

The following day he published a memorandum that: 'The refusal of the British Government to create a Second Front in Europe in 1942 has dealt a mortal blow to the whole of Soviet public opinion, which is counting on the creation of this Second Front.'

In the course of staff conversations, which took place on the 15th August, the British general, who had accompanied Churchill, continued to receive the single reply: 'A Second Front *immediately*.' And as a final touch to his courtesy, Stalin, referring to P.Q.17, asked Churchill next day if the British Navy really had a sense of honour.[3]

---

[1] Churchill, op. cit., Vol. IV, p. 286.
[2] Churchill, op. cit., p. 73.
[3] Churchill, op. cit., p. 91.

Nevertheless a joint communiqué was published after Churchill had left on 16th August. It dealt with a certain number of decisions taken with regard to the war, against Hitler Germany and her satellites.

Three days later the Dieppe raid took place.

The association was too tempting. German propaganda was quick to exploit this. It exaggerated, of course, by presenting the raid as an invasion which had been repelled. But was it so grossly mistaken, as it was hastily declared in London, that Churchill's visit to Moscow was tied up with that of the Canadians to the French coast?

CHAPTER SIX

WHERE TO RESUME THE OFFENSIVE?

IT was perhaps paradoxical to make offensive plans when we did not know where the Japanese would be halted; whether we could maintain a foothold in the Middle East, or how the Red Army would cope with the summer offensive of the Wehrmacht. But it was indispensable if we wished one day to regain the initiative.

'My centre is broken, my wings are retiring, I am going to attack!'

But when and where? This was the question. The British and American leaders were agreed on the principle of 'Hitler first'. However great the threat of the Japanese advance in the Pacific, it was the Nazis who represented the most dangerous enemy, and the one which had to be beaten first. But from there to launch an adventure at the end of 1941. . . . We could never survive the ordeal of a second Dunkirk, and that is precisely what we should have exposed ourselves to, had we tried to cross the Channel prematurely to establish a bridgehead on the enemy occupied coast.

For British strategy there was only one rational solution. To wear Germany down by the blockade, by bombing and peripheral attacks, staged by the commandos, until her military power was sufficiently weakened. Then, and only then, could they cross the water to deliver the coup de grâce – if this were neccessary.

The Americans were bolder. Possibly because they had not, like their Allies, preserved the bitter memory of contact with the German army. Perhaps, too, because they were not yet fully aware of the magnitude of the means, in men and material, which would have to be assembled before such an enterprise could be launched. They did not yet possess these means. The only trained divisions were those that formed the meagre British reserves. No doubt that the English would have had to bear the entire brunt of an attempted invasion carried out at the beginning, in other words in the spring or summer of 1942.

The different views clashed at the so-called Arcadian Conference on the 22nd December, 1941, on the initiative of Churchill. The American army point of view, represented by General Marshall, was a formal confirmation of the principle 'Hitler first'. The naval viewpoint expressed by Admiral King was slightly different. It was against Japan that the United States navy had prepared before the war, and Pearl Harbor had to be avenged. But Roosevelt, despite his sympathies for the navy, of which he had been Under-Secretary for State under Wilson, supported the military point of view, being convinced himself that Germany was enemy No. 1. The British had no problems of this type to resolve, but ambitions were for the moment modestly confined within the bounds we already know.

Meanwhile the hour of great strategic decisions had not yet arrived. America had only been in the war a fortnight, and mobilization had only just got under way. No one in Washington had as yet been able to formulate any plans in black and white. As a first step – which was carried out without delay – it was decided to send American troops to Northern Ireland. They would complete their training there, and would serve as a relief for the defence of Great Britain, thus releasing a certain number of British divisions for service overseas.

The British, on the other hand, had something to offer. In their opinion the encirclement of Germany had to be completed by the occupation of the North African coast, with or without the consent of the French Government. This was Operation *Gymnast* which could apparently be launched in the spring of 1942.

Marshall having nothing better to offer, accepted without much enthusiasm. Roosevelt seemed intrigued. There remained the question of means. More than ever now, American industry had to prepare to act as the arsenal of the democracies. All resources were pooled and a combined Anglo-American staff was created to carry out the formidable task which lay ahead.

Three months passed. Things, as we have seen, went badly. In Washington a newly promoted, and completely unknown general, was working under Marshall's orders to draw up the plans of war. His name was Dwight D. Eisenhower, and the British proposals only half satisfied him. With his team, he took it upon himself, by a process of trial and error, to find out which was the best theatre of war in which to intervene, to beat the Germans as quickly as possible and at the least cost. In succession plans for attacking through Norway, through Spain, across the Mediterranean or simply by air, were abandoned one by one. Only one satisfied him – a landing on the French coast of the Channel – as being the most direct method of piercing the heart of Germany, and the shortest road to victory.[1]

That this plan at the same time satisfied the Soviet demand for a Second Front was, in Eisenhower and his subordinates' minds, merely a happy coincidence. It seemed to them the best from purely military considerations, and it was in this spirit that they presented it to the chiefs of staff and to President Roosevelt. The latter was not particularly impressed, but Marshall and Hopkins were able to convince him.[2] The plan was accepted on 1st April, April Fool's Day, but as McNeill remarks maliciously, this Easter egg was to be short-lived.

Marshall and Hopkins flew to London on the 4th April to defend the plan before Churchill and the British leaders, with whom they hoped to achieve the same success as they had achieved with Roosevelt.

It is simple coincidence, as we know, but interesting all the same for the subject we are discussing, that at this precise moment the name of Dieppe cropped up for the first time on the desks of the officers of Combined Operations Hq. A second coincidence – the Japanese had just made a new leap – westwards this time. The Indian frontier menaced, Ceylon bombed, where would they be halted? Would they reach Suez before the Afrika Korps?

I am not exaggerating. This view was current at that moment, perhaps not in Tokyo, but certainly in Berlin and also in London, where the meeting between Marshall and Hopkins with Churchill on the 8th April, was clouded by the evocation of recent or past reverses and by the gravity of the situation in

[1] McNeill, op. cit., p. 71.
[2] Sherwood, Vol II, p. 81.

the Indian Ocean.[1] Next day news arrived of the loss of the aircraft-carrier H.M.S. *Hermes*, destroyed by Japanese aircraft off Ceylon.

In other words the atmosphere was not particularly favourable for the plans put forward by the Americans. In retrospect it must be recognized that this plan for landing across the Channel, whether in the nature of a large-scale operation (*Round-up* or *Bolero*) or a more limited undertaking, such as Operation *Sledgehammer* which merely envisaged a bridgehead in Brittany or the Cotentin peninsula, was no more than a pipe-dream in the conditions reigning at that moment.

'An attack across the Channel,' declared General Brooke, 'could only end in death, capture or ignominious re-embarkation of all the forces engaged. It would bring no relief to Russia by forcing the enemy to withdraw troops from the Eastern Front. There were already 25 German divisions stationed in France and the Low Countries. Even if the aircraft and the landing-craft were available, Great Britain had only ten trained divisions to operate on the Continent, and until the autumn the Americans could only spare two.'

The Germans laughed at the idea. Not that there were any leakages with regard to the subject under discussion – at least there has been no proof of this – but simply because they were right in their suppositions. 'Roosevelt,' declared the announcer of Radio Paris, 'has given Hopkins and Marshall full powers to provide Great Britain with all the help she might need, to try a second Narvik – *which risks ending in a second Dunkirk.*'[2]

After ten days' discussion, Churchill eventually gave his consent, convinced as he wrote 'that the study of the details (special landing-craft, etc.) and even an intensive examination of the overall war strategy would lead to the abandonment of *Sledgehammer*.'[3] With regard to his Allies, he was playing a double game – let us make a mental note – which would infuriate the Americans as soon as they became aware of it. On the

---

[1] Cf. Churchill, IV, p. 336. Roosevelt also admitted that *a priori* the eventuality of a Nippo-German conjunction in the Middle East could not be excluded. (Ibid.) p. 339.

[2] Quoted by Sherwood, 291 (my italics).

[3] Churchill, Vol. IV, p. 342.

other hand, however, the British Prime Minister had good reason for considering that an invasion would be impossible before 1943. He would have certainly been more relieved to act in North Africa or in Norway.

In view of this, the Dieppe raid which was now being seriously considered by Admiral Mountbatten, would not fit too badly into the picture, even if only to show the Americans and the Russians who were both pressing him, although for different motives, that something had to be done but that it was not so easy to set foot on an enemy-defended coast.

But this is only a hypothesis.

In short, to return to Operation *Sledgehammer*. Hopkins and Marshall returned to America, apparently convinced that their proposals had been accepted *en bloc*. In any case, Marshall calculated that it was now necessary to take the English at their word.[1]

This was the position when Molotov visited London and Washington, and it was on the strength of this assurance that Roosevelt made the promises we have mentioned to the Russian minister. Nevertheless, on the 28th May, Churchill had sent a rather disturbing cable to Roosevelt, announcing the immediate arrival of Mountbatten, whom he had briefed to explain to the American president the difficulties of 1942, to discuss a possible landing in Norway and to refresh his mind on Operation *Gymnast* (N. Africa). In actual fact the British had no wish to carry out *Sledgehammer*, the principle of which they had only accepted on one of the two following conditions:

If the situation on the Russian Front threatened an immediate collapse of Soviet resistance unless an Anglo-American attack in the west could diminish the German pressure in the east.

(a) In this case the attack could be considered as a sacrifice for the common cause.

[1] As McNeill so justly remarks, in 1942 *Sledgehammer* had every chance of being a costly failure, but, whatever the cost, the operation would in any case relieve the pressure which the German army was exercising on the Russian front. If the Red Army collapsed at Stalingrad it was obvious that a landing in 1943 would present even greater difficulties than in 1942.

(b) If the German situation in the west became so weakened that it would be a pity not to profit by it.

The latter hypothesis seemed very improbable. So long as the former was not confirmed, London would continue to raise objections. This emerges clearly from Admiral Mountbatten's remarks on his visit to Washington to discuss landing-craft, immediately after Molotov's departure, and even more from those of Churchill who arrived on the 18th June. Three days later came the fall of Tobruk. Bad news continued to arrive at an acccelerated tempo, and at the same time Anglo-American differences on the conduct of the war assumed the proportions of a grave crisis – the gravest perhaps of the whole war. Eisenhower, who had just arrived in London to take over command of the American forces in Europe, came up against a blank wall each time he tried to discuss a landing in Europe with his British colleagues. His adjutant, General Mark Clark, was grilled for a whole weekend at Chequers by Churchill in person. Finally, on the 8th July, the British chiefs of staff officially informed their American partners that the affair must definitely be abandoned.

Washington reacted violently. If this is the case, argued the American chiefs of staff, then the only thing to do was to let the English deal with Hitler in Europe and they would devote themselves entirely to the war in the Pacific.

Roosevelt had to use his tact to smooth matters over. After five days' reflection he sent for Hopkins on the 15th July, to impart the gist of his deliberations. Admittedly the position adopted by the British Government by no means satisfied him. However, if the blow against Germany in Europe had to be renounced for that year, the Pacific did not offer the best solution until the American fleet had been considerably reinforced – which demanded time. It was impossible to break with the British. He sent Marshall and Hopkins back to London, this time supported by Admiral King. They were to make sure that the British decision was really without appeal, after which they were to propose some plan for the Middle East or North Africa. The main thing was to reach a prompt decision.

Thus, despite a last offensive on the part of Eisenhower in

favour of *Sledgehammer*, preference was given to North Africa, to Operation *Gymnast*, later rechristened *Torch*.

On the 24th July Roosevelt cabled his definite acceptance. The die had been cast. France was not to be invaded that year. Eisenhower was so disappointed that he is reported to have said that this decision might ultimately turn out to be one of the blackest days in history. Nor was there to be a landing in Norway, as Churchill would have liked, because he favoured a plan devised to capture the North Cape airfields, from where the Luftwaffe harassed the Murmansk convoys. 'He saw in this the possibility of opening a second front for the Russians, of protecting the Arctic convoys and of impressing Sweden and Finland. In this way the victorious British, advancing gradually southwards by climbing in succession all the Norwegian mountain chains, would begin to roll up from the top the Nazi map of Europe.'[1]

He defended his idea for six weeks without managing to arouse the least enthusiasm. *Jupiter* – this was the name of the plan – was relegated to the waste-paper basket to join *Imperator*, another stillborn plan, so extravagant that one hesitates to believe that it could ever have been taken seriously, had Churchill himself not devoted a long note to it on the 8th June, 1942.[2]

It was a question, no more nor less, of replacing *Sledgehammer* and responding at the same time to Russia's call for help by landing a division and some armoured units on the Continent to wreak the greatest damage possible for two or three days, and to be re-embarked later – at least what remained of it. There was even talk of pushing on to Paris to raid the headquarters of the *Militärbefehlshaber in Frankreich*, on the Place de l'Opéra.

Even Churchill, that fearless character, found this a slightly tall order. He interred it without discussion.

Nevertheless, one cannot fail to observe certain points of resemblance between this fantastic project and that which was to be carried out at Dieppe in a few days' time. By and large, Operation *Jubilee*, as will be seen, was only *Imperator* on a

[1] Alan Brooke, quoted by Bryant, *The Turn of the Tide*.
[2] Cf. Churchill, IV, p. 65.

small scale. Both of them responded to political necessities, admitted in the case of *Imperator* and easy to perceive in the case of *Jubilee* – for was not Dieppe the nearest seaport to Paris ? The same conception from the R.A.F. point of view – to provoke the German fighter arm. Even to the use of tanks, envisaged for the first time for a landing. . . .

* * *

In the course of these three chapters I have tried to compile a balance sheet of the three main elements of the crisis of summer, 1942, such as it presented itself to the Allies: the gravity of the military situation in all theatres of war; the permanent obligation to aid Russia, and the imperative necessity of reconciling conflicting points of view in order to work out a common strategy. It was in this fluid atmosphere that the idea of Dieppe took shape; that it was once decided and then abandoned before being re-adopted to the full in circumstances which one has to admit, according to an expression in common usage today, entailed a certain amount of wishful-thinking.

Dieppe was not improvised in a moment of rashness, since the preparations had been under way for four months before the operation was finally decided upon. But although the circumstances of this decision are known, there has always been extreme discretion in Great Britain as to the exact motives which gave rise to it. A thousand reasons – too many perhaps – have been put forward to justify it on the military plane. It has been made out to be a costly but indispensable preliminary to the Normandy landings. Everyone agrees that politics played no part, and that it had nothing to do with the Soviet demand or the vicissitudes of the American Alliance. . . .

This may be true, since they affirm it, but one would like an explanation as to why it was necessary to lose 3,250 men and an important amount of war material to discover that tank tracks function badly on pebbles, or that it is difficult to force an entry into a ravine when the enemy commands the heights above it.

I say this more willingly than other greater men than myself who have written before me, and I shall be content to quote Field-Marshal Montgomery: 'Without a doubt the lesson of

Dieppe made an important contribution to the preparation of the landing which took place in Normandy on the 6th June, 1944. But the price of this lesson was heavy in killed and prisoners. I believe that we could have obtained the information and the experience we needed without losing so many magnificent Canadian soldiers.'[1]

[1] Field Marshal Montgomery. *Memoirs.*

CHAPTER SEVEN

WHY DIEPPE?

South of the mouth of the Somme, from the village of Ault of de la Cap Hève, the shore is formed of uniform chalky cliffs.

... When a south-westerly or north-easterly gale is blowing, particularly with a lee current, the whole coast is unapproachable. There are no anchorages.

French Instructions to Mariners.

'THE most interesting feature of the meeting between chiefs of staff this morning,' General Alan Brooke noted on the 13th May, 1942, 'was the examination of a bold raid planned in the neighbourhood of Dieppe. In the old days, when I crossed regularly from Newhaven to Dieppe, I could never have imagined that I would be studying an operation of this nature.'

As opposed to his chief, Brooke[1] had no sympathy for enterprises of this type. 'This spring,' he notes elsewhere in his diaries, 'the Prime Minister's appetite for rash expeditions has been whetted by three brilliant commando raids organized by Mountbatten's staff, one of which succeeded in blowing up the main lock gate of the submarine naval base at Saint-Nazaire.'

On the 5th May, he wrote to General Wavell: 'It is a very hazardous and difficult undertaking to try and control Churchill's initiatives.' On the 6th he resolutely opposed the dispatch of the Brigade of Guards against the island of Alderney. This project, which had been on the stocks since March, under the title Operation *Blazing*, envisaged the use of a few tanks and slightly more than 2,000 troops. Preparations were

---

[1] General Sir Alan Brooke, commanding the British Home Forces in the spring of 1941, had replaced General Dill as chief of the General Imperial Staff. He was later made a field-marshal and given a knighthood. He took the title Viscount Alanbrooke. I have retained here the name he bore at the period.

well advanced but Brooke won the day, heavily supported incidentally by Air Marshal Harris of Bomber Command, who threatened to resign. *Blazing* was abandoned with the promise that something else would be undertaken. This 'something else' was Dieppe.

It was impossible to remain idle. Not to mention the political and psychological factors we have discussed in the preceding chapter, there was a need to occupy the unoccupied soldiers in Great Britain. On this point, British and American historians are unanimous.

'The plan was accepted by the High Command for the reason which so often leads the "top brass" to accept the suggestions of their subordinates: not to discourage initiative, not to allow inactivity to undermine the morale of the troops, and to give a few formations their first battle experience,' writes the American Vagts.[1]

'Idleness in war can destroy the morale of the finest units, and the desire to help Russia fitted in well with the need to find active employment for these fine but as yet untried soldiers,' agrees the Englishman Roskill.[2]

The War Office, too, considered it essential to gain experience from a 'live raid', carried out on an enemy held coast before staging a full scale invasion. Let us add to this the desire to experiment, under fire, with the new material specially designed for attacks from the sea and, in parenthesis, of seizing the German landing-craft, 40 of which were believed to have been in the port since the days when the Germans flirted with the idea of invading England.

It is true that, in the summer of 1940, the Kriegsmarine had sent to Dieppe, for transformation into landing-craft, a certain number of the large barges which ply the canals of northern France. There were still about a score left in April 1942 but, as a particularly well informed inhabitant of Dieppe assured me – he acted as interpreter to the German Navy – there was no material of interest in the port in the summer of 1942.

After a week of discussion, writes Commander Roskill, it was decided in April that Dieppe alone afforded a military target

[1] Vagts, p. 700.
[2] Roskill, II, p. 240.

worthy of consideration. Into the bargain a radar station, the airfield, four heavy batteries and the port and naval installations could be destroyed; the loss of which would be more or less felt by the enemy.

Dieppe was also interesting from another point of view. It was within reach of the fighter squadrons based on the airfields of southern England, and the British had had plenty of opportunity to learn to their cost that air cover was an essential condition of all combined operations. Moreover the R.A.F. saw in this plan a chance of provoking the Luftwaffe into what they considered would be the greatest 'dogfight' since the Battle of Britain.

It is remarkable in any case, as the official historian of the Canadian army, Colonel C. P. Stacey remarks, that although the details of the Dieppe operation are today equally well known on the English and German sides, the documentation is very poor with regard to its origins and targets. For security reasons, no records were kept of the preliminary conversations, and historians have to base their findings on testimonies published subsequently in the memoirs of the leading actors, or collected from those who took part in the raid. A letter from Lord Louis Mountbatten, however, addressed to the committee of the chiefs of staff on the 11th May, 1942, relates that:

'Apart from the military objectives the operation will be of great training value for *Sledgehammer* or any other major operation, in so far as the actual assault is concerned. It will however throw no light on the problem of how to hold the breaches.'[1]

And finally, continues Stacey, it was an opportunity to hold an important debate on future invasion plans. Departing from the premise that it was essential to capture at an early date an important port, was it better to attack it frontally, or to land on either side at the risk of allowing the enemy sufficient time to destroy port installations, which could perhaps have been taken intact by a direct assault?

On this point at least the experience gained at Dieppe was inadequate, for three months later at Oran and at Algiers the

[1] Stacey, *Six Years of War*. Ottawa, 1955.

British insisted, in the face of American opposition, in staging a frontal attack on the ports to prevent their destruction. The cost at Oran was more than 200 dead, sacrificed in vain, and the loss of two sloops; at Algiers 100 prisoners and one destroyer for absolutely no results.[1]

*   *   *

In short, however justified these various considerations may appear, they do nothing to change the exceptionally unfavourable geographical conditions for the chosen battlefield. Let us recall Saint-Valery! And yet in 1940 Rommel's artillery had only time to rush up their guns and machine-guns to the cliff. They occupied only one of the heights commanding the beach and the port – the cliff below Saint-Valery and the cliff above Veules. This had sufficed to bar a passage to the encircled Allied troops.

Nor was it any longer a question of fortuitous emplacements. In two years the enemy had had plenty of time to post his shore batteries, and to install his defences at the entrance to passages that could be used for marching inland from the beaches. It had become, as has already been written, an iron coast, and it was obvious that the first soldier who set foot ashore would be treated in the same way as the unfortunate lieutenant whose misadventures I have related at the beginning of this book. Presumably there was no officer at Mountbatten's Hq. with sufficient curiosity to find out what had happened on this shore in 1940.

Again, at the moment of the Saint-Valery-en-Caux tragedy the weather was extremely favourable. A calm sea, no wind and no ground swell. Possibly a little fog, if we are to credit the British reports, which endeavoured to find some cause for the setback of the attempted evacuation. The French do not mention the fact.

In any case, such favourable weather is exceptional on this coast where the prevailing south-west or north-westerly winds

[1] Cf. Samuel E. Morrison, *Operations in the North African Waters*, p. 295. It is only fair to state that at Safi a similar operation met with complete success, but here the Americans profited by complete surprise and met practically no opposition.

whip up a swell as soon as they reach Force 3, in other words not an excessive strength.[1] As soon as they exceed this force the coast is practically unapproachable, particularly when the wind is blowing against the tide. In an average south-easter, an entrance to Fécamp is almost impossible, and to Dieppe a tricky proceeding.

Even in the summer months, it had to be recognized that the conditions necessary for carrying out the plan, from the nautical point of view, obtained only on an average two days a month.

But, it will be asked, what remained comparable with Dieppe, as easy to reach and to protect with fighter cover ? Not very much, admittedly. Cherbourg, a naval port, was too big a mouthful to swallow. This idea had been given up at the moment when *Sledgehammer* was abandoned. Caen, already farther away for the R.A.F., was situated too far inland. Le Havre was too big for the scale of raid which had been planned. Fécamp, on the other hand, was too small and in this respect the same objection could be raised to Dieppe, with the aggravating circumstance that the cliff there is even higher – 400 feet at Cape Fagnet. . . . And what of Boulogne ? Impossible, because of the long-range guns posted a few miles north of the town, 380 mm. batteries at Hazinguezelles, etc., barring the approaches to the coast for a radius of 25 miles.

In Brittany, apart from Brest, there was only St. Malo. Not only was this port much farther away for the air force, but its approach from the sea presented great difficulties, because it was closely commanded by the Channel Islands. There is no doubt that, in the last analysis, Dieppe was the sole objective corresponding to the target that had been fixed – a port of average importance, lying on the actual coast, which could be reached by sea within a few hours. The choice would have been perfect had the shore not presented the geographical peculiarities to which we have referred, or if the plan of operations, a repetition on a ten times larger scale to the one that had succeeded perfectly at Bruneval, had included a vast airborne landing preceding the maritime landing, destined to occupy the German defences established on the heights

[1] According to the Beaufort scale, the winds are classed from 1 to 12, Force 3 representing little more than a stiff breeze.

dominating the ports and commanding all the neighbouring indentations in the great Normandy cliff.

In default of an airborne operation, a landing from the sea should have been preceded by a powerful bombardment by big naval guns or by R.A.F. bombers. But a certain number of reasons opposed such a solution. To begin with the Royal Navy did not feel inclined to expose its big battleships to the risk of mines and bombs. Secondly, there was some doubt about the efficiency of firing from the sea against coastal fortifications.

Today we have become familiar with the numerous amphibian operations carried out in the Pacific, Africa and Europe. On several occasions during the Second World War the powerful artillery of the ships of the line, and even the lighter fire from cruisers and destroyers, intervened effectively against the land. But all these operations were subsequent to the Dieppe raid. In 1942, the most recent experiencies gained on intervention of this type dated back to the Dardanelles expedition of 1915. As is common knowledge, this expedition turned out to be a costly setback, and since then the view which prevailed in all naval schools of war was that 'the sea can do nothing against the land when well defended'. As the official historian of the Royal Navy writes:[1] '. . . long experience of engaging coast defence with warships' guns had not generally produced happy results.'

There were certain inconveniences about the preliminary bombing from the air, which might have facilitated matters. It would obviously inflict heavy losses on the civilian population. It would prematurely alert the enemy. There was a risk of pulverizing the buildings on the Dieppe front to a mass of rubble, as insuperable for the tanks as the obstacles which they were trying to destroy. And finally, taking into consideration the narrowness of the space separating the high tide line from this row of buildings, it would be necessary to cease this

[1] Roskill, *The War at Sea*, II. p. 241.
The British historian has not mentioned the precedent of the beach at Diego-Suarez where the British landed on the 5th May, 1942, to take the place from the rear, which was in fact defended by only a few mines.

bombing at the moment the troops landed, so as not to kill our own men.

To sum up, a perfectly defended port, closely dominated by cliffs, was to be attacked without a preliminary bombardment either from the air or from the sea, to neutralize its defences. All that remained was to neutralize the latter. This could only be achieved with an airborne landing or, in the last resort, with commando landing from the sea, in conditions of total surprise, which it was difficult to guarantee in advance.

This is why the first plan for the Dieppe raid, *Rutter*, envisaged as its first stage an airborne operation against the big batteries defending the town and the port. In the case of Dieppe this was certainly the best procedure. It is impossible to be wise after the event, but one wonders to what extent, by examining the facts, better results could not have been obtained and those Canadian lives spared which were to be so extravagantly sacrificed on the 19th August, 1942.

CHAPTER EIGHT

WHY THE CANADIANS?

BECAUSE the Canadians were bored. ... They had been in England for two and a half years. To be more exact the 7,449 officers and men, representing the first detachment of the 1st Canadian Division had landed in Great Britain on the 13th November, 1939. They had come to fight and for 30 months had seen nothing but training camps. A score or more had received their baptism of fire – naturally I am not talking about the stray bullets from the air battle over Britain – and for the remainder, the war had been a long series of disappointments.

Let us examine the position.

On the 26th September, 1939, the Canadian Minister for Defence had agreed to send to Great Britain a military mission to arrange the participation of the Canadian army in the war. The head of this mission was Brigadier-General H. D. Crerar. It was he who was to liberate Dieppe on the 31st August, 1944, at the head of the 1st Canadian Army ... but we must not anticipate.

The 1st Canadian Division, commanded by General McNaughton, was initially to form part of the third contingent of the B.E.F., engaged on the French front on the left flank of the 1st French Army. But events were to prove otherwise.

In actual fact, long before this movement could be carried out, the Germans invaded Norway on the 9th April, 1940, a few hours before the Allies who, for their part, had envisaged a similar operation. It was necessary to stage a counter-offensive immediately which included, among other plans, an attack on the port of Trondhjem by the 2nd Canadian Brigade under Colonel E. W. Sanson. The two best-trained battalions of this force – 1,300 men in all – left Aldershot camp in high spirits for Dunfermline, where they were to hold themselves in readiness to sail at any moment.

But on the 19th April the plan to attack Trondhjem was abandoned. The Canadians were kept for some days at Dunfermline with the idea that they might be sent to fight at Narvik. But they were sent back on the 26th April to the dreary Aldershot barracks. Two of their comrades, who happened to speak Norwegian, were posted as interpreters to a Yorkshire regiment with which they went into action near Donbas, and were nearly captured in the hasty retreat from Andalsnes.

It was an abortive coup. But the German offensive on the West Front, which was launched 15 days later, could not fail, they thought, to provide other occasions for 15,000 fighting men kicking their heels for six months in England waiting to cross to France with the 4th British Corps which, according to the plans, was to reinforce, at the end of the summer, the three army corps already affected to the B.E.F. In actual fact, on the 23rd May, General McNaughton was hastily summoned to the War Office by the British Minister for War. The situation was very serious. Three days before, the German armour had reached the sea at the mouth of the Somme. The B.E.F. was cut off from its bases; the Brigade of Guards, landed the previous night to reinforce Boulogne, was re-embarking in the worst conditions under enemy fire. The Canadian general was asked to prepare one of his brigades to sail from Dover with the least possible delay, to be transported to Calais, or possibly Dunkirk, to try and re-establish the lines of communication of the British Expeditionary Forces somewhere between Hazebrouck and Armentières.

The same evening McNaughton went aboard the destroyer H.M.S. *Verity*, which landed him at Calais.

The 10th Panzers had launched their attack the same morning and the battle was raging. It appeared very difficult to land reinforcements, and even more difficult to send them to Hazebrouck, since the Germans had completely invested Calais. McNaughton re-embarked in H.M.S. *Verity* which landed him at Dunkirk about 0330 hrs. on the morning of the 24th, after having fortunately escaped several aerial attacks. After discussing the situation with Admiral Abrial, C.-in-C. Northern Naval Forces, entrusted by General Weygand with the defence of Dunkirk, the Canadian general reported to the

War Office that his men could in fact be used on the spot to re-inforce the defence. After which he travelled to Dover where the first units of the Canadian division were beginning to assemble.

In the meantime, the War Office had seriously considered whether it was intelligent to fling these Canadian battalions in the midst of a host of more or less demoralized soldiers and a mass of even more demoralized civilian refugees. The idea was abandoned.

Two hours later there was a counter-order. General Gort, commanding the B.E.F. had asked for a Canadian brigade to defend the Dunkirk bridgehead, and it was decided that the units intended for Calais should sail on the night of the 26th/27th.

Nor did they sail this time, for the evacuation was in full swing, and grave fears were nursed as to the fate of the troops already engaged. It was ridiculous to send new units which would have to be re-embarked almost as soon as they landed. As General Dewing[1] wrote to the officer commanding the 1st Canadian Division, 'the occasion for utilizing your division will soon arise, but it must occur in conditions which will allow it to play an effective part, as hazardous as you like, but at least in acceptable military conditions.'

It was hoped to find these acceptable conditions, which neither the Norwegian campaign nor the Battle of Flanders had provided, in the Battle of France which opened the following day with the evacuation of Dunkirk. The 1st Canadian Division was incorporated with the 2nd B.E.F. which was preparing to take part in the struggle for France under the orders of General Alan Brooke, after the evacuation of the 1st. On the 12th and 13th June its 1st Brigade disembarked at Brest. McNaughton was to follow a little later with the rest of the division.

Unhappy 1st Brigade! It would have been better for it, that this trip, like those of Norway and Dunkirk, had been called off at the last moment. Taken to Brest to defend the undefend-able Breton redoubt, a myth concocted in the imaginations of the French and British Prime Ministers, it was given the

[1] Major-General R. H. Dewing, Chief of Operations at the War Office.

assembly point of Sablé on the Sarthe. It had barely time to arrive than, on the 14th June, General Brooke, after a meeting at Le Mans with Generals Weygand and Georges, telephoned to the War Office to report that in his view, all movements of British troops to France must cease without delay, and preparations made to evacuate those which were already there. General Smith received the order to bring his brigade back to Brest, where it arrived on the 16th June; it embarked on the 17th after destroying all its material with the exception of 24 field guns and a dozen Bofors. The troops were disgusted at having to scuttle all this material, without even catching sight of a German. 'Since there were no enemy less than 200 miles away, this evacuation was carried out like a rout.'[1]

*   *   *

It was eight months since these brave fellows had left their homeland. The first and most dramatic of these six years of war had ended, and the number of Canadian soldiers who had seen action could be counted on the fingers of two hands.

They were employed during the summer in preparing the defences against an invasion which was never to materialize. In the meantime the Canadian forces in Great Britain were continually reinforced. The 2nd Division went overseas at the end of June and by the end of the year the 'Canadian Corps' in Great Britain totalled more than 50,000 fighting men, still waiting an opportunity for going into action.

They tunnelled the Kentish cliffs to improve the defences. Others were sent to Gibraltar to dig holes in the famous rock. The underground hospital in Gibraltar is a monument to their work. It was all very useful, but they had not exactly left home to do this. Finally, on 19th August, 1941, just one year before the Dieppe raid, Rear Admiral Vian took 500 of them to Spitzbergen to destroy the Norwegian and Russian installations of Barentsburg on the Isfjord, before the Germans could get a foothold there. It was a remarkable firework display. 450,000 tons of coal went up in flames, floods of diesel oil set on fire or scattered into the sea, all the mining installations blown up, and

[1] *Journal of the Royal Canadian Horse Artillery.* The Germans (5th Panzers) entered Brest two days later, the 19th June.

the town of Barentsburg three quarters destroyed – incidentally by accident.

The adventure would doubtless have been diverting but it was far from glorious, since no enemy had intervened in Operation *Dauntless*, which was the name given to this operation. Moreover, it was not merely 500 men but a whole brigade which had initially been briefed, and so the importance of the expeditionary force had been reduced in the meantime – a new cause for disappointment to hundreds of Canadian soldiers.

The year 1941 was running its course. For two years the Canadian army had not yet fired a shot. The only offensive, in which about 50 of its members had been engaged, was a raid upon Hardelot, carried out on the 21st/22nd April under the orders of Major Lord Lovat; it turned out to be a complete fiasco. The landing craft carrying the Canadian commandos had not yet found their landing point, when Lovat, apparently just as disappointed, gave the signal to withdraw by firing a flare. They returned to Dover without having set foot on the French coast.

There were, however, plenty of places where there was action. In Africa, for example, where General Wavell's Imperial Forces, from December 1940 until May 1941, had inflicted shattering defeats on the Italian forces in Libya, Abyssinia and Eritrea; in Greece and Crete where the outcome had been less fortunate. The intervention by the Afrika Korps had disturbed the balance to the detriment of the British in the Mediterranean theatre, where the Canadian forces could certainly have been employed. Why were they not despatched, instead of leaving them to kick their heels in Great Britain? It was all very well that they should have been kept there at the period when the British Isles lay under a threat of German invasion, but, as the months passed, the chances of such a prospect diminished. At the end of 1941 and at the beginning of 1942, no one seriously believed that Hitler could ever invade England. There was nothing therefore to prevent the Canadians being sent to the desert. Nothing, except Churchill's solicitude for nipping in the bud the perfidious insinuations of enemy propaganda, which insisted that Great Britain was waging war in the Middle East with her Dominion soldiers. 'For a long time,' he wrote to General Auchinleck, 'I have dreaded troubles with the Australians and with world opinion, of appearing to wage all our battles in the Middle East with Dominion troops alone.' To send Canadian soldiers to Africa would only have brought grist to the mill of this propaganda.

It is perhaps idiotic, when one considers it, and the Canadian Government was entirely in agreement that their soldiers should be used wherever they could be most useful, whatever the theatre of war selected. But there are subtleties from which there is no escape and imponderables which have more weight than the most trenchant argument. There is no doubt, moreover, that the home divisions were in a minority in the African theatre of war, the only one where land warfare was actually in progress. In the 8th Army, for example, in June 1941, the XIIIth Army Corps consisted of a New Zealand division, an Indian division and a brigade of British tanks. The XXXth consisted of a South African division, against one armoured division and a brigade of British Guards. In besieged Tobruk, two Australian divisions bore the whole brunt of the defence until the day when the Australian Government insisted upon their relief, and the Royal Navy had been called upon to ensure the replacement of these 32,667 Australians by 34,113 British and Polish soldiers. It is comprehensible that Churchill, embroiled in these unpleasant discussions with the Canberra Government, should hesitate to send to Africa troops from another Dominion, which the following day might level at him the same reproaches and reclaim its men for its own defence.

Hong Kong was the scene of a very unfortunate experience. On his return from the Far East, General Grasett, formerly commander in chief of the British forces in China, had suggested reinforcing the Hong Kong garrison with two or three Canadian battalions. The idea deserved serious consideration. The question had already been asked in Washington. The British wanted to establish a kind of united defence front with the Dutch and the Americans, it being a condition that any Japanese advance beyond a certain line would constitute a *casus belli*.

But neither Admiral Stark, in command of the United States Navy, nor General Marshall, chief of the army staff, favoured this plan, which was shelved on the 3rd July, 1941. With this, all idea of a concerted defence of Western possessions in the Pacific died.

On weighing the matter up carefully, if Japan really wanted war, two or three extra battalions would certainly not be able to defend victoriously a position which was lost in advance. In any case, during August 1941, the British chiefs of staff did not consider that the game was yet lost. Japan appeared far less arrogant, *vis-à-vis* Great Britain and the United States. The garrison at Singapore had been reinforced from nine to 32 battalions. The battleships H.M.S. *Repulse* and H.M.S. *Prince of Wales* had been sent to Malaya. The dispatch of reinforcements to Hong Kong would be a powerful stimulant to the garrison and at the same time show Chiang Kai-shek that Great Britain was determined to defend herself in this theatre of war as in all the others.[1]

Churchill, who was not very keen, nevertheless agreed to put the question to the Ottawa Government, reserving the right to cancel the movement if the circumstances appeared unfavourable at the moment it was to be put into execution.

Ottawa gave its consent, without knowing the true situation in the Far East and without realizing the reservations initially made by Churchill. Since no new decisive element had intervened in the meantime, the final decision was taken on the 8th October, and the two battalions from Canada arrived in Hong Kong via Honolulu and Manila on 16th November, 1941. . . . Three weeks before Pearl Harbor!

We know the consequences. The first bombs fell on Hong Kong at 0800 hrs. on 8th December European time, and the 38th Japanese Division, reinforced by a regiment of infantry and with air support, immediately attacked the Kowloon Peninsula, the continental portion of the British colony, which fell in one week. The island itself, attacked on the 18th December, had to surrender on the 24th at 1515 hrs.

The first operation in which the Canadian army actually took place had ended with a costly setback. Of the 1,950 Canadian

[1] According to the note sent to Churchill by the chiefs of staff on the 10th September, 1941. Quoted by Colonel Stacey in the official account of the Canadian army, *Six Years of War*, Vol. I, p. 440.

soldiers who sailed from Vancouver in October, 557 never returned to their homes. 290 were killed or succumbed to their wounds, the others died of disease or exhaustion during their captivity. We can only regret with Colonel Stacey, that the British Premier had not stuck to his first idea regarding the defence of Hong Kong and the proposed reinforcement when he wrote on the 7th January: 'This is all wrong. If Japan goes to war there will not be the slightest chance of holding on to Hong Kong. It would be stupid to increase the losses we are bound to suffer. Instead of reinforcing the garrison we should reduce it to a token force.'

It is understandable that this unfortunate precedent, combined with the kind of complex which hampered the British Premier from using Dominion troops, tethered General McNaughton's Canadian corps to the British Isles. But his soldiers grew impatient. They wanted to fight, to do something; they pestered him continually. Besides, Churchill had made them a solemn promise in a speech to the Canadian House of Commons in Ottawa on the 30th December, 1941: 'The Canadian army in England today is chafing at the bit and is burning to come to grips with the enemy. But I can assure you that it occupies, and will continue to occupy, a post in the front line, a post which will allow it to fall upon the invader if he should dare to land on our shores. In a few months' time, when the season of invasions returns, the Canadian army may find itself engaged in one of the bloodiest affrays the world has ever known.'

He appeared to envisage this 'bloody affray' on British soil in the event of the Germans being able to land. The landing took place in the opposite direction, and led the Canadian soldiers to Dieppe in an operation far more costly than that of Hong Kong and which had one thing in common with the latter – that it was resumed after having been called off, just as the reinforcement of Hong Kong had been carried out later, when initially everyone had agreed that it was wrong. The result: 907 dead, 568 wounded, 1,300 prisoners, in other words three-fifths of the forces engaged. In nine hours at Dieppe, the Canadian army was to leave more prisoners in the hands of the enemy than during the 11 months of the French and German campaigns, from the landing in Normandy until the German capitulation!

CHAPTER NINE

THE ENEMY

THE end of hostilities in France in the summer of 1940 brought no notable reduction in the German forces stationed on the Channel coast. In view of operations planned against Great Britain, three Armies, the 6th, 9th and 15th forming Heeresgruppe A, remained concentrated between Ostend and Cherbourg so as to reach the appointed port of embarkation at the first signal received. The signal was never given, and on the 17th September, 1940, Operation *Sealion* was postponed to the Greek Kalends – or at least until the following spring. A new version was under review, Operation *Shark*, at the beginning of 1941, when on Hitler's decision to attack Russia, Heeresgruppe A left for a more active theatre of war on the Eastern Front. The three armies were transferred to Poland and east Germany to prepare for the campaign against the U.S.S.R., and the High Command of the Western Front passed to Heeresgruppe D.

In April 1941, the 15th Army, newly formed since 15th February from the 13th regional reserve zone (Erzatzwehrkreis) in the neighbourhood of Nuremberg, under the orders of Col.-General Kurt Haase, took up its position on the North Sea and Channel coasts from Ostend to Normandy inclusive. Haase made his quarters in Tourcoing, which was to remain the Hq. of the 15th Army until September 1944.

At this period the 15th Army comprised 17 divisions, divided into three army corps:

The size of these forces was justified by Operation *Shark*, preparations for which were in full swing. Throughout the whole of May 1941, the various formations of the 15th Army were engaged in embarkation and landing exercises in all the ports from Le Havre inclusive to the mouth of the Meuse.

But *Shark* was actually only a diversion designed to distract the attention of what was brewing in the east. The opening of the Russian campaign rendered these precautions useless. At the end of June, the German High Command ordered their cessation and General Haase gradually had to release a certain number of his large units. The first to be affected was the 319th Infantry Division, which was transferred to the Channel

Army Corps (Static)	Divisions	Sector
LXth	323rd 216th 83rd 319th	Cotentin
XXXIInd	336th 225th 302nd 332nd 716th	From Caen to Dieppe
XXXVIIth	320th 321st 208th 304th 340th 306th 227th	From Le Tréport into Belgium
Army Reserve	711th	

Islands where it remained for the rest of the war, laying down its arms on the 8th May, 1945. For a long time its soldiers, sensing that they would finish in a prisoner of war camp on the other side of the Atlantic, had got into the habit of calling themselves the 'Canada Division.'

In October the 227th Infantry Division was taken from the XXXVIIth Corps to be transferred to the Eastern Front. While other departures followed, the character of the occupation of the 15th Army took on a defensive aspect, for, in December 1941, Adolf Hitler issued his first orders for the building of the Atlantic Wall. Work actually began in January 1942.

At the period under review, that is to say at the moment

when plans for attacking Dieppe were being worked out, the organization of the 15th Army – still commanded by General Haase – had been considerably modified. The LXth Corps, renumbered the LXXXIVth Corps joined the 7th Army, and the 15th saw its sector reduced to the limits of the Orne-Meuse and with the following composition:

Army Corps	Divisions	Sector
XXVIIth renumbered in July LXXXIInd	321st–304th 306th–106th 371st	From Le Tréport to Belgium
XXXIInd renumbered in July LXXXIst	302nd–332nd 711th	Rouen–Dieppe

In addition, the 10th Panzer Division, severely tried by the Russian battles, had left the Smolensk region in mid-April to be reformed in the neighbourhood of Amiens in the sector of the LXXXIInd Army Corps. It was commanded by Lt.-General Wolfgang Fischer.[1]

The defence of Dieppe therefore fell upon the LXXXIst Army Corps (General Kunsten, with Hq. at Canteleu in the suburbs of Rouen) and more directly upon the 302nd Infantry Division, commanded by Maj.-General Conrad Haase (not to be confused with his namesake Kurt Haase, commanding the 15th Army).

From April onwards the 302nd Infantry Division, formed in

[1] Formed in Czechoslovakia in April 1939, the 10th Panzer Division had fought the Polish campaign. In 1940 it was in action with Guderian's armour, which broke through on the Somme and at Amiens in particular. Later it took Calais and in June participated in the break through from the Aisne to the Rhône. Subsequent to this it fought in Russia with the 2nd Panzer Group, suffering heavy losses at the beginning of 1942 in the Smolensk–Roslavl region. It was this division which led the advance of the German troops at the moment of the occupation of the Free Zone on the 11th November, 1942. It met its fate in Tunisia, where it had been transferred in December 1942.

Germany at the end of 1940, occupied a sector covering 40 miles of the coast from Veules-les-Roses to Le Tréport. On its left flank, to the west, was the 332nd Infantry Division (Maj.-General Hans Kessel, with Hq. at Bolbec) which held the sector from August 1941. On its right flank the 321st Infantry Division of the LXXXIInd Army Corps. In addition to the units, which by rights belonged to the 302nd Infantry Division, the reserves of the LXXXIst Army Corps were astride the sector of the 332nd and 302nd Infantry Divisions, i.e.: the III/570th Infantry Regiment, at Bacqueville-en-Caux; the I/676th at Doudeville, with the III/376th at Yvetot, and the Golle Regiment at Barentin. Dieppe formed the centre of the coastal sector of the 302nd Infantry Division,[1] but General Conrad Hasse's Hq. was at Envermeu, 12 miles from Dieppe on route Nationale 320. In the town itself was only a garrison of about 1,500 men, consisting of the staff and two battalions of the 571st Infantry Regiment (Lt.-Colonel Hermann Bartelt). At the moment of the Anglo-Canadian attack, the II/571st (Major von Bonin) occupied the sector west of Dieppe and the III/571st (Captain Schoesenberg) the eastern sector. The I/571st was in reserve at Ouville-la-Riviere.

We shall have occasion to refer elsewhere to the artillery formations posted in the Dieppe sector, but we must mention here two other important formations:

– The *Flakuntergruppe Dieppe*, which disposed of a heavy battery with emplacements on the golf course to the west of Dieppe, and a light anti-aircraft battery.

– The *23rd Schwere Funkmesskompanie* (company of heavy

---

[1] The 302nd Infantry Division was composed as follows:
  Chief of Staff, General von Steuben.
  570th Infantry Regiment, Colonel von Gzettritz and Neuhaus.
  571st Infantry Regiment, Lt.-Colonel Hermann Bartelt.
  572nd Infantry Regiment, Colonel Claus Boie.
  302nd Artillery Regiment, Colonel Helm Siggel.
  302nd Pioneer Battalion, Captain Stahl.
  302nd Detachment of Signallers, Captain Brose.
On its left flank the 302nd Infantry Division formed a common front with the 676th Infantry Regiment (Colonel Klemm with Hq. at Doudeville), which, together with the 677th and 678th Infantry Regiments and the 332nd Artillery Regiment, constituted the 332nd Infantry Division.

radar detection under Oberleutnant Weber) attached to the *Luftgau Nachrichten Regiment 51*, a Luftwaffe formation responsible for ground illumination from Belgium to the north of France. The 23rd Schwere Funkmesskompanie was responsible for air reconnaissance and the direction of the fighter arm in the sector between Les Petites-Dalles (nine miles from Fécamp), Dieppe and Saint-Valery-sur-Somme. The air information centre, *Flugmeldezentrale*, was at Dieppe. It possessed a radar type Freya 28 and two Würzburg C's. Its Hq. was at Puys.

Although unity of command was not expressly established between these various formations, some of which came from the land forces and the others from the air arm, their accord was perfect. The same applied to units of the German Navy we shall now describe, and this accord certainly bore fruit on the occasion of the attack of the 19th August, 1942.

At Dieppe there was a naval commander, Hafenkommandant, at the period Captain Wahn, subordinate to the Channel coast commander known as *Marine Befehlshaber Kanalküste*, or in short, *Admiral Kanalküste* with Hq. at Trouville. The latter in turn was subordinate to the *Admiral Frankreich*, whose Hq. were in Paris. But Wahn's authority was limited to the harbour services, the supervision of fishing, certain land defences on the sea front, etc., occupying in all about 200 men. The naval forces eventually called upon to operate in the sector formed part of the 3rd Sicherungsdivision, with Hq. at Souverain-Moulin near Boulogne, itself attached to the command of Admiral Ruge, the B.S.W. whom we have already mentioned in Chapter Two. The 3rd Sicherungsdivision consisted of a dozen flotillas of patrol boats, light and heavy sweepers (*Räum-Boote*) and monitors (*Artillerie-Träger*) stationed in the different Channel ports, according to the needs of the moment. Thus, in April 1944, the 14th Flotilla of R-boats was based on Dieppe. In 1942, there were apparently only units in transit, destined to serve as escorts for the small coastal convoys. A German U-boat was never seen at Dieppe – nothing except E-boats, the counterpart of our M.T.B.s. The most notable incidents occurred on the occasional passage of the large surface ships, raiders or blockade breakers, which moored for a night at Dieppe in the course of their crossing through the Channel along the *Rosa* route.

*   *   *

As opposed to the situation existing in France before 1939, the responsibility for coastal defence did not lie in the hands of the *Kreigsmarine*. The shore batteries of the army, *Heerenküsten Batterie* of the Seine–Somme sector, relied on *Artillerie Kommando 117*, which in the sector of interest to us, embodied the 527th Artillery Regiment from Saint-Valery-en-Caux to Saint-Valery-sur-Somme, a Le Tréport group or *Heerenküsten Artillerie Abteilung 770* with five batteries:

> at Saint-Valery-en-Caux, battery 1/799,
> at Varengeville, battery 813,
> at Berneval, battery 2/770,
> at Mesnilval, battery 770,
> at Le Tréport, battery 1/770.

In addition to these there were the field batteries of the 322nd Artillery Regiment with positions in the sector, forming an integral part of the 302nd Infantry Division and designed, in consequence, to follow its movements. All of these, as well as those of Group 770, were engaged during the attack of 19th August, but it is necessary here to describe at greater length those which belonged to the *Stutzpunktgruppe Dieppe*, in other words, to the group covering Dieppe.

Until 8th July, 1942, Dieppe had formed a defence sector, *Verteidigungsbereich*, and the Berneval battery at that time constituted an independent strongpoint. After this date, since the unimportant port of Dieppe did not seem to justify an attempted enemy landing, it had been reduced to a lower scale.

The two most important positions, since they commanded the approaches to the port for nine miles to sea, were situated at Berneval and Varengeville, both approximately six miles from Dieppe.

To the east was the II/770 Battery with its emplacements near the village church of Berneval-le-Grand. An important battery, since it consisted of four 105 mm., three 170 mm. and two 20 mm. Oerlikons for defence against aircraft and was manned by 127 men. In the immediate proximity was a radar post served by 114 N.C.O.s and men of the Luftwaffe, detached from the Sub-Flak group of Dieppe, with the additional duty of providing reinforcements in the case of an enemy landing. The 302nd Infantry Division was represented in this sector by a strong post, Feldwache, with a dozen men under an N.C.O., provided by the I/570th stationed at Assigny, five miles farther east.

As can be seen on the map, this important position was approximately half-way between the two indentations of the cliff adjacent to Co-ordinate 101 – to the east, the valley of Berneval, and to the west of Belleville-sur-Mer. This particular disposition was not without importance as we shall have occasion to see.

In most of the British documents, the Batterie II/770 appears as the Goebbels Battery. This name, in common with all the others used for the main emplacements of this sector, does not appear in any German document.

To the west of Dieppe, Battery 813, which the British dubbed the Hess Battery, was placed on the Varengeville plateau immediately north of the road which branches from the main route to reach the valley of Vasterival. This battery, commanded by Captain Schöler, consisted of six 150 mm., with no direct view of the sea because it was placed about 1,000 yards from the edge of the cliff. But a telephone cable, buried under the lighthouse at Ailly Point, ran to an O.P. from which the firing was observed by a detachment of two officers, two N.C.O.s and eight men of the battery.

The lighthouse and the Ailly coastguard station were also used as O.P.'s by the navy, manned by an officer and 50 men and 10 men of the Luftwaffe. Finally, two sections from No. 3 Company of the 571st Infantry Regiment and a group from No. 4 were stationed in the small village of Saint-Marguerite in the immediate vicinity of the Saane valley where the cliff opens out in breadth at Quiberville beach (*Widerstandnest Quiberville*).

Completing to the south what we might consider as the outer zone of defence of Dieppe, the 256th Battery, posted on the heights of Calmont above Arques-la-Bataille, three miles

south-east of Dieppe, commanded the whole of the valley of
the Arques, the port and its immediate seaward approaches. It
was attached to Artillerie Kommando 117. This is what the
British called the Hitler Battery.

In this semicircle, the 302nd Artillery Regiment had in the
first line two batteries, one to the east of the port between Puys
and Dieppe in the commune of Neuville-les-Dieppe, Battery
8/302, which the British called the Rommel Battery, and a
second to the west, behind the golf course near Quatre-Vents
farm, Battery 7/302 or the Goering Battery.

Then, to the rear, were Batteries A/302 and B/302 whose
emplacements will be seen on the map. All their guns were
105 mm. or 75 mm.

Naturally, all these units were not up to strength in this
formidable array. The material was often undergoing repairs.
Some of the 155 mm. guns had been hastily placed on concrete
platforms designed to take 105 mm. Not all of them were
adapted for firing out to sea. In any case, taking into account
the particular nature of this coast, they were largely sufficient
not only to defend the sea off Dieppe but also to command the
beaches and narrow gorges from which an invader could climb
from the shore to the plateau. On the strip of coast selected by
the British for the assault, in other words a front of 15 miles,
account was soon taken of these passages which run from east
to west – the valleys of Berneval and Belleville, the beach at
Puys, the port and beach of Dieppe (mouth of the River
Arques), the beach at Pourville (mouth of the River Scie), the
ports of Mordal,[1] Ailly, Moustiers, Morville and Vasterival
(which despite their name of port are only narrow ravines) and
the beach of Quiberville (mouth of the River Saane).

All in all, the 302nd Infantry Division, supported by its own
artillery and by five coastal batteries, was quite strong enough
to repel the Anglo-Canadian expedition on its own reserves.
Neither the army corps reserves billeted in the immediate
neighbourhood, nor the 10th Panzers from Amiens would
have any need to intervene.

*   *   *

[1] The Germans called it *Möwenschlucht*, the ravine of the gulls.

This having been said, what were the Germans expecting?

We have already seen how the Bruneval raid, coming like a bolt from the blue, had seriously disconcerted the German High Command and induced the Führer to intervene personally and to prescribe security measures in his directive No. 40. We have seen how a month later the Saint-Nazaire raid had provoked a crisis.

The Todt organization expanded and turned out hundreds of cubic yards of concrete. This was a curious concern working for the Wehrmacht with complete independence, and invariably ignoring the advice of its employers.

It is not surprising then that, 18 months later, after a tour of inspection which took him from Denmark to Hendaye and the coast of Provence, Field Marshal Rommel returned convinced that the Atlantic Wall had been erected contrary to good sense.

The Kriegsmarine had been invited to form special brigades to protect the Atlantic islands. On the 10th April Raeder drew his conclusions from experience learned at Bruneval and Saint-Nazaire. According to the Admiral they must be prepared for raids without counting too much on reinforcements. He personally did not expect any before the beginning of September, believing that the British would wait for the longer nights. The German C.-in-C. West[1] considered that from mid-April the prospect of a landing would become more and more probable, and requested his troops to keep on the alert. The German High Command shared his fears and spoke of a landing between Brittany and the River Escaut, and in particular in the Bay of the Somme.

This was good forecasting. It was a pity that it happened two years too early. There would be plenty of time to forget it before June, 1944.

*   *   *

[1] Oberbefehlschaber West, at that period Field Marshal von Rundstedt, commanding Army Group D.

[2] The possibility of an invasion by the British on the Channel coast had been the subject, long before Dieppe, of many secret notes. Alert exercises frequently took place. One interesting detail: all these documents admitted that the attack could also come from the land (Lt.-Colonel Hoffman Münster).

For a moment all this was pure speculation, exactly like the broadcasts from Radio Paris on the conversations in London between the British and American military leaders. The Germans had no precise information – or very little.[1]

At all events, towards mid-June, reconnaissance photographs of the 3rd Luftflotte began to show the presence of an important number of small landing craft on the south coast of England. By the end of July this concentration had increased considerably. In the meantime, near the Isle of Wight, concentrations of big ships had been observed, which the Luftwaffe attacked on the 17th July, as we have already mentioned.

An item of information from a Portuguese sailor who had left Portsmouth on the 13th June, reported invasion preparations on the south coast of England. Supplies of material were reported at Dover, Romney, Dungeness, Hastings, Bexhill, Eastbourne, Seaford and Portsmouth.

This was already more than was needed to confirm an impression born of logical deduction. In any case, the C.-in-C. West estimated from about the 15th June that they must take into account the possibility of an enemy operation, perhaps of major importance – at any moment and at any point along this very extensive sea coast.[2]

Whatever the reason the Führer issued a directive on the 9th July to the three services, requesting them to reinforce the western defences. It deserves to be reproduced here *in extenso*, for it gives an accurate picture of what Berlin thought at this juncture.

1. Our great and rapid victories may face Great Britain with the alternative of launching a full-scale invasion with the object of opening a Second Front, or of seeing Russia obliterated as a military factor. It is therefore highly probable that an enemy landing will take place shortly in the area of C.-in-C. West. These are the factors which indicate it:

[1] In the logbook of the 302nd Infantry Division it was noted that on the 20th May, 1942, in a shelter hollowed in the drive of a house at Criel-Plage, a letter was found announcing the landing of several parachutists between the 20th and 28th. The sender, a Frenchman from Floques, is unknown.

[2] Rundstedt's report on the Dieppe raid dated 3rd September, 1942. *Gefechtsbericht über Feindlandung bei und beiderseits Dieppe am 19.8.42.*

(*a*) The increase of reports from our agents on this point, and further data collected by our information services.

(*b*) The important concentration of transport vessels along the whole south coast of England.

(*c*) The non-appearance of the R.A.F. in the past few days.

2. The following sectors are to be considered particularly threatened:

(*a*) First and foremost the Pas de Calais, the sector between Dieppe and Le Havre and Normandy, because these regions are within the range of enemy fighters and of most of the transport barges.

(*b*) Secondly, southern Holland and Brittany.

(*c*) The main roads, airfields and headquarters are particularly threatened by parachutists, airborne troops and saboteurs.

3. In consequence I order the following measures to be taken without delay:

(*a*) The General Staff will put in a state of combat the S.S. Divisions *Das Reich* and *Adolf Hitler*, including the motorized S.S. group; the transfer of the 1st Infantry Regiment to Denmark will be postponed.

(*b*) The Army Commander and commander of the Reserves will equip for action three units of the type Walkyrie II and will transfer them to the C.-in-C. West.

(*c*) The C.-in-C. West is responsible for the security of the railways and for eventual reprisals.

4. In collaboration with the C.-in-C. West the Luftwaffe will assemble all available forces of the 7th Airborne Division and the Goering Brigade in their zones of concentration which will represent mobile units; the Luftwaffe will also transfer to France two bomber groups from the reserves of the C.-in-C. East and in accordance with his indications.

5. The Army General Staff, the Luftwaffe C.-in-C., the C.-in-C. West and the Reserve Army commander will report to me every day at 0800 hrs. the progress of measures 3 and 4 via the German High Command. These reports are to be made according to information at 1900 hrs. the previous night.

6. In the event of a landing I intend to visit the West Front in person to take over command of the operations.

*   *   *

In any event one obvious calculation had to be made: that of the periods or the combination of the tides and the state of the moon, favourable for a landing. Based on these calculations the 15th Army, in an order of the day dated the 20th July, pin-pointed three periods, from the 27th July to the 3rd August, from the 10th to the 19th August, and from the 25th August to the 1st of September.

Applying this order, General Conrad Haase placed his division in a state of alert, corresponding to a danger threaten-ing, drohende Gefahr, for ten consecutive nights, starting from the 10th August, 1942.

And finally, his namesake Kurt Haase, commanding the 15th Army, had drawn the logical conclusion of the political and strategic considerations we already know: 'Various reports,' says his order of the 10th August, 'lead us to assume that on account of the wretched plight of the Russians, the Anglo-Americans will be forced to undertake something in the rela-tively near future.' Already a few weeks earlier the LXXIst Corps had invited the 302nd Infantry Division to put in a request for the necessary personnel to bring their formations up to full complement. These requests were complied with in two drafts, and between the 11th and 12th August the division received the 1,500 men it lacked. Thus it was on its guard with a full complement when, on the 19th August, 1942, at 0458 hrs., the telephone of the staff officer on duty of the LXXXIst Corps rang at Canteleu. Fighting was in progress off Berneval. At 0510 hrs. Lt.-Colonel Sartorius, G.S.O.1 (Operations) Ia of the 302nd Infantry Division, wakened his opposite number at Army Corps Hq., Lt.-Colonel Kolbe, to tell him that Dieppe had just been bombed and that landings had been reported at Pourville and Quiberville.

CHAPTER TEN

AN UNSUCCESSFUL COUP

AT the period when a raid on Dieppe came under discussion, i.e. the 3rd April, 1942, when the subject was broached for the first time on the agenda of the Target Committee of C.O. Hq. – the office responsible for suggesting targets – it could only be considered by everyone as a purely British affair. Nevertheless, these preliminary studies coincided with the arrival in Great Britain of General Marshall and Harry Hopkins. It was difficult to keep them in the dark, even more so since, while firmly determined to attempt no important cross-Channel expedition in 1942, the British High Command was delighted to give proof that it was by no means disinterested in this theatre of war.

To be accurate, Mountbatten's staff expected the arrival of the American Mission under Colonel A. K. Truscott, the main object of which was to arrange the participation in the forth-coming commando operations of a few American soldiers, whom General Marshall wanted to gain some battle experience and their first contact with the German soldier. In view of this Truscott and his colleagues collaborated in working out the plans at C.O. Hq.

'You are a horseman and you play polo,' General Eisenhower said to Truscott when explaining what was wanted of him. 'That's perfect. Admiral Mountbatten has written a book on polo.'

An excellent introduction, but to return to Dieppe; on the 14th April the naval adviser to C.O. Hq., Captain J. Hughes-Hallett, defended the plan to a staff officer of the Home Forces. It was generally agreed that the idea was attractive and worth while, and that it should be studied in detail. A week later, agreement had been reached as to the means of putting the plan into practice – paratroops, gliders and tanks. After this, the best tactics were studied. Very much opposed to the idea of a frontal attack, Hughes-Hallett championed the indirect approach. He suggested an encircling movement carried out by troops landed on either side of Dieppe – two battalions at Pourville and Puys respectively, and tanks at Quiberville.

This plan was obviously open to criticism because it did not make sufficient use of the surprise element at Dieppe itself. But there was apparently another reason which caused this solution to be rejected.

In actual fact the Quiberville beach, one of the most important indentations on this coast, since it is more than 875 yards long, gives access to the River Saane which reaches the sea near the cliff of Saint-Marguerite. This therefore entailed a crossing followed by a second a few miles farther ahead, the River Scie which flows out at Pourville.

I am aware that in the days of the Fronde, the Duchesse de Longeville, fleeing from the citizens of Dieppe, who had remained faithful to the king, was nearly drowned in the River Scie and lost 10,000 silver crowns when crossing it on horseback (1650), but in the case of tanks I wonder what serious obstacle these brooks, which are no more than 30 feet wide, and three feet deep, would have represented? In any event, ask any of the inhabitants of the region which would appear to them the more difficult – to land tanks on a defended beach like that of Dieppe or to cross the Rivers Saane and Scie – and their reply would be unanimous.

Later, after the Dieppe raid, the Germans flooded the valley by opening the sluice gates at the points where these small water courses flowed beneath the dyke on the sea front. In 1942 they had not yet thought of taking this precaution, which had been inspired by the remarks of the C.-in-C. West in his report from the 15th Army. Nor were the bridges mined and, in the event of a surprise landing, they would have been as easy to take as all the other points of the road which runs close to the beach.

In short these two 'rivers to cross' appeared too great a problem. If necessary they would have accepted the landing of a squadron of tanks at Pourville, where there is a little more space between the mouth of the river and the cliff above the town, but this idea, retained until the 21st April, was abandoned in turn.

Finally, the broad outlines of the operation arranged on the 25th April at a meeting presided over by Mountbatten in person, adopted the frontal attack. No Canadian officer had yet been consulted and none of them was aware of what was being prepared against Dieppe. General Montgomery himself spoke five days later to General Crerar, commanding the 1st Canadian Corps, and to General McNaughton commanding the 1st Canadian Army. Neither had any objection, and it was decided that Operation *Rutter* should be carried out by units of the 2nd Canadian Division led by its commanding officer, Maj.-General Roberts. As Montgomery explained − as C.-in-C. South-eastern Command, it was his duty to supervise all these questions − it was impossible, without breaking the unity of command, to arrange a mixed Anglo-Canadian force, and of the two candidates the Canadians appeared to be the most suitable.

The 2nd Canadian Division went into training. In order to protect the secret better, it was announced that the 1st and the 3rd would follow suit.

*   *   *

The initial plan of *Rutter* defined its objectives as follows:
- The destruction of the enemy defences at Dieppe and its environs.
- Destruction of the airfield of Dieppe − Saint Aubin.
- The destruction of the radar station, the power station, the port and rail installations, the ammunition and oil dumps.
- The capture of landing-craft.
- The capture of documents from Divisional Headquarters at Arques-la-Bataille.[1]
- The taking of prisoners.

The plan included an attack on Dieppe itself, two flank attacks at Puys and Pourville, combined with airborne attacks upon divisional Hq. and the coastal batteries. These raids were to be preceded by an air attack carried out during the night on the town and the airfield, and then, at between 30 and 40 minutes after dawn, a low altitude bombing attack of the beaches

[1] We know that it was at Envermeu.

carried out by Blenheim bombers and Hurricane fighter-bombers. This air preparation was considerably reduced on the 15th May. Both the bombing of the beaches and of the town were cancelled. The bombing of the port was retained.

In the meantime, General McNaughton had reported to the Canadian General Staff at Ottawa and asked for its agreement, which was given without demur. The Canadian officers were now admitted to the discussions at C.O. Hq. The vital question remained – the point at which the tanks should be landed. Everyone agreed that the river crossing should be avoided. The L.C.T.s therefore could only be landed between the mouths of the Scie and the Arques. Now between these two rivers the only beaches that exist are those of Dieppe and a small part of the Pourville beach. In other words, the choice had been made. The advantages were studied, and in due course they were found. By landing at Dieppe the tanks would be immediately on the job, the surprise would be far greater and would certainly give both the Germans and the population a very great psychological shock. It would be easier to supply them with ammunition and to re-embark them after the raid.

This was the positive side, and it was certainly not negligible, but the adverse side was also great, and the British realized this so well that they declared themselves ready to entrust this mission to British forces. The Canadian officers would not hear of it. It was a matter of self-esteem. They would lose face before their men, if they had rejected a plan which finally offered some prospect of action, when they had been kicking their heels for so long.

The training continued. To assess the progress made, a full-scale exercise christened *Yukon* was staged at Bridport on the night of the 11th/12th June, a coastal section which resembles that of Dieppe. The results were unsatisfactory. Units were landed 1,500 yards from the point intended, and the L.C.T.s arrived an hour late.

Dissatisfied with this result Mountbatten, on his return from the United States, ordered a repeat of *Yukon* which took place on the night of the 22nd/23rd. Things went rather more smoothly, but it was still far from satisfactory. The head of Combined Operations was studying the report when Churchill, on the 26th June in the circumstances we have already mentioned, asked him to state the chances of success which he gave to a raid on Dieppe. His prudent rely is very understandable.

Nevertheless a certain optimism reigned, for after spending the 30th June on the Isle of Wight, going over the plans with General Roberts, Montgomery wrote on the 1st July that, in his opinion, the operation afforded reasonable prospects of success, provided the weather was fine, an average possibility, and provided the Royal Navy landed the troops at the hour prescribed and at the correct spot.

Montgomery, however, insisted on the necessity for keeping up the morale of the participants, and of inoculating them with an optimism which would spread to all ranks like an epidemic. Had there been, as he seems to suggest, a temporary falling off in morale? This is not impossible, for the mistakes of the first *Yukon* exercise must have made a very bad impression. But they were reported to have been rectified. And Captain Hughes-Hallett, who had not hesitated to don the uniform of a private soldier and to mingle with his men, under the name of Private Charles Hallet, to test their morale, returned at this stage convinced that the men 'would fight like hell'.

On the 3rd July General Crerar wrote to General McNaughton: 'I am entirely in agreement that this plan is a reasonable one and that it has been perfected. I should have no hesitation in coming to terms with it, if I were in the place of Roberts.'

In fact everyone was happy.

Rutter was fixed for the 4th July or one of the days immediately following this date. The C.O. Hq. posted to the Isle of Wight a great number of its officers and particularly American observers, five of whom, including Truscott, were to follow the raid in which about 60 of the Rangers were to participate. The troops began to embark on the 2nd and 3rd in the craft which were to carry them across the Channel. At the outset they were told that this was merely a repeat of an exercise they had already carried out. It was even given a name, *Klondike 1*. But Lord Louis and General Roberts in turn visited each of the transports, where each soldier was duly informed what was expected of him.

Unfortunately the weather was unfavourable on the 3rd July.

It was no better on the 4th and 5th and there was no prospect of it clearing up for 48 hours. It was therefore not until the 8th, at the earliest, that the enterprise could be attempted and, according to the tides on the 8th, there could be no re-embarkment before five o'clock in the evening. This was obviously very late – very late indeed, since it had been learnt that the 10th Panzer Division, which was believed to have been stationed at Soissons during the preceding months, was now at Amiens, a few hours away from Dieppe.

This concentration of shipping round the Isle of Wight had obviously not escaped the notice of the Luftwaffe, which despatched minelaying aircraft and bombers to attack it. Admiral James' minesweepers coped with the mines: 'My minesweepers were on the ball. They did a magnificent job and have equalled or beaten all records for the number of mines destroyed in one week. I am very proud of them.'

But there remained the bombs, and on the 7th July, the L.S.I.s *Princess Astrid* and *Princess Josephine Charlotte* both suffered direct hits; these were fortunately duds and only claimed four slightly wounded. The following day, the 2nd Flotilla of E-boats from Cherbourg, guided by the 123rd Reconnaissance Group of the Luftwaffe, appeared in these waters. While the aircraft was diverting the ack-ack, after lighting up the convoy with their brilliant flares, Kapitänleutnant Feldt's E-boats sent the tankers *Pommella* (6,766 tons) and *Gripfast* (1,109 tons) to the bottom.

This did not result in the operation being postponed, but as the former C.-in-C. Portsmouth writes: 'It was not in my power to prevent a west wind blowing, which was a decisive factor. These two-way operations are difficult to stage. Each month there are only a few days with a suitable tide and the sea must be calm enough to effect the re-embarkation. One-way passages would be far easier.'[1]

Rutter was cancelled.

The Canadian troops landed, very down in the mouth, and 'all these stout lads trained to the last button' returned very disappointed to the camps they had left so gaily for the Isle of Wight a few weeks earlier.

[1] Admiral Sir W. M. James, *The Portsmouth Letters*.

The trouble was that everybody had been informed. Now that the troops were dispersed the secret was heavily compromised. It was reasonable to suppose, as Field-Marshal Montgomery writes, that the raid had become a general topic of conversation in all the pubs on the south coast for, in addition to the 5,000 Canadian soldiers, a number of sailors and airmen had been involved. 'As soon as this force had been dispersed, I considered that the operation had been cancelled, and I turned my attention to other questions.'[1]

But C.O. Hq. was of a different opinion, and Admiral Mountbatten succeeded a few days later in having approved by the Committee of Chiefs of Staff the principles of a new expedition. Montgomery, overwhelmed by this decision, immediately wrote to General Paget, C.-in-C. Home Forces, and admitted his anxiety. 'At least,' he said, 'if they want to do something on the Continent, let them choose another target than Dieppe.'

No one listened to him. A fortnight later, on the 19th August, in Egypt at 8th Army Hq. with Churchill who had sent him to this post, he learnt that the raid had been carried out the same day.

[1] Field-Marshal Montgomery, *Memoirs*.

CHAPTER ELEVEN

FROM 'RUTTER' TO 'JUBILEE'

No one has ever given a really satisfactory explanation why, from the 14th July, the plans of Operation *Rutter* were brought out again from the cupboard to which Montgomery hoped they had been banished for ever. Naturally the immediate origin of the report of the operation, i.e. the bad weather, entailed nothing definite. The tidal tables and the moon phases during the course of the summer offered other favourable conjunctions. The Germans had made a note of them, and the problem was no more difficult for the British. What disturbed Montgomery was the compromising of the secret.

Was this the only reason? Did he not see in it an excellent opportunity of abandoning a raid for which he had never shown anything but lukewarm enthusiasm. He does not explain this in his memoirs.

What he does explain, without beating about the bush, concerns the modifications which were brought to the initial plan when it was vigorously resumed under the name of Operation *Jubilee*.

Certain modifications had been introduced into the revised plan. The most important of these were, firstly, the elimination of paratroops and their replacement by commandos, and secondly, the elimination of the softening up bombing by aircraft.

'I should certainly not have agreed with any of these modifications. The commandos, if considered necessary, could complete but not replace the airborne troops. The demolition of the enemy defences by a preliminary bombardment was essential (as was the case in Normandy in 1944, before the troops landed on the beaches). My feeling with regard to the Dieppe raid is that there were far too many authorities involved; it lacked a single leader responsible for the operation from the beginning to the end.'

The cancellation of the raid had left serious repercussions. 'It was felt to be a defeat,' Hughes-Hallett wrote later, 'and it was for this reason that so much value was attached to its resumption and execution.'[1]

For his part, Truscott – in the meantime promoted to General – who had spent this period of waiting aboard a destroyer, has recorded the consternation which the utterances of Captain Hughes-Hallett had caused at C.O. Hq. To hear him speak, this cancellation signified that the leaders were incapable of carrying out, or the staff of Combined Operations of conceiving and mounting, a large scale operation which was realizable.

However, not everyone shared this point of view. The basis of all these raids was a controversial matter. If it were a question of training – let that pass – although in the last analysis the training was of equal advantage to the enemy. But if it were merely a question of occupying idle troops, it was no longer justified.

'The Germans are delighted by these raids, for nothing shows them better the weak points in their defences than an attack launched with limited targets. Each time we unmask a weakness on his coast, and it is obvious that he will take advantage and reinforce the shore from both sea and land.'[2]

But on the other hand the fervour shown at C.O. Hq. coincided perfectly with the great urgency for making a gesture in favour of the Russians. Although it is nowhere on record, it is beyond doubt that the pressing solicitations of the staff of Combined Operations, combined with all these political considerations, created the climate needed to win a decision. This at least appears in a note from General McNaughton, repeating a conversation which he had on the 25th July with Lord Louis Mountbatten.

'Apparently Stalin has cabled the Prime Minister asking what he intends to do in the way of launching diversionary raids against the Germans. The Prime Minister was pleased to be able to indicate in his reply that something was brewing,

[1] Rear Admiral J. Hughes-Hallet, *The mounting of raids*, in the Journal of the United Service Institution, November, 1950.

[2] Truscott, *Command Missions*, p. 35.

and suddenly gave his consent that first priority should be accorded to the preparations for *Jubilee*.'[1]

In the meantime, it had been decided to change the code name of the operation, possibly in the hope of affording better security to an affair which had become too public. It was intended to make people think that it was really another operation, and this is also one of the reasons cited to explain the modifications brought to the original plan.

Some of these modifications were only of minor importance. Weather permitting, there was no difficulty in embarking part of the troops in their landing craft in England, instead of transshipping them in view of the French coast, as had been foreseen in *Rutter*. It was actually a simplification. A decision which turned out to be more serious was that of replacing the airborne troops by commandos landed from the sea. The reasons put forward by Colonel Stacey do not appear very convincing. According to him the use of airborne troops was abandoned because this demanded really fine weather – but then the whole operation demanded this fine weather – and that no one was certain whether there was sufficient time to train the paratroops for this mission. But had they not already been briefed for *Rutter*? Or else, if others were chosen, could they not be made to do the job in double quick time when told what was expected of them?

We already know the reasons which weighed against a preliminary bombing – the risk of putting the enemy on his guard and of piling up masses of insuperable rubble in the path of the tanks, not to mention the losses to which the civilian population would have been exposed. Furthermore, at neither of the two periods envisaged for the raid, i.e. between the 18th and 23rd August and between the 1st and 7th September, would the moon be favourable for a night bombing attack, and Air Vice-Marshal Leigh-Mallory, commanding the aerial forces engaged in the operation, could guarantee no precision. 'Very much to the contrary,' wrote General Roberts, 'because since it had always been insisted upon that this bombing should be carried out at night, imprecision was guaranteed.' However, the commander of the 2nd Canadian Division, who after all

[1] Quoted by Stacey, *Six Years of War*, Vol. I, p. 141.

was to have the responsibility of the land operations, does not appear to have been particularly disturbed by the conditions in which his troops were to be engaged. Colonel Durnford-Slater, who was to lead a British Commando at Berneval, seems to have been struck by his passiveness during the preliminary discussions. 'General Roberts took practically no part when asked to say whether the plans suited him. Like the rest of us he was convinced of the possibility of carrying it out but, as opposed to Leigh-Mallory, he did not raise the least objection.'[1]

The final plans were complete on the 31st July, but the participants were not to be notified until the last moment. To put the tank crews, which had to be trained to embark in the L.C.T.s, off the scent the 2nd Canadian Division announced on the 10th August a course of training to begin on the 15th, lasting a month. These exercises were designed in the main to test the procedure used to ensure the buoyancy of the tanks, which had been equipped with a very original type of elevated exhaust pipe, and a host of technical problems. What type of ammunition to issue to the infantry, how to protect the combatants from the effects of water, how to dress the men who would undoubtedly get drenched. Was it advisable to dress them in canvas or was it not better to let them wear the regulation battledress? What was the best way of getting radio sets and their batteries, etc., ashore, without their being ruined.

On the 11th August, General Crerar reported to General McNaughton that he had no revisions to make to the final plans. The latter approved them on the 14th, on the 16th units of the 2nd Canadian Division, detailed to participate in the operation, were despatched to their embarkation points.

According to the words of a British admiral, 'the Royal Navy is a gun whose projectile is the British Army'. Now the gun was loaded against Dieppe, but the projectile was Canadian. The entire C.O. Hq. had its finger on the firing cord, waiting for the order to fire to be given. In accordance with a chain of commands, from the 2nd Canadian Division (General Roberts), the 1st Corps (Crerar), the 1st Army (McNaughton) and the commander of the British Home Forces (Paget) to

[1] Durnford-Slater, *Commando*, p. 99.

the committee of the Chiefs of Staff, the final decision rested with the British War Cabinet and, in practice, with Churchill. We know how his time was spent during the first 15 days of August: he was in Moscow and Cairo. In both places, he had to cope with a host of troubles and difficulties. . . . It was the most unfavourable setting for a decision, which had taken long to ripen and had been coldly calculated.

CHAPTER TWELVE

THE NEW EQUIPMENT

I STILL have a delightful recollection of the first amphibian operation in which I took part. Firstly, because I was only 23, and secondly because it took place on one of those marvellous June nights, peculiar to the coast of Provence – and, I almost forgot to mention, because it was only a peacetime exercise. My gear had been stowed for a week in the battleship *Lorraine*, and I was rather proud of this, because she was the flagship of the Mediterranean Squadron. The purpose of the exercise was to blow up a culvert on the Nice–Marseilles railway in the neighbourhood of Golfe-Juan, and the most redoubtable enemy consisted of a cactus bush upon which I sat in the dark.

In those days the landing of a detachment from a large ship entailed a ceremonial in which the part of the enemy was of only conventional importance. The boats were lowered into the water; the men, wearing gaiters and helmets, embarked in them, carrying their muskets, with a rattle of metal and yells from the petty officers who, in order to silence the ratings, had to outshout them. As soon as everyone had installed himself in the darkness, and there was no one to jostle, and no hands to crush scrambling down a rope ladder, a steamer spitting a rain of sparks took the convoy in tow in line ahead – large sloops, canoes, and armed whalers which even at night flew the national flag. On their arrival at the beach, the sloops anchored a few yards off shore in order not to run aground. Then the lighter whalers moored alongside their bows and, if the man-oeuvre had been well executed, the landing plank in the bows, held by two bare-foot topmen with bell-bottoms turned up, reached the dry sand, allowing everyone else to jump ashore without getting their feet wet.

This is how a landing was carried out in the thirties. Not very different from what it must have been a hundred years earlier when Admiral Duperre's fleet carried the Algerian expeditionary force to the beach at Sidi Ferruch.

Precisely the same way in which the landing had been effected on the Gallipoli beaches in 1915. And since the Dardanelles expedition had left a nasty taste in the mouth, everyone was convinced that there would never be any more landings in force. In other words, these landing exercises were not taken very seriously, but were considered good enough to absorb some of the superfluous energy of the marines.

Every navy, however, including the French Navy, had been forced to experiment with landing-craft of a slightly better quality. We had three at the outbreak of war – three motor launches built specially for the Lorient school of marines. They came to a sad end at Le Havre, where they had been sent at the beginning of June 1940 when there was still hope that the Germans would be halted on the Somme, and when the idea of making a landing in their rear had been under review.

The first landings under fire on 14th May, 1940, at Bjervik, during the Narvik campaign were carried out with British material. The number of amphibian craft was less than a dozen – a few L.C.A.s (landing-craft assault) for the troops, two or three M.L.C.s (motor landing-craft), forerunners of the L.C.M.s (landing-craft mechanized), each carrying a tank. In one of them serious difficulties were encountered on account of a ramp that refused to descend, but the tanks were finally put ashore at the same time as the Béthouart legionaries, and the Germans were obliged to flee into the mountains. A fortnight later, thanks to this successful landing, the Allies entered Narvik.

Thus their first victory in this war was an amphibian operation.

*   *   *

Nine L.C.A.s and two L.C.M.s participated in the Dunkirk operation, where five of the former and two of the latter were lost together with the vessel carrying them. But the four remaining craft returned to England, somewhat damaged, but delighted that they had managed to evacuate 2,000 men from the beaches.

By and large the results were encouraging. Orders were given for 64 L.C.A.s, 4 L.C.M.s and 6 L.C.S.s (landing-craft support) at the end of September, followed by a second order for 104 L.C.A.s.

At the same time the Americans perfected the L.C.P. (landing-craft personnel) designed by a particularly talented engineer named Higgins. The British thought well of him and ordered 136.

L.C.A., L.C.P. and L.C.M. were not sea-going craft. For long-range operations the British transformed into L.S.I.s (landing ship infantry) a few small steamers capable of carrying approximately a battalion, and six L.C.A.s and two L.C.M.s to put the men ashore on the chosen beach. According to the size of the vessel they were classified as L.S.I.(L.) (large), L.S.I.(M.) (medium) and L.S.I.(S) (small).

None of these, however, solved the question of transporting tanks; for the L.C.M., the only craft capable of carrying one, was considered inadequate for crossing the Channel. Moreover it was impossible to lower it into the water loaded in an L.S.I. A craft was urgently needed, capable of beaching like the L.C.M. and sufficiently large to be sea-worthy. In this way was born the L.C.T. (landing-craft tanks), the first of which underwent its trials on the Tyne in November 1940. It was subsequently to be replaced for lengthy expeditions by the L.S.T. (landing-ships tanks), large sea-worthy craft capable of beaching with a displacement of 4–5,000 tons when fully loaded. The first of them, the *Bachaquero*, a re-fitted tanker, landed its tanks without trouble in a few minutes on the sandy beach at Courrier near Diego-Suarez on 5th May, 1942, but it must be remarked that this was on a practically undefended shore.

As a complement to the L.C.T.s, Admiral Mountbatten required in 1942 a raider capable of transporting 200 men by sea across the Channel and of landing them directly on the beach. His answer was the L.C.I. (landing-craft infantry), which the Americans agreed to build. The first batch was ready in December, naturally too late to take part in the Dieppe raid, for which there existed as yet only L.C.A.s, L.C.P.s, L.C.M.s, L.C.T.s and L.S.I.s.

But in order to guarantee the protection of these 'engines of war' and to engage the coastal defences at point-blank range, it was indispensable to have craft equally capable of beaching, or at least of sailing, in very shallow waters. On the initiative of Churchill, who had accompanied King George VI on an inspection of the training centre for amphibian craft at Inveraray, two L.C.T.s were transformed, decked and equipped, one with two 4 inch guns, the other with eight 2 lb. mortars, and the other with four 20 mm. Oerlikons. These were the first L.C.F. (landing-craft flak). Later many others were built. Six of them took part at Dieppe.

To complete the different types of landing-craft which took part in Operation *Jubilee* mention must be made of the L.C.S. (landing-craft support), much smaller than the L.C.F. and armed for close combat. The following are the specifications of the different craft.

L.C.A.: Landing-craft Assault

An all-British conception, this craft, capable of being transported by big ships, was designed to put ashore a platoon of infantry in less than two feet of water. More than 2,000 of them were built during the war. The hull was laminated with lateral plates, an armour-plated door to stern of the ramp and two lateral decks to give cover to the passengers. Two 65 h.p. Ford V.8's drove the twin screws.

Specifications

Length – 12·65; beam – 3·10; total draught – 0·55 to 0·70.
Displacement: 9 tons light, 13 tons fully loaded.
Speed: 7–10 knots; radius of action 90–100 miles.
Transport capacity: 35 men and 875 lb. of equipment.
Armament: 1 heavy machine-gun (Bren gun).
Crew: 4 men plus 1 officer for 3 L.C.A.s.

L.C.M. (1): Landing-craft Mechanized (Mark 1)

Designed to carry a light tank or two motor vehicles. Used for amphibian operations, originally for putting ashore the first vehicles, and later to act as lighters between the transports and the beach.

Specifications

L. – 13·60; b. – 4·27; t.d. – bows 0·46, stern 0·84.
Displacement: 21 tons light; 35 tons fully loaded.
Speed: 6 knots, 5–7·5 knots.
2 60 h.p. petrol engines, Chrysler or Thorneycroft.
Radius of action: 80 miles, 6·5 knots.
Transport capacity: 1 tank or 1 self-propelling machine-
    gun, or 1 truck of less than 16 tons, or 6 jeeps, or 2
    Bren carriers.
Partially protected by its own weapons.
Crew: 1 officer and 6 men.

L.C.P.(L): Landing-craft Personnel (Large)

Derived from the American R-boat, these small landing
barges built entirely of wood had no collapsible ramp, but
low-decked bows from which the troops left when landing.
When carried by the L.S.I.s they could be lowered fully loaded
by means of catheads. No protection.

Specifications

L. – 11·17; b. – 3·30; t.d. – bows 0·74, stern 1·07.
Displacement: 6·5 tons light, 9 tons fully loaded.
A single Hall-Scott engine.
Speed: 7·5–9·25 knots.
Radius of action: 150–320 miles.
Armament: 1 Lewis machine-gun.
Transport capacity: 25 men or 4 tons of material.
Crew: 1 officer and 3 men.

L.C.S.(L.): Landing-craft Support (Large)

Designed towards the end of 1940 for the dual purpose of
being carried by an L.S.I. and as an anti-tank weapon.

Specifications

L. – 14·30; b. – 3·84; t.d. – bows 0·71; stern 1·30.
Displacement: 24·5 tons, 2 165 h.p. Gray diesel motors,
    twin screws.
Speed: 10·75 knots. Radius of action: 100 miles.

Armament: 1 anti-tank 40 mm. gun in the tank turret.
             2 12·7 machine-guns.
             2 7·6 machine-guns.
             1 4 inch smoke-laying mortar.
Protected against 12·77 mm.
Crew: 1 officer, 11 men.

L.C.F.(L.): Landing-craft Flak (Large)

The L.C.F.(L.) was the largest landing-craft used for the
Dieppe landing. Derived from the L.C.T., it had been designed
to ensure the protection of the assault forces against low altitude attacks from the air, and against surface attacks before
and during the landing, and to be able to direct its fire against
enemy machine-gun emplacements or concrete pillboxes.

Specifications

L. – 48·55; b. – 9·45; t.d. – 2·20.
Displacement about 400 tons.
Diesels, twin screws. Speed: 11·5 knots.
Bridge and gun turrets.
Armament: on the 6 L.C.F.s used at Dieppe, the L.C.F. 1
             had twin 4 inch and 3·20 mm. Oerlikons; the L.C.F.s
             2–6 carried 8 40 mm. pompoms and 2 Oerlikons.
Crew: (variable according to the armament). On an
             average 2 officers and 79 men.
In addition, for Operation *Jubilee*, most of these craft
             carried a doctor.

L.C.T. (Landing-craft Tank)

A large barge enabling tanks and vehicles to be landed on
sloping beaches of a minimum of 1 in 3 gradient.

Specifications

L. – 43·75; b. – 9·45; t.d. – light 0·58, bows 1·52, stern
             loaded 1·12 bows, 2·13 stern
Displacement: light 296 tons.
2 engines, 2 screws V. Speed: 11 knots.
Transport capacity: 3 40 ton tanks.
No protection.

Armament: 2 pompoms.
Crew: 2 officers, 10 men.

L.S.I. (Landing-ship Infantry)
Various Specifications
(a) L.S.I.(S.)

Prince Charles, Prince Albert

Displacement: 3,600 tons.
Speed: 22 knots.
Capacity: 8 L.C.P.(L.) or L.C.A. or L.C.S. 270 men.
Crew: 200.

(b) L.S.I.(L.)
Glengyle, 13,000 tons, speed 19 knots.
Capacity: 12 L.C.A. or L.C.S. 700 men.
Crew: 280.

*   *   *

Such was the new equipment which the whole of England, led of course by C.O. Hq., was burning to try out on a grand scale. Although the choice of Dieppe for this experiment finally turned out to demand an appalling price in human life, we must not lose sight of the lessons learnt. On the other hand one cannot compare the value of this costly experiment with the knowledge which was to be gained later in the Mediterranean. As Forrest Pogue wrote: 'It was thanks to the Mediterranean operations in 1942–43 that the future leaders had time to work out a new strategy and to apply the lessons learned in battle.'

This is also the opinion of the famous American critic Hanson Baldwin, who considered that North Africa was a training ground, a military school for the Allies, a dress rehearsal for a more important and more difficult play that was still to be performed.[1]

[1] These two questions are taken from R. W. Thomson's book, The Price of Victory.

Part Two

THE 19th AUGUST

PROLOGUE

Jo LOVEGROVE made no comment when Jean-Albert Errard, at the moment of leaving, asked her for two days' sandwiches. Then, as she watched him go, swallowed up beneath an incredible amount of gear, she was seized by a sudden presentiment. She ran up to her bedroom to look for a precious souvenir to give him, and returned with a small silver ship.

'Take this, it will bring you luck,' she said, handing it to him.

Reserve Leading Seaman Errard had been mobilized in 1940 and joined the sloop *Commandant Delage*. He was present at the evacuation of Dunkirk, and sailed his ship between the sprays of bombs and corpses floating in the water. On his return to Brest on 11th June, he learnt that he had been transferred from the *Delage* to another aviso of the same class, the *Boudeuse*, but the latter left without him and he found himself without a ship. Eight days later, to escape the invasion, he embarked at Camaret in a fishing boat which took him to Plymouth. A few days later he joined de Gaulle's forces and exchanged his cap badge for that of the Free French Naval Forces.

This step had led him to a thousand adventures, to Dakar, to the Gaboon and to Syria. . . . Then, in the summer of 1941, bored to death in the Levant, he had put in a request to return to England where, at the beginning of 1942, he went into training with the 1st Battalion of Marines, a commando created by Lt. Kieffer.

The training was tough, but life was not without its charm, for these volunteers led a very special life. No barracks, complete liberty outside the hours of service, and quarters among the local population. With three of his comrades, Errard had been billeted in a small boarding house kept by Jo Lovegrove in a charming villa rented from a cousin of Lloyd George at Brynhenllan, Criccieth, North Wales. From here they left every morning for their training ground, and often on a Saturday, in full battledress, carrying heavy kit, they left for long route marches from which they returned in the evening completely exhausted.

This is why Jo was not greatly surprised to see him leave that Saturday, 15th August, with his kit. But the provisions for two days, and the fact that he left on his own, suddenly made her think that all these exercises must one day or another lead to something serious. Now Jo, who was a good hostess to her four lodgers, had a particular weakness for Errard. She was eventually to marry him and to leave North Wales for the Latour-Maubourg district of Paris.

Her presentiments were correct. The mascot she gave to her sailor proved efficacious, for Errard returned safe and sound from an expedition in which, according to the statement of the leader of No. 4 Commando, Lt.-Colonel Lord Lovat, he had every chance of becoming a corpse.

Kieffer, at the request of the British, had selected 15 men to participate in the Dieppe raid. Once before, at the beginning of July, an M.P. had taken Errard from the arms of Jo in a dance hall. This was for Operation *Rutter*, but he had known nothing about it; for him, the raid had turned out to be a simple trip in a truck and the expedition had been called off before he was given any information. This time things appeared more serious. From the training centre, the men were entrained and on Sunday, 16th they arrived in London with four hours leave, which naturally could only end in a pub. Time to swallow a few whiskies and then on their way as the clock struck 12.

On arriving at Newhaven they were sent to a hush-hush camp. They were shown pictures of coasts and a spot whose name they were not told. 'This is where you will land, just at the foot of this cliff. Here's the entrance to the ravine. Look out for the machine-gun which is posted where I've placed my cane.'

And they embarked on the 18th.

*   *   *

One who might have found the time drag more than the former ex-leading seaman of the *Commandant Delage* was Petty Officer Paul Voisin. With a little luck he might have left Dunkirk in Errard's boat or on some other. Surviving the offensive on the Meuse with some units of the 5th Motorized Infantry Division, he had waited three days at Bray-Dunes in vain for an opportunity to escape. With a few comrades on the morning of 4th June, 1940, the last morning of Dunkirk, he had launched an abandoned sand-locked boat to try and cross the Straits. The colonel had told them that they would not get far. They rejected his advice, but the current proved too strong. They sailed two miles, then gave up, and were brought back to the beach where the Germans arrested them.

This was now two years and two months ago, and sometimes the time seemed very long in this lost village of Ziegenheim in Westphalia.

Sergeant Voisin did not consider his lot to be worse than any of the others. In his wisdom he had considered it preferable to agree to plough the land, rather than languish behind the barbed wire of Stalag IX, to which his rank entitled him. Billeted with about 60 of his comrades in a commando hut, he went every morning to the farm, ate his fill and worked at a profession which was, after all, not very different from that which he practised in peacetime at Hautot-sur-Mer near Dieppe on the property of which he was in charge.

But this was not quite the same thing! And perhaps that Tuesday, 18th August, 1942, as he walked at nightfall along the path leading to Kommando No. 487, he thought with a trace of sadness of the gentle light which at nightfall bathes the incomparable plain which stretches as far as the eye can see before his little house at Hautot. How did his plain look that evening? How were his garden and his trees? What was the weather like? When would he see his own folk again – a year, two years – who could tell. At the speed things were going. . . .

He would certainly have been very surprised had anyone told him that they would be fighting near his home on the following day and that, thanks to this battle, he would be home in three weeks!

18th August, 1942. 2100 hrs. The slow train from Rouen had

just stopped in the station of Petit-Appeville, the last halt before the tunnel through the wall of chalk which separated Dieppe and the valley of the Arques from the valley of the Scie. A woman got out, accompanied by her two children, a boy and a girl of between twelve and thirteen. Darkness had begun to fall, but the evening was exceptionally mild, and the silence so profound and complete that Madame Mirabaud was struck by it.

What disturbed her, above all, was not to see the cart of Papa Quilan, the Varengeville baker, whom she had asked to come and meet her that evening at the station. Her fears proved groundless. She heard the sound of horses' feet on the road. It was the baker. He picked up her baggage and set out. It was so peaceful that it was sad to think of the war. More so, in occupied territory on a coast heavily guarded by an enemy army, which had to be borne because no one had been able to prevent it coming, looking out on such a strangely empty sea, and in the far distance a friendly coast hidden beneath the veil of darkness which had descended since the invasion. . . . 'The far shore,' as the British called it. It had never appeared so remote. . . .

The horse trotted along the sunken road which, avoiding the hairpin bends of Le Havre road, led to the top of the plateau. During the First World War Indian troops had taken up their quarters in this gully. Traces of their sojourn remained in the shape of concrete foundations from which the huts had long since disappeared.

They reached Varengeville. Madame Mirabaud and her children could no longer go to the large white house at the edge of the cliff above the port of Ailly. The Germans had commandeered it. They had had to rent a room in a small boarding-house, where they arranged their lives as best they could. The children fell asleep, but Madame Mirabaud was unable to sleep. She seemed to have dropped off for a few moments when the crackle of machine-guns awakened her. The flak was in action. The sound of bombs and an appalling crash. . . . Less than 1,500 yards away the British had just blown up the ammunition dump of the Varengeville battery. At the same moment, had Papa Quilan forgotten her that evening, Madame Mirabaud would have met at the Havre cross-roads, wearing the same 'shaving dish' which the leader of the Indians had worn in 1914, the soldiers of the Queens Own Cameron Highlanders of Canada.

*   *   *

For the inhabitants of this coast, that evening of the 18th August had been no different from any other evening, except that it was slightly more beautiful. The German occupation was doubtless oppressive, but it was not particularly rigorous at Dieppe. The people of Normandy are cautious and cunning. They refrained from arousing for no reason the anger of their conquerors, and in general did not approve of the hopeless manifestations which some of the resistance groups had begun to stage. Not that they were indifferent, but they love efficiency. It was useless causing trouble unless you created the same for the enemy. This is why the occupying authorities had not yet been seriously disturbed by the behaviour of the population. A telephone cable cut here and there. Sometimes an old sporting gun undeclared, but generally unserviceable. . . . This was about the extent. . . .[1]

Their greatest worry so far had come from the R.A.F., whose raids on the coast were more in the nature of a provocation than a systematic offensive, and were characterized by a sort of irregular time-table.

On consideration, however, these raids had clearly multiplied for some time. In the month of June, five attacks had been made on the town, one of which, on the 5th, was particularly long and violent and had caused serious damage in Dieppe. At sea there was a great deal of machine-gunning. Confined one imagines to the German shipping, it unfortunately did not spare the French fishing boats. On the 18th June, for example, two naval recruits were killed in the trawler *Alexandrine-Grand*. To offset this, on the 17th July, the target was better chosen, since a German patrol boat was sunk three miles off Mesnilval. One of the German sailors was killed and the others were picked up by the French barques, *André Marie* and *Inter-Nos*.

In July there were a good half dozen attacks. No more

[1] Unfortunately there were exceptions. An inhabitant of Saint-Nicolas d'Alliermont, arrested on the 16th June, 1942, for concealing a weapon, was shot on the 19th September.

bombs. The tactics had changed. The R.A.F. had started to 'prang' trains at the expense of the French railway personnel.

The beginning of August, however, had been remarkably calm. No alert was reported during the first fortnight, either on land or at sea at the expense of the fishermen. On the 16th, however, a Spitfire was shot down at Bréauté, in the sector of the 332nd Division, and the same day a little before 2000 hrs. a German patrol vessel returned to port with five wounded, one seriously.

There was nothing particularly significant in these sporadic attacks. Nothing of course comparable with the methodical strategic offensive which took place two years later, during the months prior to the Normandy landings. Nothing either which could herald the formidable air battle which developed on the 19th August over Dieppe – the most violent and bloodiest since the Battle of Britain.

There was, however, a new indication. The first American Flying Fortresses had just appeared over Rouen. For weeks German propaganda had taunted the U.S. Air Force – 'Where are your Americans?' asked leaflets dropped in their hundreds on all the British airfields, within range of the Luftwaffe.

'Reassure yourselves! Here they are.' On the 17th August at 1756 hrs. General Ira Eaker took off from Grafton-under-Wood airfield in Great Britain, in the B.17 *Yankee Doodle*, with 11 other Fortresses, escorted by R.A.F. fighters. This was the first time that the American airmen had shown themselves in the air over occupied France. The target was the marshalling yards of Sotteville-lès-Rouen. For most of the crews of No. 97 Bomber Group, it was their baptism of fire. They had just taken up their quarters in Great Britain, at Polbrook in East Anglia. A new enemy had arrived for the flak and the German fighters. The experience was conclusive. The 12 Fortresses passed unharmed through the bursts of flak. A few fighters from Jafu 3 had managed to take off.[1] They could not prevent Eaker giving his signal: 'bombs away'. Twenty-five large bombs fell on the target in the marshalling yards, which incidentally was otherwise unaffected, but that is another story.

The Germans suffered 12 dead and 32 wounded. This would

[1] *Jagdfliegerführung* (Fighter Group).

have been perfect had the civilian population not been sorely tried with 51 dead and 82 wounded.

The 12 Fortresses returned intact to the great satisfaction of General Sparks, commanding the 8th American Air Force in Great Britain, who had anxiously awaited their return on the airfield. Everyone was delighted. The American airmen, intoxicated by their success, would be able to play their part in the great aerial circus planned for the following day, 19th August.

*   *   *

On the Dieppe coast everything was calm. The normal routine. . . . The inhabitants were allowed to visit certain beaches and there were plenty of bathers about in this fine weather. A young woman from Hautot-sur-Mer had arranged to meet her friends to bicycle to Pourville, that Wednesday morning, 19th August. A stray bullet, fired by a plane, broke her leg just as she was getting on her bicycle, and in this way prevented her from coming face to face with the Cameron Highlanders.

The fishermen had been out on the 18th from morning to nightfall, within the three-mile limit laid down by Captain Wahn. Only in the Pas de Calais was the night of the 17th disturbed by a raid from British M.T.B.s, covered by the battery from Saint-Margaret's Bay on the Kent coast which replied to the guns of Griz Nez and Boulogne. Twenty-eight large shells fell on the French coast, doing little damage, but the encounter at sea was more serious, and the 18th Flotilla of German patrol boats clashed with the British coastal forces. On returning to port they claimed at least one of the enemy sunk and probably a second, and two others set on fire. There must have been an element of truth for these claims, since that night the navy lost M.T.B. 43 off Gravelines and M.T.B. 218 farther out to sea in the Straits of Dover. On the other hand, the 4th E-boat Flotilla, which had come out to sweep mines, had to break off its operations because of the fog.

1945 hrs. German time. Before going aboard Lt. Bögel visited the harbour commander's office in Boulogne. He was informed in a few words of the night's incidents. Nothing but routine. . . . 'Any special orders for my convoy?'

'Nothing for the moment. Your three coasters are ready to sail. The *Rosa* route as usual. . . . Nothing reported from "over there"; Dieppe is expecting you at 0500 hrs. Oh, I forgot, after the moon sets the Ailly lighthouse will flash for three minutes every quarter of an hour. Keep a good look-out, too, because there must be two or three patrol boats in the neighbourhood. Have you today's recognition signals?'

'Yes, would you like to check them?'

'All in order. Good luck . . . and no unpleasant encounters.'

The lieutenant boarded his U.J. (Ubootjäger). The convoy totalled five ships – one heavy minesweeper, two light R-boats and two U.J.s escorting the small convoy. He was in command.

Aboard everything was shipshape. Ropes singled, engines trimmed. His second-in-command awaited him in the cabin. Gangway raised. Bögel ran up to the bridge. A glance ahead, a glance astern. . . .

Leinen los! Cast off!

CHAPTER THIRTEEN

INTRODUCTION TO THE COMBAT

DIEPPE was therefore to be attacked directly without preparation from the air, without a naval bombardment and without the intervention of paratroops. We already know the name of the commander-in-chief of the land forces – General Roberts, commanding the 2nd Canadian Division. On 17th July the command of the naval forces was entrusted to Captain Hughes-Hallett, R.N., whom we have already met as technical adviser to C.O. Hq. Both men sailed in the destroyer H.M.S. *Calpe* in which Hughes-Hallett struck his flag. On the other hand, Air Marshal Leigh-Mallory, in command of the aircraft engaged, remained at No. 11 Fighter Command Group Hq. at Uxbridge, where he was joined by Admiral Mountbatten and General Crerar. He was represented on the *Calpe* by Air Commodore Cole who remained in constant radio communication with No. 11 Group. At Portsmouth, Admiral Sir William James, whose lot was to dispatch the expedition, was in a fury. It would happen that on this particular Tuesday, at this awkward moment, one of those V.I.P.s should arrive out of the blue – Admiral Stark, U.S.N., head of the American naval liaison mission whom he was bound to receive.

'As soon as the American had left I rushed to the Fort and discussed the operation with Mountbatten and Leigh-Mallory. We had a mass of meteorological information, sometimes contradictory, but we finally decided to give the signal for the raid to proceed. I remarked to Mountbatten that one should never tell the experts anything about an operation for which they had been consulted. It was only too human for these 'met' fellows to see the worst side of things as soon as they were told that an important operation, jeopardizing thousands of human lives, depended upon the way in which they interpreted the weather chart.'[1]

[1] James, *Portsmouth Letters*.

The American observers had taken up their positions in different ships of the naval force. General Truscott was aboard H.M.S. *Fernie*, the reserve Hq., together with Brigadier-General Mann, G.S.O.1 of the 2nd Canadian Division, with half his staff, the other half having embarked in H.M.S. *Calpe* with General Roberts. This was more than enough to fill the little space available in these small destroyers. An operational headquarters had been arranged in the wardroom, whose walls were covered with maps. On a table a plan of the coastal sector where the raid was to take place, radio sets in all the corners. . . .

The battle order and the plans had been dictated by the geography and the organization of the enemy defences. They can be listed as follows:

In the centre the main objective Dieppe, with its beach and port flanked by two cliffs, both of which were powerfully fortified. To the east the cliff bore the name of the Bismarck position, to the west, below the town, was the Hindenburg position.

The 1,500 yards of beach extending between the fairway into the harbour to the east and the cliff of Bas Fort-Blanc to the west were arbitrarily divided into two parts – Red beach on the port side and White beach on the Bas Fort-Blanc side.

The two beaches framing Dieppe, to the east Puys and to the west Pourville, from where the fortified Bismarck and Hindenburg positions could be attacked, were christened respectively Blue beach and Green beach. On each of these two Canadian battalions were to land. At Dieppe itself three battalions and one battalion of tanks were detailed to land.

There remained the two outer batteries of Berneval and Varengeville which, according to the *Rutter* plan, were to be taken by paratroops. In Operation *Jubilee* they were given as targets to No. 3 Commando (Berneval) and No. 4 (Varengeville). Both of them were to be attacked from both flanks at the same time, so as to be caught between two fires. No. 3 Commando, therefore, was to land partly on the Berneval beach (Yellow 1) and partly on the Belleville-sur-Mer beach (Yellow 2). No. 4 Commando would use the beaches of Vasterival (Orange 1) and Sainte-Marguerite (Orange 2).

The batteries of Saint-Valery-en-Caux, 1/779 and of

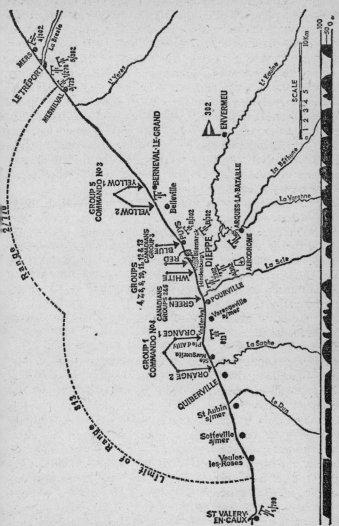

The five sectors of attack and the German coastal batteries

Mesnilval, 3/770, were ignored as being too far apart. In fact they would not intervene directly against the landing zones. Actually the 1/779 was to fire sporadically against the ships on the right wing of the British naval force, and the 3/770 at Mesnilval fired 227 150 mm. shells against its left wing.

All in all, five landing zones and, therefore, a minimum of groups to organize except the transportation of the first wave.

Each landing force consisted of one or more troop transports (L.S.I.) with its L.C.A.s, L.C.S.s escorted by small support craft (S.G.B.s, L.C.F.s, M.L.s and M.G.B.s). Incidentally No. 5 Group, detailed for the Yellow beaches, had no L.S.I., No. 3 Commando having embarked directly at Newhaven in the L.C.P.s of the 1st and 24th Flotillas, to be put ashore without transhipment.

Now there remained to organize the remote support of the landing-craft.

In 1942 there did not, as yet, exist any definite doctrine for the support of operations against the land. The memory still remained of the Dardanelles when the British and French cruisers, entrusted with the task of reducing the Turkish batteries, had blown up one after the other on the mines generously sown by the adversary. The Channel with its shallows, was an admirable field for sowing classic buoy mines as well as magnetic mines. This was one of the reasons why the big ships had not been used, and why the main Naval support was represented by a modest contingent of eight Hunt class destroyers, whose main armament was confined to four 4 inch guns, and whose torpedoes were of no interest for this particular operation.

Seven of these destroyers were from the Royal Navy, and the eighth from the Polish navy.

H.M.S. *Calpe*, Lt.-Commander J. H. Wallace, R.N. (the flagship of Captain Hughes-Hallett and General Roberts).

H.M.S. *Fernie*, Lt. W. P. Willett, R.N., Reserve Hq. (the actual commander, Lt.-Commander Ackworth had been wounded the previous day).

H.M.S. *Albrighton*, Lt.-Commander R. J. Hanson, R.N.

H.M.S. *Berkeley*, Lt. J. J. S. Yorke, R.N.

H.M.S. *Brocklesby*, Lt.-Commander E. N. Pumphrey, R.N.

H.M.S. *Bleasedale*, Lt. P. B. North-Lewis, R.N.

H.M.S. *Garth*, Lt.-Commander J. P. Scatchard, R.N.

O.R.P. *Slazek*, Kmdr. Popov R. Tyminski.

To these eight destroyers must be added two sloops or gun-boats, H.M.S. *Alresford*, Commander R. E. C. Dunbar, R.N. (Retd.) and H.M.S. *Locust*, Lt.-Commander W. J. Stride, R.N. (Retd.); 12 motor gunboats (M.G.B.), four steam gunboats (S.G.B.) and 20 motor launches (M.L.) designed for close quarters support. And finally, a special mission had been given to seven French chasseurs, three of which were commissioned by the Royal Navy and four by the Free French Naval Forces:[1]

Chasseur 14, Lt. W. H. P. Loftie, R.N.

Chasseur 43, Lt. Boju, F.F.N.F.

Chasseur 42, Petty Officer Parc, F.F.N.F.

Chasseur 13, Lt. E. G. Egerton, R.N.

Chasseur 41, Lt. J. E. Syms, R.N.

Chasseur 10, Sub.-Lt. Chanlieau, F.F.N.F.

Chasseur 5, Lt. Ibarluccia, F.F.N.F.

These 53 ships represented the total of the support forces. The amphibian flotilla for the transport and the landing of the troops consisted of:

- 9 L.S.I. carrying all told 60 L.C.A., 8 L.C.S and 7 L.C.M.
- 78 L.C.P.
- 6 L.C.F.
- 24 L.C.T.
- 7 L.C.M.

in all, 191 landing-craft, bringing the total up to 244, not including the minesweepers which were to clear the waters ahead of the expedition.

These different 'engines of war' were divided into 13 groups:
- Group Nos. 1–6 for the landing of the commandos and the Canadian infantry (one per sector and two for Pourville);
- Group No. 7 reserve afloat;
- Group Nos. 8–11, L.C.T.s for the landing of the tanks;
- Group No. 12, L.C.T. for the staffs of the 4th and 6th Brigades and the Medical Corps.

[1] An eighth had been briefed, Chasseur 11, Lt. Montador. As will be seen later, it was unable to put to sea.

– Group No. 13. Gunboats and chasseurs to force the entrance to the port, to capture any German war material to be found there and to destroy the port installations.

This was far the most important expedition of all those which had so far been staged. Its assembly and dispatch naturally demanded great care. They took place in the five ports of Shoreham, Newhaven, Southampton, Portsmouth and Gosport, the latter being specially devoted to the embarkation of the tanks, which began on the evening of the 17th on receipt of orders to prepare, whereas the troops, totalling 6,086 men, did not embark until the afternoon of the 18th on the final order issued on that date at 0010 hrs. by Admiral James.[1]

The landings were to take place nearly at high tide, for two reasons: firstly the extent of the uncovered beach would be reduced to a minimum and secondly, the beaching of the landing craft could be carried out in the best conditions. In actual fact the beaches of the Dieppe coast at low tide consist of strips of sand alternating with rocks, with a very slight slope. At high tide, on the contrary, the sea lashes the 20 feet wide bank of pebbles along the edge of the cliff, with a very much steeper slope. These pebble beaches are greatly disliked by the summer visitors, for they are hard on tender feet. But at least they are without surprises. At high tide, in fine weather, an L.C.A. can approach right up to the cliff or the dyke, and its passengers can land with dry feet. At low tide they would have been forced to wade ashore for some distance up to their waists in water, across ground which was full of obstacles.

On the 19th August, 1942, high tide at Dieppe was at 0303 hrs. G.M.T., i.e. 0403 hrs. English summer time and 0503 hrs. German time. The sun rose at 0505 hrs. In other words, by landing at about 0500 hrs., it was at the start of the ebb tide, in a dawn which had risen at 0430 hrs. Zero hour was fixed at 0450

---

[1] Unfavourable weather reports apparently caused the operation to be postponed for 24 hours from the date planned, the 18th. But when the readiness signal was given on the evening of the 17th, the forecasts were reasonably favourable for the next 48 hours. These forecasts proved to be true.

hrs. for the flank landings and at 0520 hrs. for the main objective, Dieppe.[1]

The sailing of the forces was therefore arranged in stages, the distance to be covered varying between 65 and 120 miles according to the ports of departure, but the itineraries had been arranged so that all groups would be obliged to follow fairways which had been swept at the last moment in the minefields, which the Germans were believed to have laid in the middle of the Channel, approximately parallel to the French coast. On the map reproduced will be seen the limits of this suspected zone, the itineraries of the different groups, the fairways swept, as well as the site of the German minefields actually sown in the summer of 1942.

Four points, respectively marked by the letters DD, LL, FF and QQ, denoted the channels swept half-way between Newhaven and Dieppe. The sweeping of these channels had been entrusted to the ships of the 9th and 13th Flotillas,[2] which sailed separately from Portsmouth on the afternoon of the 18th, assembling at about 2130 hrs. at the point of rendezvous N.N., eight miles south of Newhaven, where four M.L.s with orders to serve as markers awaited them.

The sweeping took place at midnight and was carried out without incident. Each channel, four cables wide (780 yards) was carefully marked with buoys. Not a single mine was seen but some were spotted on the afternoon of the 19th, by the ships returning from Dieppe. They caused no mishap.

Groups No. 1 (Orange), 2 (Green), 3 (Blue), 4 (Red and White), 8, 10, 12 and 13 arrived from the Isle of Wight ports, Portsmouth and Southampton. Their rendezvous was a point eight miles S.E. of Portsmouth. The other groups, which left Shoreham and Newhaven, were to meet at N.N. after a much shorter crossing. They were therefore the last to sail.

[1] In the report of C.-in-C. West, in the section 'Information', we read that the German Command did not consider a landing at daybreak probable. This shows, continues the report, that one must be prepared for everything, even the improbable.

[2] 9th Flotilla, Commander H. T. Rust, R.N., *Sidmouth, Bangor, Blackpool, Bridlington, Bridport, Bude, Rhyl* and *Tenby*.

13th Flotilla, Commander L. J. S. Ede, *Blyth, Clacton, Eastbourne, Felixstowe, Ilfracombe, Polruan, Stornoway* and *Rothesay*.

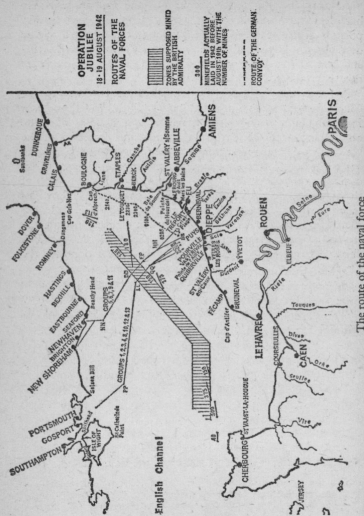

The route of the naval force

At 2115 hrs. the *Queen Emma* was the first to cross the barrage of nets which enclosed the Solent, and took up her position at the head of Groups 2, 1, 3 and 4, followed by the destroyers in line ahead, flanked on either side by the S.G.B.s and M.L.s. The moon in its first quarter set at 2316 hrs. After this they sailed in complete darkness.

At 0100 hrs. H.M.S. *Calpe* reached the entrance to the Channel west of the minefields (LL-QQ), but the *Queen Emma*, by failing to observe the signals, continued as far as the east passage (DD-FF), reserved in principle for ships of the Newhaven–Shoreham sector – without incidentally causing any confusion. Other ships missed the mineswept channels but came to no harm. At 0300 hrs. one entire force were south of the suspected zone. No unfortunate encounters. . . . The element of surprise appeared to be guaranteed. The L.S.I.s set their course for the points assigned them for transhipping the troops in the L.C.A.s, i.e. the points SS, GG, RR and BB, situated respectively ten miles from the coast opposite the Orange, Green, White and Red, and Blue beaches.

Three-quarters of an hour later, when the craft began to make for the shore, a dogfight broke out unexpectedly between the German and British sailors, who were equally surprised by the incident.

CHAPTER FOURTEEN

AN UNEXPECTED ENCOUNTER

WHEN Sergeant Errard arrived at Newhaven quay that Tuesday, the evening of 18th August, a score of L.C.P.s lay moored there, awaiting the personnel of No. 3 Commando, Lt.-Colonel Durnford-Slater, whose mission was to put out of action the Berneval battery. In the craft in which he embarked were two other French sailors, two American Rangers, a few British and Canadian soldiers, in all a dozen men. The other landing-craft had a similar crew.

The 23 vessels of the 1st and 24th Flotillas of L.C.P.s, commanded respectively by Lt. D. R. Stevens and Lt.-Commander D. L. Stork, R.N.V.R., constituted the Assault Group No. 5, under the orders of Commander D. B. Wyburd, R.N., who, as we know, had to make the crossing direct without transhipment.

Wyburd sailed with Durnford-Slater in S.G.B.5, commanded by Lt. Hummel, R.N.V.R. His group comprised the L.C.F. (L.1) commanded by Lt. Foggett of the Australian Navy, and M.L.346 commanded by Lt. Fear, R.N.V.R. After passing the channels marked in the minefields he took up his position to port of the naval force, setting a course for the Yellow beaches, guarded on the flank by the two destroyers *Slazak* and *Brocklesby* which were weaving four miles to the north-east, ready to repel any intervention on the part of the German E-boats.

The moon had set since 0100 hrs. and the approaches were carried out in total darkness. It was now a little after 0340 hrs., and according to the reckoning of Captain Wyburd, Group No. 5 should now be not more than six or seven miles from the coast, which could not as yet be distinguished. Absolute calm reigned and the surprise seemed to be total.

Suddenly at 0347 hrs., the darkness was rent by the flashes

of tracers. Group No. 5 had just run full tilt into a small German convoy, sailing quite peacefully from Boulogne to Dieppe. Its escort, commanded by Lt. Bögel, did not take long to react when the look-out men spotted the outlines of the intruders against the horizon.

Slazak and *Brocklesby* spotted the firing, but instead of setting course for the action, Commander Tyminski, the senior officer, thinking that the firing came from the shore, saw no reason to modify his patrol, and did not interfere in the engagement.

Captain Wyburd, for his part, leading his formation from S.G.B.5, considered that he must remain at his post to try and keep his L.C.P.s in formation. This was very courageous on his part, because for ten good minutes the small gunboat was subjected to the concentrated fire of all the enemy escort vessels, which as Admiral Ruge wrote: 'Gunned and drew alongside anything which came within range of their stem-posts.'[1] But as Captain Hughes-Hallett remarks in his report: 'he would probably have done better to profit by the superior speed of his vessel, to lay a smoke-screen, which would have masked his landing-craft. As was inevitable, S.G.B.5 was soon out of action, her guns reduced to silence, her boilers pierced by five shells and half the crew wounded. To stern the L.C.P.s had scattered in complete confusion.'

On the other hand Lt. Foggett, observing that the enemy only seemed to have eyes for S.G.B.5 which was directly ahead of him, made a sudden flank attack with his L.C.F. 1 and in a few seconds his 202s has registered several direct hits. M.L.346 came up in turn and Lt. Fear competed with his Australian comrade in bravery. Foggett set fire to the submarine-chaser, UJ.1404, which had to be abandoned by its crew. Its burning wreck was spotted about 0530 hrs. by the *Brocklesby* who picked up the 25 survivors before sinking it. The UJ.1404 exploded at 0645 hrs., four miles north-north-west of Berneval. A little later Fear was to settle accounts with the small armed coaster *Franz* (200 tons), which appeared on the scene from the west at the moment when some of the landing-craft were trying to land their troops on Yellow 1 beach. Abandoned by its crew,

[1] Vice-Admiral Friedrich Ruge, *The War at Sea*.

the *Franz* ran aground at Penly, where the crew of M.L.346 had the satisfaction of capturing its flag.

Bögel had to take his convoy to Le Tréport where the crew of the *Franz* also arrived in its lifeboats. He claimed to his credit the destruction of a big assault craft carrying 30/40 men, which had been gunned and rammed by UJ.1411, and believed furthermore that he had seriously damaged two other landing-craft.

The surprise had been total on both sides. Neither had been able to raise the alarm because most of the radio sets had been put out of action at the start of the engagement. But the noise of the gunfire and the flashes of the firing had been enough to arouse the attention of those who witnessed the scene. The Berneval observation post was not long in sounding the alarm in its sector, with the result that at all the points planned for landings, the assailants had logically to expect an enemy well on its guard, when they arrived at 0550 hrs., in other words approximately an hour after this most unfortunate skirmish.

In every account so far published on the Dieppe raid, this chance encounter between the craft of No. 5 Group and the small vessels of the German Boulogne convoy is blamed for the fact that the British lost the benefit of surprise, and that it was largely responsible for the setback to the operation.

This is true to a certain extent, but it is wrong to over-simplify matters. In actual fact matters were far less obvious. If it be true that the passage of the Boulogne convoy was part of the risks inherent in every foray, the presence of a patrol vessel on duty off Dieppe had to be taken into account. Now there was not only one but three, and the craft of the other groups had every chance of meeting them had the Boulogne convoy not forced this encounter. The strange thing is that, although these three patrol vessels realized that something abnormal was taking place, they were content to observe that the attack was out to sea and to return to port.

Having said this, what were the consequences of the first alert given by the Berneval post? If we are to believe the reports of the LXXXIst Army Corps and of the C.-in-C. West, the first result of the engagement was to alert the whole coast. This was certainly the case at Berneval where, within ten minutes, the entire post was at action stations, but certainly not at Pourville where the first wave landed at 0450 hrs., without receiving a shot, and where the men of the mess at La Maison Blanche were strangled in their beds. Nor at Puys where the hero of the German defence, a certain corporal, leaped for his machine-gun, wearing only his helmet and a white nightshirt, which was certainly not the rig of a soldier who had been alerted an hour before.

The report of the 302nd Infantry Division indicates, moreover, that even in Dieppe the 571st Infantry Regiment was only called to action stations (*Gefechtbereitschaft*) at 0500 hrs., in other words, ten minutes after the first landings.

These are the details which can be read on this subject in the logbooks of the 302nd Infantry Division and the LXXXIst Army Corps:[1]

302 Infantry Division

0345 hrs. – Sentry post at Berneval hears fighting at sea.

0357 hrs. – The men of the *Sondergerät* (Luftwaffe) east of Berneval take up their action stations.

0405 hrs. – The 571st Infantry Regiment reports a violent naval engagement about 12 miles from Dieppe.

0410 hrs. – The 572nd Infantry Regiment reports an engagement at sea nine miles from Criel-Plage.

0425 hrs. – The 571st Infantry Regiment reports that since 0345 hrs. one of our convoys is being attacked by enemy naval forces, eight or nine miles off Dieppe.

0430 hrs. – Enemy launches reported off Puys. The II/302 Artillery Regiment orders *Sperrfeuer vor Puys* (barrage fire off Puys).

0450 hrs. – Berneval reports ships in front of the ravine.

LXXXIst Army Corps

0458 hrs. – First report from the 302nd Infantry Division. General alarm for the engagement of the convoy.

[1] All the times recorded in the original documents are one hour in advance of those published here. To simplify matters I have, in principle, except when otherwise stated, adopted British summer time, one hour in advance of G.M.T. but one hour later than German summer time. (G.M.T. plus 1 in the first case, and G.M.T. plus 2 in the second.)

0510 hrs. – Lt.-Colonel Sartorius of the 302nd Infantry
Division, G.S.O.3 (Ic.) announces enemy landings at
Pourville and Quiberville and the bombardment of
Dieppe.

0520 hrs. – Lt.-Colonel Kolbe transmits the news to 15th
Army Hq.

0540 hrs. – The LXXXIst Army Corps reports landings at
Berneval and Dieppe to 15th Army Hq.

0545 hrs. – Nothing to report in the sectors of the 33rd and of
the 711th Infantry Divisions. The Army Corps reserves
alerted. . . .

The first legend to be destroyed, as has been done discreetly
by the official historian of the Canadian army.[1] In the last
analysis this unexpected skirmish did not immediately 'alert
the entire coast'. It compromised the British at Berneval, but
above all because the L.C.P.s of No. 5 Group were dispersed,
and it was insufficient to prevent less than a mile away the
landing of Major Young and his men at Belleville. In view of
this, if No. 3 Commando did not manage to capture Battery
2/770, Young's team at least was able to neutralize it for an
hour and a half, in other words, for the whole time corresponding to the critical period of the landings. We shall see how this
happened in a later chapter.

What emerges from this chronology is the fact that the
engagement occurred at 0347 hrs., and that the alert was not
sounded on the coast until 0458 hrs. By that time No. 4 Commando had already landed at Vasterival and Quiberville, 15
miles farther west.

The truth is, that even at Berneval, although the enemy was
immediately alerted by the gunfire at sea, they by no means
realized at once that an operation against the coast was in progress, and as soon as the skirmish was over they thought quite
naturally that nothing more would happen. In a later chapter
I have published the testimony of Canon Lemercier, curé of
Berneval-le-Grand since 1923, and of M. Pierre Courtin, at the
time captain of the Fire Brigade. The Germans, whom they
met shortly after the bombing attack which at about 0500 hrs.
accompanied the attempt of No. 3 Commando, did not appear

[1] Stacey, op. cit., p. 359.

to suspect anything. At the moment the British troops arrived fully armed at the outskirts of the village, they still believed that it was merely a normal air raid.

* * *

But this is only one aspect of the question. In actual fact, the German defences should have been alerted and informed of an amphibian attack more than an hour before the chance encounter at Berneval, just as on the British side, Hughes-Hallett must have known, since about midnight, that there were Germans at sea.

For in both camps the electro-magnetic detection (radar) had functioned perfectly. Had the information been correctly transmitted or interpreted, it is very possible that at Dieppe today there would be no street bearing the name of 19th August, 1942, nor a well-populated Canadian cemetery on the heights of Janval. Either the British naval force normally informed of the presence of the Boulogne convoy should have purely and simply put about, or the German coastal batteries, particularly the two most powerful units at Berneval and Varengeville, duly alerted, should have barred any approach to the shore.

We shall now examine successively the two camps to follow the vagaries of 'this night of dupes'.

Eight months earlier at Pearl Harbor, Sunday, 7th December, 1941, the G.I.s Joseph Lockard and George Elliot had finished their spell of duty at their radar which, according to orders, had to function from 0400 to 0700 hrs., during the uncertain hours of dawn which are most favourable for surprise attacks.

Having nothing better to do, while awaiting the arrival of the truck which was to take them back to barracks, Elliot, a recruit who was anxious to complete his training, continued to function the apparatus, after the hour his watch should have ended. Suddenly at 0706 hrs., a particularly strong echo appeared on the radar screen, so strong in fact that Lockard thought that the instrument had broken down. But no, everything worked perfectly. It recorded a mass air formation 137 miles from Pearl Harbor, 3° east of north.

The news was immediately telephoned to the anti-aircraft information centre, where Lt. Tyler happened to be alone, waiting to be relieved at eight o'clock. Tyler, impressed by the message which the telegraphist brought him, called the radar station. There was no possible doubt. At 0715 hrs., Elliot and Lockard plotted the formation at 92 miles . . . about 50 aircraft flying towards Hawaii at 180 knots.

As ill luck would have it, the officer suddenly remembered that some Flying Fortresses were expected at Hawaii.

'They're friends,' he said, 'don't worry,' to Lockard.

Twelve Flying Fortresses were in fact at that moment approaching Pearl Harbor, but what Elliot and Lockard had picked up was far more important – 98 Japanese bombers, 48 torpedo-carrying aircraft, with an escort of 43 fighters. At 0755 hrs. they arrived over the target, taking the American Pacific Fleet completely by surprise. The rest of the story is well known.[1]

The reaction of the *Kriegsmarine* at Dieppe was exactly the same as that of Lt. Tyler when, at 0232 hrs. on the 19th August, 1942, the *Flugmeldezentrale* passed on the news that the big Freya radar 28 reported 'numerous targets' at 21 miles off Dieppe. 'O.K.,' replied the sailors, 'it's the Boulogne convoy, which is expected at Dieppe at 0500 hrs.'

Experience had taught the Germans that, although the Freya gave accurate bearings, its precision at distances between 11 and 21 miles (its extreme limit) left much to be desired, could therefore only indicate the approximate speed of the target. It was enough, however, to alert the three patrol vessels of the 2nd *Sicherungsdivision*, which at that moment were at sea off Dieppe. But what was the point of disturbing them since they were awaiting friends?

But it was not the Boulogne convoy which the Freya radar had picked up. These very numerous targets were in fact Hughes-Hallett's ships disengaging from the minefields – a little less than 25 miles from Dieppe to be precise.

For about an hour these targets remained in the same position, then at about 0330 hrs. they were seen distinctly to form into different groups, which appeared to concentrate in the

[1] Cf. Walter Lord, *Pearl Harbor.*

direction of the Dieppe coast. A few minutes later began the naval engagement we have already described, but the German naval command, still having no clear picture of the situation, was satisfied with the idea that it was merely an attack by British M.T.B.s, a normal occurrence. At 0410 hrs., the radio station at Le Havre reported: 'Surface forces attacking our convoy three miles off Dieppe.' The *Marinegruppe West* informed Heeresgruppe D and the 3rd Luftflotte that it was in all probability a routine attack. Had not one, in fact, taken place the previous night?

This was by no means the opinion of Lt. Kohn, head of the central information (F.M.Z.), who, confident of his apparatus, remained at the telephone. Noting the incredulity of the sailors, he alerted the 23rd *Funkmesskompanie* which, in turn, alerted the Ic. of the division who referred the matter to the army corps. Only then did Lt.-Colonel Sartorius take it upon himself to order a general alert for all units of the 302nd Infantry Division. It was a little after 0400 hrs., but the transmission of the alarm was relatively slow, since a large proportion of the front line units were still not at their action stations at the time of the first assault.

Therefore rather it was the radar which had picked up the naval skirmish at Berneval that alerted the 302nd Infantry Division – but with a certain delay. There is no doubt that, without the reticences of the *Kriegsmarine*, the artillery could have opened fire much earlier and in greater concentration. It would be interesting to know what Hughes-Hallett would have done then.

Fire was not opened until 0441 hrs. by the 7/302 Battery at Quatre Vents farm near Pourville. Varengeville did not open fire until six minutes later, in other words, three minutes before the first landing. As for the Berneval battery, it only fired 14 shells on the craft at the entrance to the ravine between 0500 and 0510 hrs. After this it remained silent, apparently unaware that there were more than 100 ships off Dieppe, nor did it open fire again, except in its own defence, until 0555 hrs. Had all these batteries concentrated their barrage simultaneously at 0400 hrs., at the moment when the Freya indicated the suspect formation was heading for the shore, one wonders if the British sailors would have felt entitled to persist.

In any case it must be recognized that neither the report of the C.-in-C. West, nor the war diary of the *Seekriegsleitung* (direction of the war at sea), admit that the radar provided valuable information before the start of the naval engagement at Berneval. But I have obtained my information from Lt.-Colonel Carl Otto Hartmann of Münster, serving at the time with the 23rd *Funkmesskompanie*, who was kind enough to give me a circumstantial account of the events of that night culled from the archives of the *Luftgau Nachrichten Regiment*. Information, incidentally, confirmed by the report of the artillery regiment on Hill 527, attached to the batteries of the Le Tréport–Saint-Valery-en-Caux sector.

'The indications provided by the radar, which was able to follow the progress of the approach, did not reach the coastal artillery, presumably because, at the moment the British naval forces arrived, the engagement with the convoy also occurred. This is precisely what emerges from Hoffmann's account. The radar played its part; it was the exploitation of its information which was at fault.'[1]

Why should we be surprised in these conditions that Captain Wahn, naval commander at Dieppe, did not include in his intelligence report this information which was not taken seriously by his services and only bore fruit after a considerable delay. . . . Doubtless the defence was not yet trained to use the information given by a recently installed apparatus, some of which installations were not yet complete.[2]

Installed far earlier and serviced by better-trained men, the British radar had played its part to perfection. Not so much on ships at sea, only one of which made certain contact, but in the British coastal stations where the apparatus was naturally far more powerful. From 2040 hrs. on the 18th, the German convoy had been picked up on the Dover radar half-way between Boulogne and Etaples. An hour later it was picked up between

---

[1] To my knowledge only Admiral Lepotier in his book, *Raiders from the Sea*, p. 188, makes a short allusion to the indications given by the radar.

[2] This was also the case of the reconnaissance post of the Kreigsmarine at the lighthouse on Ailly headland.

Etaples and the mouth of the River Authie. At 0040 hrs. Portsmouth took over. At 0100 hrs. on the 19th, it was located off the Bay of the Somme 15 miles north of Le Tréport. One hour before the engagement it had been located 10 miles north-west of this port.

Naturally Admiral James, whose staff centralized all this information at Portsmouth, could not know either the composition or the exact destination of these ships, which sent back their echoes on his radar screen. Possibly they were merely patrol vessels. Perhaps, too, these patrols would penetrate Hughes-Hallett's zone of operations. In any case, it was worth while sending a signal. James sent two. The first at 0127 hrs. and the second at 0144 hrs.

It was a waste of time. The first warning was apparently received by no one, in any case not by H.M.S. *Calpe*, since Hughes-Hallet does not mention it in his report, nor by the *Slazak-Brocklesby* group, which was best placed to intercept the German convoy, to destroy it or push it back beyond the Bay of the Somme, far away from the major part of the British naval force. As for the 2nd signal, it was duly received aboard H.M.S. *Fernie* which, it will be remembered, served as the second Hq. afloat, but nobody had any idea that the *Calpe* had failed to receive it, and no one took the initiative of transmitting the signal to No. 5 Group, which at this moment (0244 hrs.) was only five miles from the enemy.[1]

In this way an almost perfect detection system served no purpose to the British as a result of faulty transmissions. Hughes-Hallett knew nothing of the approach of the German convoy. He received echoes of the engagement, but he had to wait for more than two hours before learning what had happened. Admittedly orders authorized the commander of No. 5 Group to break radio silence if, as the result of a delay or of excessive losses, it appeared that a successful landing on the Yellow beaches was seriously jeopardized. But Wyburd was in no state to use the radio. The radio sets of S.G.B.5 were

[1] It appears that throughout the whole raid, H.M.S. *Calpe* had some difficulties with her wireless apparatus. A little later, Brigadier General Mann explained to General Truscott that this destroyer with two damaged wireless apparatus had to relay its communications with the land through H.M.S. *Fernie*. Truscott, op. cit., p. 68.

destroyed one after the other, and it needed more than two hours to transmit messages to H.M.S. *Calpe* by a M.L. It was 0600 hrs. when Hughes-Hallett finally received accurate information about this night skirmish during which it had been impossible for him to communicate with his flagship, the *Calpe* being unable to abandon the protection of the ships of No. 4 Group, particularly of the *Glengyle*, the largest of the L.S.I.

At 0600 hrs. the attack was in full swing; there was no question now of a retreat.

CHAPTER FIFTEEN

VICTORY AT VARENGEVILLE

0645–0700 hrs. – *Frühsport* (morning P.T.).
1045–1145 hrs. – *Geschutz Exerzieren* (gun drill).
Daily orders for No. 813 Battery for Wednesday,
19th August, 1942.

The crew of S.G.B.9 had been given double rations and been
ordered to be in readiness for the 16th August. It was ready a
good week in advance and the reward was a week's leave. This
leave was only relative for the commanding officer, Lt. Peter
Scott, R.N.V.R., who had just been sent a docu~~nt of 60 to
70 pages with an impressive number of photographs and maps
to digest – the orders for Operation *Jubilee*.

On 18th August at 2037 hrs., just as the siren sounded the
'All clear' after the classic evening air reconnaissance, the small
steam gunboat slipped its moorings, crossed the Portsmouth
narrows and entered the Solent to take up its position alongside the *Prince Albert*, which was to be her companion as far
as the swept channel through the minefields.

They were the fourth of the completely new series of steam
gunboats which had come into service to participate in the
operation – S.G.B. 5, 6, 8 and 9. There was to have been a
fifth, No. 3, that of the group leader, but it had not been ready
in time and Lt. George Pennell, R.N., so as not to miss the
'party', had to sail in Scott's boat. The S.G.B.9 was attached
to No. 1 Group under the orders of Lt.-Commander Mulleneux, R.N. It apparently consisted of only three boats – the
Prince Albert, already mentioned, S.G.B.9 and M.G.B.312.
This was only in appearance, for on arriving without incident
at 0258 hrs. at the moorings assigned to her, the large L.S.I.
lowered from her cathead six L.C.A.s and one L.C.S. destined
to land No. 4 Commando under Lt.-Colonel Lord Lovat in
charge of the operations on the Orange beaches, at Vasterival

and Quiberville beaches, to attack the Varengeville battery.

Just as the *Prince Albert* was about to cast anchor, Scott's attention was drawn to flashes ahead, three flashes every 20 seconds, characteristic of the Ailly lighthouse, which the Germans had allowed to function for a few minutes every quarter of an hour, to guide the Boulogne convoy. The British officer could not believe his eyes. Better still, a few miles to the east a few of the red and green lights of the Dieppe jettyheads were on.

While the Commandos were getting into the L.C.A.s the scene suddenly lit up in the east at 0350 hrs., exactly one hour before the time fixed for the landings. This was the start of the naval engagement at Berneval. At the same time three suspicious shadows could be seen outlined against the coast, travelling east; they did not seem to be aware of the presence of No. 1 Group off Ailly Point. These were the three patrol vessels of the 2nd Sicherungsdivision setting their course in the direction of the firing.

For the moment the men of No. 1 Group had nothing better to do than speculate on the destination of the enemy formation which had passed without spotting them. Led by M.G.B.312, Lt. Rye, R.N.V.R., in which Commander Mulleneux had struck his flag, the landing-craft proceeded in two lines ahead for Orange beach 1 (Vasterival) and Orange beach 2 (Quiberville) respectively. Scott took up his position to stern in S.G.B.9 to be ready to give them the support of his guns. Some way off the destroyers *Bleasdale*, *Albrighton*, *Berkeley* and *Garth*, protected them against an eventual irruption by the enemy from the west – a rather comfortable protection against a rather problematical danger. In actual fact the only danger from the west was from Battery 1/799 at Saint-Valery-en-Caux which, despite the distance, could have given them a lot of trouble . . . provided it had been alerted.[1]

The German destroyers at Cherbourg – if there were any there – were really too far away!

Straight ahead was the Varengeville battery which they had come to attack. But Varengeville had not yet fired. Battery 813 had lost a fine opportunity of carrying out some magnificent

[1] This battery subsequently fired 57 shells.

firing practice on the *Prince Albert*, immobilized during the lowering of her landing-craft. When it opened fire at 0447 hrs. at Vasterival as at Quiberville, the two parties of L.C.A.s had arrived at the beach, where both were protected by the cliff and out of the angle of fire of the six 150 mm. guns.

*   *   *

I have retraced on foot the route followed that night by the two groups of No. 4 Commando charged with capturing the battery, from the front and the rear. I have sailed along this coast and walked along the shore at low tide in order to study, at a distance, what kind of obstacle the cliff with its indentations presents.

Projecting into the sea with a reef of rocks marked by a bell buoy, Ailly Point separates Orange 1 and 2, between which there is a main difference. To the east of Ailly – unmistakable since the light was lit that night – the indentations of Morville and Vasterival are practically invisible from the sea. They can only be seen at close quarters. They are however fairly simple to spot thanks to a small minaret, an Edwardian kiosk on the roof of a house built at the edge of the cliff. To the west there is no difficulty in recognizing the Quiberville beach. The only problem for the Commandos was to make for the right bank of the Saane and to land on that part of the beach which is still called Sainte-Marguerite Plage. In both cases the sailors were able to beach with precision and without hesitation. At zero hour precisely, 0450 hrs. – at Quiberville for Lovat and his men, and three minutes later at Vasterival for C Company of No. 4 Commando led by Major Mills Roberts. At the same moment the R.A.F. fighters sprayed the installations of Ailly Point. No one could have wished for a better orchestration.

At Orange 1 everything went according to plan. Mills Roberts' 70 men met with not the slightest opposition. The tracers which left their wake in the sky, were obviously directed against the R.A.F. Bostons and Hurricanes, but no one was expecting them either at Morville or at Vasterival.

The choice now had to be made of one or the other of these

two indentations in the cliff about 300 yards away, from which it was possible, even easy, to reach the edge of the little wood which climbed to the heights immediately opposite Battery 813. Mills Roberts decided upon Vasterival and the Morville ravine which was narrower and apparently impractical because of the thick barbed wire entanglement defending it. Not that the Vasterival gorge was free, but, with a few Bangalore rockets, there was every chance of cutting a passage through the wire, and luckily the explosion of the charges coincided perfectly with the first R.A.F. attacks and passed unnoticed by the enemy.

But what enemy ? As we have seen, there was not a single German soldier on the shore between the port of Mordal and the observation posts at Ailly lighthouse. Farther inland the crew of Battery 813 was far too busy and the guns far too noisy to lend an ear to the explosions of a Bangalore at the bottom of a ravine nearly a mile away.

The time needed to climb about thirty steps, to negotiate the sunken road, and the commandos were on the plateau. ... They even took the liberty of exploring a few houses in the valley, not to forget the Hôtel de la Terrace, whose owners still remember that memorable night with pleasure. It was agreed to search the area and then to form a perimeter for the withdrawal of the whole force (Lovat and Mills Roberts parties) round the galley area. No shot had been fired, no challenge received from a sentry when Lt. Ennis installed his mortars three paces from the edge of a little wood directly opposite Battery 813, which was busy laying a barrage out to sea. Behind him Lt. Style had deployed his section. If their comrades who had landed at Quiberville had been as lucky, the battery position would be caught between two fires according to plan. The problem facing Mills Roberts was not to reveal himself too soon. The fire group was to approach the battery and engage at 0615 hrs. but it had to rush forward and engage at once as the battery had opened fire earlier than the planners had anticipated. And then, they had to engage not only the big guns themselves but the secondary defensive armament consisting of heavy machine-guns and also mortars and remain for 40 minutes. Face and hands daubed with green paint to be less obvious in the darkness,[1] L/Corporal Mann took up his position in the bushes, a stone's throw from the battery. He could not miss.

At 0550 hrs. the mortars went into action. The third shell caused a fantastic explosion. By a piece of great good luck it had fallen directly on a munition dump. Moreover, the accurate and skilled small arms fire against not only big guns but also secondary armament was the main factor in silencing the battery.

No. 813 Battery was already virtually out of action. At least it was to play no further part that day as a coastal battery, i.e. to fire seawards. The mortars unleashed a furious affray almost at point blank range, but this was only a hors d'oeuvre, for in a few moments the Germans were to find themselves in an even worse position.

Lord Lovat and his men had wasted no time. As we have seen, the four L.C.A.s had landed at the appointed time at the eastern extremity of Quiberville beach, naturally beyond the mouth of the Saane which it will be remembered was considered to be an insuperable obstacle. Lt.-Commander Mulleneux had sailed in the L.C.S. which accompanied them. The approach of the five craft had been peaceful until the moment when a white flare rose in the sky and a hail of machine gun bullets swept the beach. *Widerstandsnest* Quiberville was obviously on the alert. Scott leaped ashore from his S.G.B.9 and, at approximately 1,000 yards, opened fire with his 3 inch cannon at the spot from which the firing seemed to come. The enemy was silenced, fired once more only to be silent for good after a few salvoes from S.G.B.9 and the L.C.S.

In the meantime, the landings had begun. The first man to leap ashore was Lt. Veasey followed by a strong patrol. Climbing the cliff, which fell away at this point, without difficulty, they rushed forward, grenades in hand, to clean out the enemy post and to cut his telephonic communications.

The 'party' was not quite over, however, for just as the rest

[1] A detail which struck the defenders. We read in the report of Lt.-Colonel Wagener commanding a neighbouring battalion, the II/556: 'This morning very early Battery 813 was attacked by *geschwärzten Männer* (men with black faces) who blew up the guns and immediately disappeared . . .'

of the Commando was making its way through the barbed wire, a German mortar shell burst among the group. Had the mortar continued to fire, Lovat and his men might have found themselves in a difficult situation, but fortunately it decided to change target and to fire at the landing-craft, which promptly disengaged and put to sea. This lucky diversion enabled a most dangerous crossing to be made. In a few moments No. 4 Commando had negotiated the barbed wire and crossed the road to attack at the double along the little path which, at this spot, follows the meanderings of the Saane on its right bank.

Presumably the Germans of *Widerstandsnest* Quiberville must have thought that they had definitely wiped out the intruders. From this direction they saw and heard nothing more. They were presently to send reinforcements to Battery 813, when they heard the sound of the battle unleashed by Mills Roberts.

Lovat now advanced under the shelter of the slope which descends gently from the plateau to the river, cut in places by deeper glens, hollowed out by the small tributaries of the Saane, which today have disappeared. About 1,500 yards from the shore the third of these glens led directly between ploughed fields and cornfields – stubble at the time, for the harvest had been gathered – to the little wood at Blancmesnil-le-Bas, where the British were to find perfect cover for the final approach.

At the moment they infiltrated this wood, a scout on the left wing sighted the reinforcements which were making their way unsuspectingly through Sainte-Marguerite wood towards the battery, where the battle was in full swing. This troop was immediately dispersed by the fire of the British tommy guns.

On arrival at the northern fringe of the wood, the Commandos found ahead of them a small farm on the edge of the main road, the last shelter before the open country and the perimeter of the battery. Some of the American Rangers accompanying them were able to climb on to the roof from which one was flung to the ground, unhurt, by the blast from a bomb which the R.A.F. had aimed at the battery. He climbed back to his O.P. without delay.

It was now 0610 hrs. It was exactly eighty minutes since the

L.C.A.s had reached beach Orange 2 – in other words, about the time it would take an ordinary walker to cover the distance. Lovat and his men had also had to land and to fight a battle.

A flare rose into the sky, and Mills Roberts from the other side of the battery knew that all the actors were in place for the final assault. Half a mile away at the Café du Val d'Ailly, M. Abraham, the Mayor of Varengeville put his nose outside, to find out the cause of all this din.

One of his clerks came up. 'The British are here,' he said.

'Are you crazy?'

'Well, what's this?' replied the man showing him a packet of English cigarettes.

The Varengeville battery had originally been posted on some grass land dominating the descent to Ailly port. Later it had been transferred to Mesnille where, since the 19th March, 1942, it had been promoted to the rank of *Stützpunkt*, a strong point which was to defend itself with its own weapons against any air or land attack. In front of it was no other friendly force, except the personnel of the sentry posts and O.P.s at Ailly Point, and it could only expect reinforcements from 571 battalion in reserve at Ouville, which also had to provide a company of reinforcements in the sector Quiberville–Ouest–Saint-Aubin-sur-Mer. Like the 302nd Division, it had long since notified the commander of the coastal artillery that it was not in a state to give the battery the protection of its infantry.

From 0447 hrs., the Varengeville battery had been firing sporadically to sea.

The following are the details taken from the report of the German artillery commander (*Artillerie Kommando 117*):

0447 hrs. – 6 shots, not observed, on ships sighted off Quiberville (presumably aimed at Group 1 and in particular at the *Prince Albert*).

0459 hrs. – 2 shots, range 6,800 yards.

0515 hrs. – 18 shots at ships off Dieppe and Pourville.

0530 hrs. – 3 shots at ship off Dieppe, range 6,200 yards.

0538 hrs. – 24 shots, range between 4,300 and 11,000 yards.

0554 hrs. – 8 shots. Hit registered on a landing-craft.

Barrage of 24 shells.

0600 hrs. – 6 shots on Pourville.
>   10 shots, range between 7,600 and 5,500 yards.
>   22 shots on the ships off the Dieppe jetty.

These were the last shots fired out to sea. At 0635 hrs. the six guns had to swivel and lower the range from 9,200 to 330 to defend themselves at point blank range.

0635–0645 hrs. – 13 shots range between 330 and 380 yards in
>   defence of the battery.

And then silence. . . . 813 no longer answered. Because, pressing ahead, the Commandos had at two places crossed the breaches cut by the Bangalore rockets in the barbed wire encirclement, to attack the guns in the open. This was the most dramatic moment of the assault. Captain Pettiward of the Bedfordshire and Hertfordshire Regiment and Lt. Macdonald of the Royal Dragoons were killed leading their men, but on their heels, Major Porteous, R.A., wounded three times, led his men in a ferocious bayonet attack. They were soon joined by their comrades of B Troop who, more fortunate or more sheltered, had forced a passage with their hand grenades and reached the very heart of the battery. Only four Germans remained alive. The rest were dead or had fled. Captain Schöler, the commanding officer, was seriously wounded. A few minutes later the six 150 mm. guns were blown up.

It was 0655 hrs., or according to the daily orders taken from Schöler's desk, the hour when the German gunners should have been doing their P.T. This was no time to dally! The British Commandos wrapped up their dead in Union Jacks before taking to their heels to stumble down the Vasterival glen by which everyone had to retire. Commandeering their four German prisoners as stretcher bearers, they were able to bring back their wounded leaving behind them 12 dead and a similar number missing, which from a total of 250 men represents about 10 per cent of the troops engaged.

Seated on a rock, Lord Lovat supervised the re-embarkment of his men; he was easy to recognize because he was the only 'paleface' in this band of black-faced men. He was delighted. 'We did our job spot on,' he said to the war correspondent of

The Times. 'Up and at 'em with bayonets . . . we hacked them to pieces.' At this moment a mortar shell caused a piece of the cliff to fall not far away. 'It's beginning to hot up,' he said, 'I'm going aboard.' He took up his position at the rear of his men who were hastening towards the L.C.A.s, carrying their wounded on their Mae Wests or on pneumatic rafts. He was soon in the water up to his knees. 'Hi,' he shouted to the nearest craft, 'why don't you draw in closer? You don't expect me to get my knees wet do you?'

But the tide was now too low and the slope too slight. Lord Lovat was obliged to take a bath.

Towards 0815 hrs., the two last landing craft bringing back the victorious No. 4 Commando, left beach Orange 1 which was now completely deserted. At 0850 hrs., its leader reported to General Roberts aboard H.M.S. *Calpe*, while the wounded were taken aboard H.M.S. *Fernie*, and the little flotilla of L.C.A.s returned to Newhaven where it arrived at 1745 hrs. under its own steam.

*   *   *

It was not until 0702 hrs. that the 302nd Infantry Division was informed by a message from Major Wastl, commanding Coastal Artillery Group 770 (H.K.Abt. 770), that No. 813 Battery had been engaged in a hand to hand combat. It already knew at this moment that the 1st Battalion of the 517th Infantry Regiment in reserve at Ouville, had dispatched a section from No. 2 Company to reconnoitre towards Varengeville and Pourville – it was dispersed by Lovat's troop – and believed that the attempted landing at Quiberville had been repulsed. At 0714 hrs. it gave the order to the commander of the I /571: 'In the event of battery 813 being threatened, send a company of infantrymen to counter-attack.' At 0726 hrs. it ordered the III /570, in reserve of the Army Corps, to advance on Ouville where the I /571 had no troops available,[1] to relieve it in its mission of counter-attacking in the valleys of the Scie, the Saane and the Dun. The O.C. I /571 was to make immediate contact with the commander of III /570, and the division

---

[1] In the meantime the I/571 had received orders from its colonel to proceed to Hautot and counter-attack at Pourville.

wanted to receive news of the battery as soon as possible.

This news was somewhat delayed. Not until 0910 hrs. did *Widerstandsnest* Quiberville see a dispatch-rider arrive to announce that the battery had been completely encircled, and not until 1000 hrs. did the division finally know that the enemy had retired, leaving the battery '*fast aufgeriesen*' (completely wiped out).

In the meantime at the Ailly lighthouse, the 80 airmen, sailors and gunners of the observation post were totally unaware of the fighting that was taking place less than a mile away. On the other hand the 302nd Division knew from a radio message from the *Flugmeldezentrale* that all was quiet at the lighthouse.

The German reports stated that No. 813 battery had still fired six shots after being reoccupied by the defenders, but the British and Canadian authors dispute the fact, arguing that in their casualty lists, the same Germans admitted the six guns of the Hess battery as total losses. Whatever the truth, from 0635 hrs. onwards, not a single shell was fired against the British ships crowded on the beaches.

At a relatively modest cost, No. 4 Commando had carried out its mission beyond all expectations and, according to the official report, in an exemplary manner.

*   *   *

The 28 German soldiers, killed in the course of this action, were buried at Varengeville in a plot of land facing the sea against the marvellous background of a coast which was not theirs, but to which fate had summoned them to die for Germany. Doubtless believing that they had done something magnificent, some unknown persons on the eve of the liberation of Dieppe stole the wooden crosses which marked the place of their burial.

Despite this futile outrage, the defenders of No. 813 battery rested in peace in the most beautiful of all marine cemeteries, beside the local dead until the day the German government undertook to recover the remains of all its soldiers who had fallen in Normandy.

This was in the autumn of 1960. The appalling rainy

weather hastens the erosion of this crumbling cliff, which every year loses about 16 inches as a result of the sea's infiltration. In this freshly dug square of earth, the rainwater filtered at its pleasure, and the disturbance caused grave landslides.

After 18 years, this was the last wound inflicted on Varengeville by Operation *Jubilee*.

CHAPTER SIXTEEN

BERNEVAL

The curé of Saint-Berneval-la-Grand had heard nothing of the gunfire which took place out to sea slightly before five o'clock in the morning – German time, which he, in common with all the other inhabitants of the occupied zone, was obliged to observe. He was awakened an hour later by the sound of exploding bombs which, for an inhabitant of the Channel coast, was by no means an unusual occurrence in the year of grace 1942.

The trouble was that this explosion was immediately followed by a vivid flash. A house went up in flames a stone's throw from the Presbytery. The curé was not long in doubt. He flung a few belongings into a suitcase, dressed in all haste and left his house.

Some two or three hundred yards away the Fire Brigade was busy carrying out the orders of its Captain, Pierre Courtin. The Germans did not seem particularly worried, and two of them who passed with their rifles slung and wearing forage caps stopped for a moment to look at the firemen with the air of experts. They even lent a hand to get the flames under control. Abbé Lemercier had nothing special to do now in this part of the world. After a glance at his delightful little eleventh century church[1] hardly discernible in the darkness, he made his way calmly towards the pond at the Berneval–Dieppe juncture of the coastal road and the road from Graincourt to Berneval.

He had not gone a hundred yards before he came to a halt in amazement. Ahead of him at the roadside stood two British

[1] Spared by the raid on 19th August, 1942, the church – and incidentally nearly all the village of Berneval-le-Grand, was flattened on the 3rd June by a bombing raid, presumably intended to support the landing which took place three days later in the Bay of the Seine. The official target for this raid was the wireless station. The bombers dropped 541 tons of H.E. and a ton of incendiaries.

soldiers, their faces and hands covered with black grease. They made a sign to him which is comprehensible all the world over – the forefinger to the lips.

A few minutes later, these Britons, who had come out of the blue, would have run across the German soldiers who were certainly miles from suspecting the enemy in the neighbourhood. At Berneval-le-Grand no one was yet aware of anything, whereas less than 1,500 yards away at the bottom of the Petit-Berneval valley, the battle was already in full swing.

* * *

Apparently the alert had not been given to all the German posts of the Berneval sector, when the L.C.P.s of No. 3 Commando, or to be more accurate those which had not been dispersed by the naval engagement against the small Boulogne convoy, prepared to land. Possibly since a certain time had elapsed, the German defences were strengthened in their idea that it was strictly a naval occasion and did not imagine that anything could be happening ashore.[1]

It is certain, however, that on one of the two beaches at least, the British profited by complete tactical surprise.

Of the 23 landing-craft of No. 5 Group, half a dozen were to have landed at Belleville, where the commandos approached Battery 2/770 from the rear in precisely the same conditions as those enjoyed by Lord Lovat at Varengeville. In actual fact only one arrived, L.C.P.15, commanded by Lt. Buckee, R.N.V.R., fortunately carrying the leader of the expedition, Major P. Young of the Bedfordshire and Hertfordshire Regiment. All the rest had disappeared, dispersed by the action. . . .

When Buckee arrived on his own, five minutes ahead of time off the Belleville gorge, hardly discernible in the darkness, he gave Young a questioning look.

'My orders are to land, I am carrying them out.'

They were 20 in all; three officers and 17 men. The time 0444 hrs. Not a shot fired.

[1] It will be remembered that the first salvoes of the naval engagement were exchanged at 0347 hrs. The first commandoes did not land at Petit-Berneval until 0515 hrs., but at Belleville on the other hand at 0545 hrs. – British summer time.

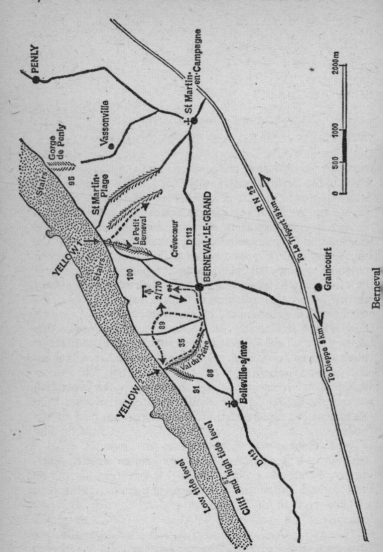

PENLY

Gorge de Penly

Vassonville

St Martin-en-Campagne

St Martin-
Plage

Stairs

95

YELLOW 1

Stairs

Le Petit
Berneval

Crévecœur

BERNEVAL-LE-GRAND

D 113

R N 25

To Le Trégort 19 km

Graincourt

100

2/770

89

35

Val du Prêtre

88

91

Belleville-s/mer

YELLOW 2

Low tide level

Cliff and high tide level

D 113

To Dieppe 3 km

Berneval

There are several routes up to the plateau from the Belleville gorge. The most westerly leads to the village of Belleville by a path which affords little cover. Young took the narrow, enclosed central path which leads, via the Val du Prêtre to departmental road D.313, to within about 500 yards of Berneval-le-Grand.

The only land mines were under the barbed wire at the entrance to the gorge. Thus, according to the German report: 'With the aid of ladders and other climbing gear, they were able to climb up the slopes of the gorge, to skirt the minefield, which extended only as far as the entrance to the gorge, and attack the battery.' Traversing the slope the 20 men had soon overcome these obstacles. The worst was behind them. They reached the plateau at 0530 hrs., just as the R.A.F. arrived over the battery they were to attack. It was this bombing which had woken Abbé Lemercier and called for the intervention of the Fire Brigade. An excellent diversion, for Young and his men were able to reach the church without meeting anyone except the curé. The battery was a few hundred yards ahead, partially masked by houses. After casting an envious glance at the steeple, which would have constituted an ideal perch for their snipers, but which unfortunately was inaccessible for lack of a ladder, the little group turned about and crossed the fields, to emerge 200 yards to the west of the target, which was now unobscured and within range of small arms. These were somewhat meagre: a few rifles and tommy-guns, and a 2-inch mortar and six shells. They had been forced to leave their 3-inch mortar on the beach, because it was too heavy for a single man to carry; nor would it have been possible for him to negotiate the barbed wire.

Just before 0600 hrs., Young revealed his presence by opening fire on Battery 2/770, silent at that moment after having fired 14 shells between 0500 and 0510 hrs. at the landing-craft approaching Petit-Berneval.

Surprised by this unexpected attack, the commander swivelled his guns in the direction of the intruders. But the latter were so close that they were below the angle of fire, even when sighted at point-blank range, and the 105 mm. shells passed well over the heads of the British.

At the 12th shot, the Goebbels battery fell silent, but not for good – it was out of the question for Young to destroy it with such feeble weapons – but in any case for more than an hour and a half. We can read in the report of the commander of the 117th Artillery Regiment that, after firing 12 shots at 0554 hrs. in direct support, Battery 2/770 did not continue to fire seawards until 0745 hrs.[1]

This was because the fire from the British sub-machine-guns prevented the German artillerymen from firing their guns. Had a single section attacked with sub-machine guns and grenades the affair would have been over. But Young had distributed his men so intelligently that the Germans certainly did not realize how few their adversaries actually were. In addition to this, as we shall see, a part of the gun crew had been sent into the Berneval gorge to deal with the invaders.

But everything has an end. Ammunition began to run out. At any moment the small group would be captured by German reinforcements who must already be on the way. In actual fact, as we shall see, this was far from being the case. At 0730 Young decided that the moment had come to break off the engagement. The small troop retired step by step, firing as they went, following the cliff westwards, then plunging into the ravine which debouches in the Val du Prêtre near the sea. The gallant Buckee was there with his L.C.P.15, which had had to take avoiding action for some time in view of the strong enemy fire, but he had returned at the appointed hour to take off the 20 men whom he was able to re-embark under the protection of M.L.346. No one was missing and they had only one wounded.

At 1230 hrs., Young and his men were the first to arrive at Newhaven. Together with Lovat's men they were the heroes of the day. Their exploit had actually had an influence on that of the Varengeville commando, for with a mere 20 men they had

[1] The following is the firing time-table of the 2/770:
    0500–0510 hrs. – 14 shots at the ships off the Berneval creek.
    0554 hrs. – 12 shots in direct support of the position.
    0745 hrs. – 22 shots at the ships at sea, and 63 at a transport.
    0830 hrs. – 40 shots at an M.T.B. off Dieppe.
The battery fired its last shells between midday and 1230 hrs., in all 558 shells of 105 mm. and 47 of 170 mm.

neutralized a battery of seven guns served by about 200 men, for an hour and a half – which surpasses the bounds of any normal imagination.

* * *

Could it have been foreseen that it would have been better to abstain from carrying out the attempt directed simultaneously against Yellow beach 1, in other words against the Petit Berneval gorge?

As will be seen from the map, this gorge lies at the end of a track descending from Berneval-le-Grand to end in a stairway hollowed in the cliff. Farther east, a second gorge, the Fond de Morval, descends towards this same gorge from the wooded heights of Crèvecoeur. Two hundred and twenty yards farther to the east is the indentation which gives access to the beach of Saint-Martin.

Closely watched by the sentry post and the relatively important garrisons of Battery 2/770, by the radar and radio stations, this access to the sea had neither barbed wire nor mines. Moreover, until 19th August, the civilian population was allowed to go down to the sea.

At 0454 hrs. the post at Petit-Berneval and the look-outs of Battery 2/770 observed four small ships making towards the coast, together with a small coaster which replied to their recognition signals. (This was obviously the *Franz*, the fate of which we already know.)

'Surging up from astern it, the four small assault craft sped towards Petit-Berneval, too close for the battery posted 100 yards above sea level to be able to fire at them. On the other hand, the post opened fire with rifles and machine-guns. Five minutes later two of the craft were burning, under the enfilade fire from the post. Sheltering behind them, the enemy managed to land in a concealed sector of the shore, and climbed in the direction of the eastern gorge, in other words, the Fond de Morval, which was mined.'

This is how the Berneval landing must have appeared to the German defences, according to reports I have been able to examine. The overall British accounts agree in the main.

It will be remembered that the naval engagement against the

Boulogne convoy had completely dispersed No. 5 Group. Leaking like a sieve, S.G.B.5 had been able to withdraw at six knots with two fifths of its complement out of action. Commander Wyburd had had to be trans-shipped to an L.C.T., to try and report to Hughes-Hallett. Neither he nor Colonel Durnford-Slater were therefore on the spot to direct operations. L.C.F.1, which had bravely stuck to its post, also had to retire at about 0450 hrs., in other words at the moment the landing should have taken place. All its officers and most of the crew had been killed or wounded. The officer in command decided that it was out of the question to try a landing. He set course for H.M.S. Calpe, in company with three L.C.P.s, rallying four others on the way. Four more ships, damaged during the battle, had set course for Newhaven, one of them piloted by a sergeant of the Hampshire Regiment, who took the helm after the whole crew had been killed or wounded, navigating with a simple army compass. Four and three makes seven, and four makes 11. Together with that of Buckee, who was on his own at Belleville, this makes 12, and of the 11 missing to arrive at the total of 23, three or four had been sent to the bottom during the engagement.

Remained the indomitable Lt. Fear with his M.L.346. Twenty-five minutes before zero hour, he rallied four and soon five L.C.P.s which he resolutely led to the beach, without bothering to think what might have happened to the rest of Group No. 5. A sixth was to join him a little later.

At first his approach was relatively comfortable. As the German report explains, the Berneval guns were powerless against these small ships sailing below the cliff. After firing 14 shells without result between 0500 and 0510 hrs., the battery commander ordered the cease fire and sent an officer with a few men and a machine-gun into the gorge. Others were posted on the edge of the cliff and the moment the L.C.P.s reached the shore 20 minutes late at about 0510 hrs., bursts of machine-gun fire, grenades and rifle shots literally pinned down the commandos as they tried to enter the gorge. Lt.-Commander Corke was mortally wounded together with most of his crew aboard L.C.P.42 which had to be abandoned. It was in this craft that Errard was sunk after three fruitless attempts to beach.

However, M.L.346, blazing away with all its guns, repelled an armed sloop which had just appeared on the scene – doubtless one of the three patrol ships from Dieppe – and at 0535 hrs. settled accounts with the *Franz* as we have already related. At 0600 hrs. L.C.P.85 put its passengers ashore under heavy fire. These heroic actions served no purpose. With the exception of one small group which, according to statements from the inhabitants seemed to be confirmed by the German report – was able to reach Crèvecoeur wood by the Morval gorge and kill four Germans in a small pillbox, none of the assailants made much progress. Pinned down at the foot of the cliff, with all the officers killed in quick succession, including the American lieutenant Loustalot, who took over from his British comrades, they were all doomed to death or captivity.

At 0615 hrs., a quarter of an hour after the last landing, the commandos fired a flare to recall the landing-craft. Four were able to approach, protected by M.L.346. Of the three which were successful, one foundered on the rocks and had to be abandoned, while the second could only disengage with the greatest difficulty. But they found no one to evacuate apart from the beach troop. Crouching against anything that could afford them cover, or hiding in the nearest houses, the commandos were unable to approach. After waiting until 0730 hrs. in a critical situation, the landing craft had to withdraw.

The German reinforcements arrived. As soon as the landing at Berneval became known, the 302nd Division had given orders to Major von Blücher, commanding the detachment of anti-tank chasseurs, to counter-attack in the direction of Berneval with the cyclist squadron stationed at Saint-Nicolas-d'Aillermont and the 3rd Company of Engineers from Arques-la-Bataille, with any vehicles they could procure. No. 3 Company had set out at 0550 hrs. from D'Assigny, headquarters of I/570, and its scouts reached Vassonville at 0650 hrs., while the main body arrived at 0715 hrs. at Saint-Martin-en-Campagne. Recce troops of the 570th Infantry Regiment explored the edge of the cliff from Criel-Plage as far as Penly.

The first of these units arrived at Belleville via Graincourt at 0710 hrs. The 302nd P.Z. – jg.-Abt. missed intercepting Young and his men. It could easily have crossed the Belleville

gorge which was only 1,600 yards away at 0710, and which was
not occupied until 1000 hrs. Young had passed at 0745 hrs!

But at Berneval itself, the affair was virtually over when
Blücher arrived. He had only to pick up the prisoners, who
surrendered one after the other until 10 o'clock in the morning.[1] Those who had hidden in the houses were denounced by
the manager of La Potinière. He was in the pay of the Germans
since he had been placed there by the Austrian Foetzer, whose
misadventures in 1940 are related at the beginning of this
book.[2]

Eighty prisoners were taken the same day to Envermeu,
where, later in the evening, they were to rejoin their comrades
who had been taken at Dieppe or at Puys. They were billeted
in the church, where the population did all it could for them,
some of them displaying such tokens of friendship that the
Feldgendarmerie made three arrests.

Fourteen Germans had been killed at Berneval. The mayor
was asked to bury them, but the authorities changed their
mind and the pit dug was used for three dead commandos,
whose bodies had been lying in the first-aid chapel at Petit-
Berneval. On the 20th August a Requiem Mass was said for
them by Abbé Lemercier, assisted by the curé of Saint-Martin-
en-Campagne. Although only the two mayors had been notified, 200 of the inhabitants turned up with flowers. The
Germans, it is believed, were far from satisfied and according
to the local inhabitants, it was as a reprisal for this manifesta-

[1] Among them was a Frenchman, Sergeant Maurice César, who was
caught at the end of the afternoon trying to return to the beach.
Having shed his battledress and beret, he was able to pass for a French
Canadian.

On 20th August, in the train which was taking him to a prisoner of
war camp, César took advantage of a slowing down to jump. He was
fired on unsuccessfully and was able to hide in a wood. Then marching
south he reached Evreus where he remained for a month and a half on a
farm. From here he went to Paris and then to St. Quentin, where his
family lived. In June 1943, César was able to regain England, in
company with a British airman.

[2] This individual, whose name is of little importance, extricated
himself from the affair before the Rouen Court of Justice after the
liberation, by pleading that he had merely asked the Germans what
he was to do with a wounded Briton who was lying outside his door.

tion that the French prisoners from Berneval were not freed like those of Arques-la-Bataille or Hautot-sur-Mer.

This is not impossible, but we might remark that the prisoners from Varengeville were not released either.

Would this not rather be a mark of their annoyance that at Varengeville the commandos had effectively destroyed the guns of Battery 813, and that at Berneval before Battery 2/770 they had, as the report of the Heeren Küsten Artillerie Regiment 527 recognizes: '. . . succeeded in forcing the battery to defend itself in close combat, thus diverting it for an hour from its mission which was to fire at targets out to sea.'

CHAPTER SEVENTEEN

THE DISASTER OF PUYS

ONE need only have arrived once at Dieppe on a cross-Channel steamer, or simply to have walked along the front, to realize that the conquest of the Le Pollet cliff was essential to a successful landing on Dieppe beach. No spot on this wide open space can escape the observer posted at the Neuville coastguard station or at the foot of the chapel of Notre-Dame-de-Bon-Secours. With two or three well-placed machine-guns, a platoon of infantry established at this observation post would suffice to prevent the least movement on the beach. Even by landing at high tide, and presuming the esplanade to be free – whereas it was barred by a heavy barbed wire entanglement – there was still 50 yards to cover in the open, before gaining the shelter (?) of the seafront buildings.

In the course of the preliminary discussions, everyone at C.O. Hq. agreed that a frontal attack on the Dieppe beach would have no chance of success unless control had previously been obtained of this cliff above the town and unless the famous battery, which the British called the Rommel battery and the Germans B /302, could be silenced. On the map can be seen the exact position of this battery which consisted of four 105 mm. guns. The cliff above Dieppe dominates the entrance to the port like a vertical wall some 160 feet high. It was therefore out of the question to try and scale it. On the other hand a successful landing at Puys beach, 1,600 yards as the crow flies, would allow indirect approach. It was also from Puys that one might hope to reach, apart from the Rommel battery, the power station and the gas works situated close behind the port at the foot of Neuville-lès-Dieppe Hill.

Hence the interest in the operations staged against Blue beach, entrusted to a battalion of the Royal Regiment of Canada under the orders of Lt.-Colonel Catto, reinforced by three companies of the Black Watch (Royal Highland Regiment). The transport of these units was ensured by the L.S.I.s of No. 3 Group – *Queen Emma* and *Princess Astrid* and by the *Duke of Wellington* attached to No. 4 Group for the crossing.

Lt.-Commander Goulding, R.N., was responsible for the landing of the Royal Regiment of Canada. He had sailed in S.G.B.8 commanded by Lt. Friffiths, R.N. M.G.B.316, Lt.-Commander Cartwright, R.N.V.R., and two L.C.S. carried by the L.S.I.s participated in support of the landings.

The beach at Puys is hardly more than 270 yards long. It is not easy to recognize on a dark night or in cloudy weather, and every inhabitant of Dieppe remembers the disaster that overtook the Newhaven packet, which one day ran ashore, having mistaken it for the entrance to Dieppe. In short, although the big transports had anchored correctly at 0320 hrs. at the point prescribed in RR, and the trans-shipment to the landing-craft was carried out without incident,[1] Goulding beached at 0506 hrs. – in other words, 16 minutes late. Protected by a smoke-screen laid by the R.A.F., the L.C.A.'s arrived to within a hundred yards of the shore, without being molested. The Germans revealed themselves just as the first wave landed, and many officers and men were killed or wounded on the actual ramps. More serious still was the presence of a nine to 12-foot high wall, impossible to scale under the murderous fire of a machine-gun camouflaged in what appeared to be an innocent villa half-way up the cliff, and which swept the whole beach at point-blank range. This was possibly the heavy machine-gun of the corporal in his nightshirt mentioned by Colonel Hoffman.[2]

In fact the whole defence of Puys was carried out by relatively few, but admirably placed, Germans on the cliff up the coast near what is known as Caesar's camp: a detachment of

[1] This seems extraordinary when we consider that at the moment of this trans-shipment, large scale fighting was going on at Berneval, a few miles from RR.

[2] This reaction, by and large, improvised by the defenders of Puys would certainly have been less effective a quarter of an hour earlier, which gives strength to the remark of Captain Hughes-Hallett when he writes on this subject: 'I am afraid that this delay of 15 minutes was partly responsible for the very strong opposition encountered by our forces as soon as they landed, literally pinning them to the spot.'

the 15th Company of the 52nd Luftnachrichten Regiment
serving the Würzburg radar, and a section of the 9th Company
of the 571st Infantry Regiment, in all 150 men under the
orders of Lt. Willi Weber, commanding the 15th Company.

The presence of the British off Puys, however, had been
spotted for some time before the landing of the first wave, since
the IIIrd Group of the 302nd Artillery Regiment, as we know,
ordered a barrage to be laid down at 0430 hrs. But in actual
fact the artillery played no role in the defence of the beach, and
this fell to the lot of a few well-placed automatic weapons. 'At
0515 hrs.,' writes Lt.-Colonel Hoffman, 'the first wave was
defeated and wiped out.' This was precisely the view of a
Canadian witness, Captain Browne, when he wrote that it
needed a bare five minutes to transform an attacking battalion
into less than two companies, forced to go over to the defensive,
overwhelmed by fire whose direction they could not locate.

Witnesses of this carnage, the small L.C.S.28 and 8, which
accompanied the assault craft, had opened fire at point-blank
range, but without great effect, on the houses or pillboxes from
which the firing seemed to be coming. They were soon reduced
to silence.

But the second wave approached 'as calm and resolute for
this baptism of fire despite the first gleams of breaking dawn'
writes Captain Browne, 'as though they were on manoeuvres.'
It approached at 0525 hrs. and was greeted like the first with
fire from machine-guns, mortars and anti-tank guns handled
by the radar defences.

Nevertheless, to discover the extent of the operation, Lt.
Weber sent a motorized patrol in the direction of Berneval to
make liaison with the neighbouring formation Luftnachrichten
Regiment 51. When his scouts returned they declared that the
coast was free of the enemy as far as Berneval – doubtless after
the departure of Major Young – Weber was able to withdraw
two heavy machine-guns from the right wing of his radar post,
and direct their fire against the enemy which was trying to
break through the barbed wire on the extreme west of the
beach. The intervention of Focke-Wulf 190s and Messer-
schmitt 109s made things easier.

It was already daylight at 0545 hrs., when the third wave

advanced under fire from the Rommel battery. It consisted of a company of the Black Watch led by Captain Hicks, carried by the *Duke of Wellington*'s L.C.A.s. L.C.M.99, which carried the beach party, was seriously damaged and although they were transferred to L.C.A.208, their leader found it impossible to land, so intense was the enemy fire.

It would therefore have been better had no one landed, for the Black Watch could do nothing but increase the number of dead, wounded and potential prisoners, already huddled under the cliff at the western extremity of the beach, which afforded relative cover. To cross the wall and the barbed wire seemed out of the question. The only ones to succeed, shortly after 0600 hrs., was a small troop of 20 men led by Lt.-Colonel Catto in person. Cutting a passage in the barbed wire at the western extremity of the wall, they were able to scale the cliff, mop up two houses on the way and advance west in the hope of making liaison with the men of the Essex Scottish, who had landed at Dieppe on Red beach. They were never destined to meet them for this reason: after skulking for a certain time in a copse near the villa once inhabited by Alexandre Dumas, they had to surrender at four o'clock in the afternoon.

*   *   *

At 0600 hrs., therefore, about 600 men had landed at Puys, a score of whom alone had managed to cross the beach and the game could now be considered as lost. The only consolation – the R.A.F. at the outset supreme in the air, but which was soon to have this supremacy disputed by the squadrons of Jafu 3. The only hope now was to try and retire. The trouble was that no one realized the true situation aboard H.M.S. *Calpe*, where Lt.-Commander Goulding reported at 0700 hrs. that the Royal Regiment of Canada had been landed. This was a fact, but at this very moment a message was received from H.M.S. *Garth* transmitting a message received from Blue beach: 'Is there any chance of getting us out of here?' This message was unmistakable. Goulding jumped into a M.L. to try and lead the landing craft to Puys. They were subjected to heavy fire and several were sunk. By 1145 hrs. Goulding realized that, after several hours' effort, he was unable to reach Blue beach and that no one had been taken off. Another attempt was made by four L.C.A.s from the *Princess Astrid*. One was sunk and the others had to retire. On their return they reported that they had seen no sign of life on the beach. Moreover from 0835 hrs., the 571st Infantry Regiment had been able to report to the 302nd Infantry Division that Puys was firmly in German hands and that the enemy casualties already amounted to 500 prisoners or killed.

According to the testimony of Lt.-Colonel Hoffmann, the Canadians began to surrender at about 0930 hrs. and the action was finished at 1050 hrs. Collecting the wounded went on until 0200 hrs. of the following night, disturbed at the outset by machine-gunning from R.A.F. aircraft which, according to Hoffmann, killed about 15 wounded Canadians. The air-sea rescue launches of the Kriegsmarine picked up a few soldiers and sailors struggling in the water.

The defenders of Puys had suffered infinitesimal losses – two dead and nine wounded. Our losses were 152 dead and 465 prisoners, including 19 officers. The booty consisted of six heavy and 16 light mortars, four machine-guns, 62 submachine-guns, 12 anti-tank guns, 304 rifles and two British flags, not to mention explosives, grenades and equipment.

The figures given by Colonel Stacey, according to the Canadian records, are approximately the same. The number of Canadian soldiers landed at Puys amounted to 655. Of this number only about 100 men returned – in practice those who had been unable to land. 208 were killed in combat, two died of their wounds in England and 18 in captivity. All the rest were taken prisoner.

More than any of the engagements fought that day, the battle of Puys shows the incredible difficulties that this coast opposes to a landing from the sea. Doubtless this should have been foreseen. With a few well-placed machine-guns, 150 men stopped more than 600. Admittedly these 150 men knew how to fight! 'I congratulate you on your soldiers, sir!' said a Canadian captain in bad German to Lt. Weber.

Field Marshal Sperrle, commanding the 3rd Luftflotte, was of the same opinion, for he arrived on the following day to present the Iron Cross First Class to Lt. Weber and to decorate 28 of his men.

Awards that were well deserved for it was at Puys, in fact, as Hughes-Hallet writes, that the fate of the Dieppe raid was decided. 'There is no doubt that this was the main cause for the failure of the military plan.'[1]

[1] Hughes-Hallett report.

CHAPTER EIGHTEEN

PARTIAL SUCCESS AT POURVILLE

SITUATED in the vast indentation at the mouth of the River Scie, between the gulf of Dieppe, framed by the heights of Caude-cote to the east and the woods of Varengeville and Hautot to the west, the little summer resort of Pourville has no blemish except for the appalling style of its Edwardian houses. It has a charming casino and a beach which, at low tide below the pebbles, offers a vast extent of sand unencumbered by the rocks which plague its neighbours. The cliffs that flank it on either side are less steep and the bends of the Dieppe road afford views of the coast perhaps even finer than that which can be seen from the marine cemetery at Varengeville.

With no scalings to be foreseen and no narrow gorges to cross, the Canadians of the South Saskatchewan Regiment had plenty of room for setting foot on these 900 yards of beach, with the reservation, that Combined Operations Staff fearing, as we have mentioned, the crossing of the River Scie, wished to land the greatest number of men on the right bank of the river, which reaches the sea through a tunnel not far from the cliff above the town.

We already know the dispositions of the coastal batteries which ensured long distance defence from the sea. Close quarters defence to the west was practically nil as we have seen – a small detachment – *Feldwache* – provided by No. 6 Company of the 571st Infantry Regiment to watch the coast from Pourville to Ailly headland. No fixed defences. The only military establishments were represented by the Kommandan-tur, stationed opposite the casino, a small first-aid station in a villa on Varengeville beach and a mess at the Maison Blanche, a large villa on the edge of the cliff, 140 feet high at this point. In the casino were billeted the 'conscripts' of the Todt organi-zation, men of all nationalities. Access to the beach was for-bidden.

The danger came from the cliff above the town where were to be met with in succession from west to east:

- A section of No. 6 Company of the 571st.
- A group of No. 8 Company, billeted below the Dieppe coast.
- A section of the 6/571 and a group of the 8/571 protecting Battery 7/302.
- On the cliff nearer Dieppe, not far from the golf course, a heavy flak battery, a radar post and its armament, personnel of the 52nd Luftnachrichten Regiment, etc.

In this sector, too, was the Hq. of the O.C. 11/571, responsible for the western defences of Dieppe (Major von Bonin), and that of Colonel Bartelt, O.C. 571st Infantry Regiment, on the esplanade of the old castle. In fact, the whole of these heights which lie between Dieppe and the River Scie constituted a regular fortified redoubt, defending both Dieppe and its harbour and Pourville and its valley.

The conquest of this redoubt, although to a lesser extent than that of the cliff above Dieppe, determined the conditions for the success of the main landing. The mission was entrusted to the South Saskatchewan and the Queens Own Cameron Highlanders of Canada, to whom had also been allotted more ambitious objectives, in particular the occupation of the airfield, the destruction of Battery 265 at Rouxmesnil-Calmont and finally a raid on the divisional Hq. which was believed – wrongly as we know – to be at Arques-la-Bataille, i.e. three and a half miles from Dieppe as the crow flies, and a good six miles from Pourville.

*   *   *

The first wave had been transported by No. 2 Group which, in the formation on leaving the minefields, brought up the rear of No. 1 Group. The South Saskatchewans had sailed in the L.S.I.s *Princess Beatrix* and *Invicta* which together carried ten L.C.A.s, two L.C.S.s and two L.C.M.s protected by S.G.B.6 and M.G.B.317.

At 0300 hrs. the two transports anchored at point GG. The

landing-craft were lowered and the troops embarked. Three-quarters of an hour later everything was ready, and the small flotilla set out to cover the last ten miles. There was no opposition from the shore. The landing was carried out with mathematical precision at 0452 hrs., but farther to the west of the River Scie than had been planned. This was tiresome, not on account of the obstacle this rivulet represented, but simply because it meant a longer distance to be travelled over open country to reach the Dieppe shore, below the cliff above the town. Hence a certain delay in attacking this position – a delay which partially forfeited the benefit of surprise, for naturally the defences soon showed themselves. Hardly had the Canadians landed than a machine-gun opened fire. There were a few casualties among the followers.

Nevertheless, at the west end of the beach, C Company had enjoyed almost complete surprise. M. Sadé, the owner of the Hôtel la Terrace which was about 50 yards from the dyke opposite the little Pourville chapel, was sleeping peacefully, when he was awakened by an unusual bustle in the hotel. Seeing lights outside he called out to his guests:

'What the hell are you doing with those lights ? You'll get us all into trouble.'

'But don't you know. The Tommies have landed, you'd better take shelter.'

Everyone rushed down to a cellar.

M. Sadé was not the only one to be taken by surprise. At the Maison Blanche there had been a party the previous evening, probably to celebrate some promotion. A dozen or so of the revellers or their orderlies were sent to their eternal rest, stabbed by a party of Canadians whom Lt. McIlvin had led in silence along the steep cliff path leading directly to the villa. The casino was occupied without difficulty, then a small group of houses opposite and the cottages where, in peacetime, the luxury shops of Paris displayed their wares during the season. Hastily barricaded with planks and mattresses the Maison Blanche became for some hours a Canadian pillbox. The rest of the company infiltrated into the neighbouring gardens and woods of Hautot-sur-Mer. In fact the situation had been swiftly taken in hand at the River Scie, but from this side there was little to fear, and the most important targets lay to the east.

A Company alone, with the mission to capture the radar station on the cliff 1,600 yards away, had been landed correctly on the right bank of the Scie. It had no difficulty in mopping up two pillboxes which housed the anti-tank weapons, principally a 47 mm. gun, but in trying to advance farther along the cliff above the town it ran into serious difficulties. B and C Companies, too, whose target was the battery 7/302 at Quatre Vents farm, lost a great deal of time crossing the valley, and it needed all the heroism of Lt.-Colonel Merritt, the battalion commander, to lead his men under increased fire to the perimeter of the radar station and the battery at Quatre Vents. The destroyer H.M.S. *Albrighton*, which was to give covering fire with its four 100 mm. guns, could not fire effectively, because the artillery observer who had landed with the troops did not give the gunners the correct range.

The Pourville attack consisted of a second wave launched by the battalion of the Queens Own Cameron Highlanders of Canada, Lt.-Colonel Gosling, which was to be put ashore half an hour after the first South Saskatchewans. This battalion, like the Berneval commando, embarked direct at Newhaven in the L.C.P.s, to approach the beaches without trans-shipment. Twenty-eight landing-craft of the 2nd, 6th and 7th Flotillas of L.C.P.s, under the orders of Colonel McClintock, R.N., forming No. 6 Group, supported by two motor launches. . . .[1]

As the result of a navigational error, the L.C.P.s of No. 6 Group reached Pourville beach half an hour late – at 0550 hrs. instead of 0520 hrs. It was broad daylight when the Cameron Highlanders landed to the sound of the bugle, but the enemy's reactions were not very swift. Swift enough, however, to kill Lt.-Colonel Gosling the moment he put foot ashore. Major Law took over and the battalion infiltrated into Pourville, detaching a reinforcement company for the attack on the cliff above the town, while the rest tried to force a passage by the

[1] 2nd Flotilla, nine L.C.P.s, Lt. Byerley, R.N.V.R.
6th Flotilla, nine L.C.P.s, Lt. Murray, R.N.V.R.
7th Flotilla, ten L.C.P.s, Lt. Garrard, R.N.V.R.
M.L.190, Lt. Ball, R.N.V.R.
M.L.194, Lt.-Commander Whitfield, R.N.V.R.

left bank of the Scie towards its final objective, the airfield of
Dieppe–Saint-Aubin.

As can be seen from the map this airfield was situated on the
heights two and three-quarter miles from the Paris–Rouen
road but in the commune of Saint Aubin-sur-Scie. To reach it,
therefore, Law had to cross the River Scie at the hamlet of
Petit-Appeville in the valley a mile from Pourville, then climb
the slopes dominating the right bank to reach Vertus wood and
join the tanks, which in the meantime it was hoped would
have been able to land at Dieppe.[1] All this represented a far
longer distance to cover than if they had landed directly on the
right bank. On the other hand, the woods, which partially
covered the heights on the left bank, provided the men with
adequate cover against the battery of Quatre Vents, by which,
we must remember, the South Saskatchewans were being
strafed. It was no great task to reach Petit-Appeville. The
great thing was to arrive before the Germans.

This would perhaps have been possible had the Camerons
landed at 0520 hrs., the appointed time. In actual fact the reinforcements of the 1/571, alerted at Ouville at about this
time, did not leave until 50 minutes later, taking nearly two
hours to reach Hautot, for their overloaded bicycles collapsed
one after the other. Nevertheless they had been in position
three-quarters of an hour, preparing their counter-attack on
Pourville, by the time the Cameron Highlanders, at 0845 hrs.,
reached the Petit-Appeville crossroads – it has now been
renamed the Canadian crossroads – after several encounters in
Hautot and Bernouville woods. Law remained under cover
waiting for the appearance of the tanks at Vertus wood which
was directly opposite him on the heights. Nothing to be seen.
Not a Canadian was to reach Vertus wood . . . except as a
corpse.[2]

The hour of the rendezvous had long since passed and the
time for re-embarkation was drawing near. The crossing of the

---

[1] A very ambitious programme, when we consider it. Even suppos-
ing that the tanks had landed safely, they could only reach Vertus
wood by the boulevard Gambetta and the main road, or through a
maze of steep streets, remarkably easy to defend.

[2] The dead of 19th August, 1942, were all taken to Vertus cemetery.

River Scie turned out to be impossible. All that could be done was to retrace their steps, and pray to heaven that the South Saskatchewans had managed in the meantime to keep the route open for their retreat.

They had done so, and Law was able to reach the beach in good order. He arrived there at 1000 hrs. with 80 per cent of his forces intact. This was not bad. Unfortunately there was not as landing-craft in sight.

* * *

It is a mile from Pourville to Petit-Appeville. This mile represents the maximum advance made by the assailants, and it was for this sector, in the course of that afternoon, that the German command showed its greatest apprehensions. Had it been known aboard H.M.S. *Calpe*, it might have been possible to exploit this partial success by rushing to Pourville the reinforcements which were to be sacrificed at Dieppe. But the transmission functioned as badly as possible, and in any case, as the Germans would notice when studying the captured British plans, the development of Operation *Jubilee* was so rigid in detail that it left no scope for any initiative.

In fact there have been no battle in Dieppe. There were five or six clashes with no other liaison than those envisaged in these unrealistic documents.

These plans foresaw that in the event of success, after reaching their targets and destroying everything that had to be destroyed, all the troops landed at Puys, Dieppe and Pourville would return and re-embark at Dieppe. At 1000 hrs, the fate of the Royal Regiment at Puys had already been sealed. Dead or as prisoners they had no need of boats. Now it was a question of improvising the evacuation from Pourville an hour earlier than had been planned – and it had to be done quickly because the enemy continued to receive reinforcements.

No news of the Camerons was as yet known on H.M.S. *Calpe* at 0900 hrs. when General Roberts decided to withdraw.

An L.C.A., dispatched to Green beach to obtain news, was repulsed at 0930 hrs. by the fire of the German defences. A second, at 1000 hrs., found the beach deserted. The commandos, cowering against a wall, were trying to escape the heavy fire from the cliff above. A man who tried to cross the beach was killed in a few seconds. The L.C.A. withdrew. Others returned at 1045 hrs., including a number which had been detailed for Dieppe. They put about as soon as they realized their mistake. Of the rest a number were sunk or disabled. The destroyers, *Albrighton* and *Bleasdale*, came as close inshore as they could to shell the cliffs from where this murderous fire was coming. The 1/571 had now reoccupied the Mordal cliff at the Maison Blanche, abandoned by McIlven. From the embrasure of one of its windows a machine-gun sprayed the beach, and the destroyers themselves were constantly spattered by the machine-gun bullets. One of them managed to silence it with a lucky shot.

The situation was hardly more favourable for the troops ashore than for those in the landing-craft off the beaches. The tide had turned since 0500 hrs. It was now almost low tide and several hundred yards had to be covered before they could embark.

Defended by a rearguard of 100 men led by Lt.-Colonel Merritt in person, the Pourville bridgehead resisted until 1130 hrs. when the last square had to surrender, having exhausted its ammunition. When the L.C.A.s 250 and 315 finally arrived at 1215 hrs., nothing could be heard on this beach, which was strewn with corpses and hulks, except the explosions of the German shells. The two small craft withdrew under a hail of fire.

Nevertheless the sacrifice made by Merritt, who was to be awarded the V.C. for his heroism, had not been in vain. The fact that 268 out of 503 men of the Camerons and 357 out of 523 of the South Saskatchewans were able to re-embark at Pourville, was as much thanks to him as to the crews of the landing-craft. But in these two battalions alone, the total of killed was 151 and the number of prisoners 266. If we add the 269 wounded taken back to England, the total losses amounted to 686 out of 1,026, in other words, more than 65 per cent.

And this in a sector where one could justifiably consider the operation a partial success.

At 1337 hrs. the 571st Infantry Regiment reported: Pourville is firmly in our hands.

It is miraculous that there was not a single casualty among the civil population of Pourville, which had no shelter, most of the cellars being flooded. A strange fact – the German Command did not bother to prevent civilian circulation, and as at Berneval, the flowers seemed to bloom spontaneously on the newly dug graves of the Canadian soldiers, who were temporarily buried in the Casino garden.

CHAPTER NINETEEN

THE DIEPPE BEACHES

WHEN the experts from C.O. Hq. had elaborated the details of Operation *Jubilee* they counted on the fact that at 0520 hrs., at the moment the main force arrived off the Dieppe White and Red beaches:

- The two outer batteries of Berneval and Varengeville would be in the process of being put out of action.
- The forces landed at Puys and Pourville would be taking the Hindenburg and Bismarck positions on either flank of the port.

It was to give these troops time to carry out their missions that the landing at Dieppe was planned for half an hour after the others.

Now at 0520 hrs. precisely the fighting at Puys had ended in the disaster we have already described. In the Pourville sector, the South Saskatchewans met with insurmountable resistance on the slopes of Caudecote. Operation *Jubilee* was virtually damned. Lord Lovat's victory at Varengeville, and Young's remarkable tactical success at Berneval, would merely limit the losses at sea where, taken all in all, the German shore batteries would have only a very limited success – far below its estimates. They would not change the situation on the beaches – which incidentally did not come within the field of fire of batteries 813 and 2/770 – against which the intact medium batteries could only fire at point-blank range.

Hughes-Hallett and Roberts, who knew nothing of the skirmish at Berneval, before the first flank landings, were also uninformed before the main landing of the serious turn of events at Puys and to a certain extent at Pourville. Worse still, at 0640 hrs. on the strength of a signal, the origin of which has

never been clarified, General Roberts thought that the Royals
had not landed at Puys and gave orders that they were to be
sent to Dieppe. At this moment they had already suffered
martyrdom for an hour and a quarter on their beach.

Even if Hughes-Hallett had been informed immediately, it
is difficult to see how he could have changed the course of
events. How could he stop – even had he wanted to do so – the
30 landing-craft, which were already under way, or the R.A.F.
squadrons which were about to bomb the defences of the sea
front and lay a smoke-screen over the beaches? How could he
have resigned himself to humiliate these troops, who had been
kicking their heels in England for so long, by refusing to attack
an obstacle? It was unimaginable, and doubtless such a
suggestion would not have been accepted by the commander
of the 2nd Canadian Division, whom we shall see later successively engaging all his reserves in a battle which was irremedi-
ably lost.

The wheels had been set in motion. To the glorious but
barren sacrifice of the Royals, the South Saskatchewans and the
Camerons was to be added that of the Royal Hamiltons,
the Essex Scottish and the Mont-Royal Fusiliers . . . and the
Royal Marine Commando only partially escaped catastrophe
by the skin of its teeth.

*   *   *

At 0550 hrs. precisely, five squadrons of Hurricanes – about
50 machines – hedgehopping above the Dieppe front, attacked
with cannon and machine-guns all the German defensive
positions, whose emplacements had been spotted well ahead,
with a precision which aroused the admiration of the enemy
commander when he was finally able to examine the maps that
fell into his hands. Four destroyers, and the gunboat *Locust*,
were to have opened fire at the same time. The *Locust* was not
at the rendezvous, for she had been delayed en route, but for
ten minutes the 16 102 mm. guns of the destroyers fired with
precision, while the aircraft laid their screen above the shore.
Dieppe disappeared in the smoke.

Inadequate to reduce the German defences, as we shall see,
this perfectly synchronized air and naval preparation –

according to some eye-witnesses terrifying[1] − greatly facilitated the approach of the landing-craft of No. 4 Group bringing its troops to the White and Red beaches. In fact, there were no losses when the first wave landed, but things deteriorated rapidly.

Group 4 comprised three L.S.I.s, H.M.S. *Glengyle*, H.M.S. *Prince Charles* and H.M.S. *Prince Leopold*, transporting 28 L.C.A.s, three L.C.S.s and one L.C.M. Immediate support was assured by M.G.B.326, Lt. Russell-Roberts, R.N.V.R., M.L.291, Lt. Lumsden, R.N.V.R., and H.M.S. *Locust*, Lt.-Commander Stride, R.N. (Retd.), a river gunboat whose shallow draught allowed it to come well inshore. She had won her laurels at Dunkirk by engaging a German battery and evacuating 2,239 Allied troops in five trips, the last of which was carried out at the very last moment.

The troops transported belonged to the 4th and 6th Brigades, commanded respectively by Brigadiers Lett and Southam, embarked with their staffs in the L.C.T.s. The former was seriously wounded before he had even waded ashore; the latter, slightly less seriously wounded, was the only officer of his staff able to disembark. Thanks to a radio set installed aboard a scout car landed at the same time as the tanks, he was able to keep up a rather precarious contact with H.M.S. *Calpe* until the moment he, too, was taken prisoner.

The first wave consisted of a battalion of the Royal Hamilton Infantry, Lt.-Colonel Labatt, for White beach, and a battalion of the Essex Scottish, Lt.-Colonel Jasperson, for Red beach. The objective of the former was the cliff west of Dieppe where it was to make contact with the South Saskatchewans under cover of the tanks; the objective of the latter was the occupation of the fort and the protection of operations, which were to be carried out there by the Royal Marine Commando.

It had been planned that the tanks should intervene at the precise moment the air and naval preparations finished, so that

[1] This was not everyone's opinion. General Truscott found this bombardment far less severe and impressive than he would have wished. Neither H.M.S. *Fernie*, his flagship, nor H.M.S. *Calpe* took part, for it was feared that the firing would disturb the functioning of the radio apparatus provisionally installed in these two flagships.

the infantry would not be without protection at the moment when the Germans, recovering from their momentary inaction, would start up a very violent fire. This would be all the more murderous since, after setting foot ashore, the soldiers would have a hundred yards to cover in the open, to cross the front which bristled with barbed wire.

As a survivor of the Royal Hamiltons was to write later: 'The German sniper is a real specialist, and there were snipers on all the roofs. The same applied to the trench mortar men whose shells fell exactly where they wished. The beach was perfectly covered by light machine-guns installed in the houses, and heavy machine-guns, which enfiladed us.'[1]

It was precisely against these defences that Churchill tanks of the 14th Battalion the Calgary Regiment, Lt.-Colonel Andrews, were engaged. Their 75s should have had an appreciable effect on this redoubtable defence and should have been useful in aiding the infantry's advance. Unfortunately the tanks arrived late.

The tanks had been loaded in three's on the craft of the 2nd and 4th L.C.T. Flotillas, which were split into four groups. (Groups No. 8, 9, 10 and 11, Group No. 12 carrying the brigade staffs.) Immediate cover was assured by the M.L.s and L.C.F.s.

It happened that the first wave of three L.C.T.s of No. 8 Group, conveyed by H.M.S. *Fernie*, by drifting to the west, took approximately ten minutes to regain the position assigned to them. Ten fatal minutes during which not only the infantrymen were mowed down like rabbits, but the German gunners could take all the time they needed to set their sights. As soon as they emerged from the smoke-screen, the L.C.T.s were greeted with an inferno of fire. By now it was about 0535 hrs.

L.C.T.145, Lt. Reynolds, R.N.V.R., was the first to beach, and landed its three tanks at the eastern end of the beach. But it was set on fire and soon reduced to a burning hulk, which had to be sunk. No. 127, Captain McPherson, R.N.R., arrived at the beach with half his crew out of action, but was able to land his tanks and withdraw. No. 159, Sub-Lt. Cooke, R.N.V.R., was hit before he could even beach and was never able to

Quoted by Buckley, op. cit., p. 235.

disengage. No. 121, Lt. Brookes Hill, R.N.V.R., also remained on the beach. No. 126, Lt. Cheney, R.N.V.R., arrived in flames, landed its tanks, and sank. Aboard No. 163, Captain Cooke, R.N.V.R., three men in succession were killed at the helm, and it was only at the fourth attempt that the craft beached in shallow water under cover of No. 145.

On one of the L.C.T.s the chain supporting the ramp snapped just at the moment the leader's tank was about to disembark. The tank sank in eight feet of water. The others crashed against the wall bordering the beach and only four managed to cross it and reach the esplanade, for the sappers landed from the L.C.T.s to breach the wall with explosives had either been killed, had been unable to land, or found themselves with their material either soaked or burnt and in any case useless.[1] The second wave arrived at this juncture. At 0605 hrs. as planned, the four L.C.T.s of Group No. 9 arrived at the beach with their 12 tanks. The firing had not diminished. L.C.T.124, Lt. Gwinner, R.N.V.R., landed his three tanks and sank as he withdrew. No. 125, Lt. Roberts, R.N.V.R., had to take avoiding action after landing the first tank, and when he made a second attempt three-quarters of an hour later, his entire crew was either killed or wounded. Led by the second officer, it managed to land a second tank on the beach and to withdraw under its own steam, to be taken in tow by the sloop *Alresford*. No. 165, Captain Barber, R.N.V.R., and No. 166, Sub-Lt. Alanson, R.N.V.R., were able to land all their tanks, the former suffering serious damage, and the second with no trouble.

Eleven out of 12 tanks landed by the second wave following 17 out of 18 by the first was not a bad performance in the conditions reigning on the Dieppe beach. True that it was paid for by the loss of five L.C.T.s, half the craft of this type which had effectively approached the beach. For in view of the turn of events, the following landings were cancelled and Groups No. 10 and 11 put about.

Of these 28 tanks landed, 12 were immediately put out of

---

[1] Of the 352 officers and men of the Royal Canadian Engineers landed from the various landing-craft to make the necessary breaches, 189 were killed or seriously wounded before setting foot ashore.

action on the beach, seven crossed the wall and four penetrated
the town. It is not clear what happened to the others. According
to Stacey some of them arrived on the front. The German
reports are conflicting on this point, and the British were unable
to obtain information from the survivors of this group, because
of all the crews of the tanks landed, one signaller alone returned
to England on the evening of 19th August.

There has been great talk of the 'surprise' in store for the
assailants – the bank of pebbles covering that part of the beach
left free by the sea at high tide. The word is inaccurate. There
are plenty of pebble beaches in England and all the necessary
experience had been gained. But these experiences had not
foreseen that the sappers charged with facilitating the passage
of the tanks across these pebbles would be almost entirely wiped
out. Left to their own devices, three-quarters of the tanks lost
their tracks and were paralysed. In this respect it can be
admitted that Dieppe was a 'victory for the pebbles'. The
presence of the Churchills, however, was not entirely of no
avail to the infantry. Reduced to the state of fixed batteries, im-
pervious to the 37 mm. German anti-tank guns, some of them
remained manned by their crews until after midday, and contributed largely to the salvage of everything that could be saved.

But what did turn out to be a surprise was the unexpected
strength of the concrete walls built by the Germans at the end
of the streets leading to the beach.[1] These obstacles not only
hampered the Canadians, but made it impossible for the
Germans to reinforce the seafront with anti-tank artillery.
A strange thing – neither of the adversaries thought of over-
coming this difficulty by using the courtyards or the gardens
of certain buildings with large carriage doors leading to the
front, or into the Descelliers which runs parallel to it.

*   *   *

But what had happened in the meantime to the Royal Hamiltons and the Essex Scottish?

At the west end of the front, where the Rue de Sygogne
debouches beneath the castle, was the Casino which the Germans had started to demolish barely a week before. On 19th

[1] 'Unexpected strength of blocks at the ends of streets.' Churchill.

August, only the south-west wing of the building had been destroyed, and the rest was occupied at the moment of landing. It needed the Royal Hamiltons a good hour to master the situation. This was learned at 0712 hrs. aboard H.M.S. *Calpe*, where good news certainly arrived faster than the bad.

It was all the same a strongpoint gained, for apart from the Casino which offered a certain cover, it directly commanded access to the Rue Sygogne and the nearby buildings. A small group of 15 men, led by Captain Hill, took advantage of this to penetrate into the town where, without gaining much ground, since they did not go beyond the church of Saint-Rémy, they managed to hold on until 1000 hrs. The arrival of German reinforcements forced these men to fall back on the Casino. Together with another small group, which burst into the town hall, this appears to be the only detachment of the Royal Hamiltons which managed to cross the front and infiltrate into Dieppe itself.

Deprived of the sapper support, which was to cleave a passage through the obstructions, the Royal Hamiltons were greatly handicapped. The guns and machine-guns posted on the other side of the channel, on the Neuville heights, did the rest as can be read in the official report.

'This appalling enfilade fire made the capture of the beach impossible and all the rest of the plan fell to the ground.'

At 0600 hrs., according to this plan, the Royal Hamiltons should have joined up with the South Saskatchewans who had landed at Pourville. They were far from doing this.

On Red beach, the Essex Scottish were in an even worse position for, like the Royal Hamiltons, they did not enjoy the relative protection of the Casino. Here the battlefield was totally dominated on its flanks by the two cliffs, and ahead by the buildings of the boulevard de Verdun. At the near end of the west jetty, a small pillbox housed an anti-tank gun. Not far away an old Renault tank, model R.17-18, had been placed on the quayside behind a concrete wall. These two emplacements alone, which the Canadians were never able to capture, sufficed to block all movement on this part of the front. The Renault tank fired 90 armour-piercing and 95 H.E. shells. Its crew obtained a lucky hit in the engine of a Churchill tank, Conger, whose 51 mm. armour plating had been pierced by a 37 mm. shell. Having exhausted its ammunition, and with no chance of receiving any more, the crew took shelter behind a concrete wall and continued to fire. It had the satisfaction, a little later, of receiving the surrender of a dozen Canadians.

From the whole Essex Scottish battalion, a single group of ten men led by an N.C.O., Cornelius Stapleton, managed to infiltrate the buildings of the boulevard de Verdun. They reaped a bloody harvest and pushed on through the small streets of this district to the maritime station from which the Germans dislodged them at 0815 hrs.

According to the report of Captain McCrae, the only officer from this battalion to return to England on 19th August, 20 minutes after landing the losses of the Essex Scottish had already amounted to between 30 and 40 per cent. It was no longer a question of delivering an organized combat. Huddled against the beach wall, as in a trench without a parados, the survivors could only fire at random. They managed to fling a few grenades into the tobacco factory, which was on their list of targets for destruction. For some obscure reason, the British command believed that it was used as an ammunition dump. It was a calumny of this peaceful building, whose walls housed only perfectly innocent material. The smokers of Dieppe, reduced like their compatriots to a meagre ration of six packets of cigarettes a month, were in despair when they saw all this treasure go up in flames when the factory caught fire.

*   *   *

Witnesses of this desperate fighting, the sailors did all they could. The destroyer *Albrighton* began by silencing a flak battery which was firing in the direction of Pourville and then lifted its fire to the factory. *Bleasdale* and *Garth* harassed the German positions on the cliff above Dieppe. But it was obvious that their guns were ridiculously under-calibred. It was, moreover, a surprise to the Germans to note that their enemies did not possess a more important naval support. This was also the opinion of Admiral James, C.-in-C. Portsmouth: 'A battleship or a cruiser might have made all the difference.'[1]

[1] James, op. cit., p. 187.

Arriving shortly after 0600 hrs. off the entrance to the port, H.M.S. *Locust* had a duel with a cliff battery above Dieppe, but was forced to withdraw four minutes later after a direct hit on the bridge. The crew of L.C.F.2 distinguished itself particularly by its valiance. Its commanding officer, Lt. Graham, R.N.V.R., had approached almost within point-blank range to give the infantry the support of his pom-poms and Oerlikons. His guns were put out of action one after the other. Graham was killed, and later all the ship's officers. Without a moment's hesitation the M.O. Lt. Martin, himself wounded, took command of the vessel until it finally sank, riddled with shrapnel like a sieve. Picked up by H.M.S. *Calpe*, Martin resumed his medical duties until he collapsed, by tending, together with his colleagues of the *Calpe*, the wounded which the L.C.A.s had brought back in their dozens aboard the flagship.[1]

In short, at 0700 hrs., the situation at Dieppe was grim in the extreme. The Canadians had retained a foothold on the beach, but in the most difficult conditions, exposed to an enemy fire which showed no sign of abating. Apart from the few exceptions already mentioned, no penetration of the town had been achieved. A small group which tried to climb the cliff below the town was wiped out.

General Roberts knew nothing of all this. Furthermore, shortly after 0630 hrs. he received a signal announcing that the Essex Scottish had established themselves on the beach and in the neighbouring houses. What was the source of this information? Possibly an earlier message from the Essex addressed to the Royal Hamiltons reporting the raid by Cornelius Stapleton. Whatever the answer Roberts, calculating that the situation was well in hand on Red beach, decided to send in his reserves, i.e. the battalion of Mont Royal Fusiliers, embarked in the L.C.P.s of Group No. 7, and whose commanding officer, Lt.-Colonel Ménard, had been aboard H.M.S. *Calpe* for half an hour.

Group No. 7 comprised of Nos. 4 and 5 Flotillas of L.C.P.s (Lts. Wallace and Roulston, R.N.V.R.) had sailed direct from Newhaven under the orders of Lt.-Commander Datham aboard

[1] Apart from the members of the crew, 278 wounded soldiers were treated aboard the *Calpe*.

L.M.214 which ensured the close protection of the group together with No. 230, Lts. Lyle and Nees, R.N.V.R.

At 0700 hrs., the 26 landing craft which had so far remained off shore in reserve, now set their course in line ahead for Dieppe beach. The Germans could observe them perfectly. All the shore batteries concentrated their fire on these 'mosquitoes', all the machine-guns hidden along the front swept the beach ahead of them, while from the chateau hand grenades and mortar shells rained down upon them. Two L.C.P.s were lost as they beached and a third had to withdraw. In all these craft the losses were heavy and the French Canadians, virtually pinned to the spot, could do nothing. Moreover, the greater part of the battalion landed at the extreme western end of White beach, whereas Roberts had intended to send them as reinforcements to Red beach near the entrance to the harbour. Blocked under the Bas Fort Blanc cliff, with no egress towards the town, the fusiliers could only hold on as best they could, and ultimately surrender when there was nothing else to be done. Their complement was 484, and 111 perished in this sinister adventure. Only 125 returned to Great Britain, including 50 wounded. All the rest fell into the hands of the enemy. Let us recall here the name of Sergeant Dubuc who, at the head of a small group, penetrated as far as the port where he caused considerable damage, was caught, gave his guards the slip and was able to re-embark.[1]

---

[1] Cf. Thompson, *Dieppe at Dawn*. Dubuc began by mopping-up two pillboxes near the Casino. Then, spotting an abandoned tank which the ebbing tide had left high and dry, he took up his position inside it and fired all the ammunition he could find at the positions on the cliff below the town. After this he entered the town by the Rue de Sygogne and, via the buildings on the sea front, reached in succession the Duquesne basin, which he found empty, and then the Canada basin where he captured two German landing-craft, but was obliged to abandon them later since he could not sail them away. Making his way back to the town by the railway line which served the port, with no ammunition left, he encountered a strongly armed enemy patrol to whom he was forced to surrender. The Germans, not content with disarming their prisoners, removed their shoes and confident that they were thus powerless, left them to be guarded by a single fighting man.

Dubuc, having managed to distract the attention of his guard, made a sign to his men, who strangled the German with their bare hands.

*   *   *

But there were still victims to sacrifice – the British this time, a whole commando of Royal Marines, 18 officers and 152 men under the orders of Lt.-Colonel Phillips, R.N., who had sailed in the chasseurs of Group No. 13.

According to the plan this group was to have consisted of eight chasseurs and the gunboats *Alresford* and *Locust*. These chasseurs were small French craft of about 150 tons, armed with a 75, a few machine-guns and anti-submarine grenades, which, after playing a heroic part in the defence and evacuation at the French ports from Dunkirk to Cherbourg during the 1940 invasion, had retired to the British ports. Impounded on the 3rd July by the Royal Navy they had been refitted to form part of the Free French Naval Forces.

A particularly exciting role had been planned for them in Operation *Jubilee* – to force the harbour entrance, to remove everything afloat and to destroy the rest. The hero of Saint-Nazaire, Commander Ryder, R.N., was to direct operations personally aboard H.M.S. *Locust*.

On the night of the 9th/10th August, Chasseur 11, Petty Officer Montador, F.F.N.F., during a night patrol, had been in collision with Chasseur 14, manned by British ratings, which had prevented her from taking part in the operation. Then, during the night of the 18th/19th, Chasseur 42, Chief Petty Officer Parc, F.F.N.F., was delayed in the minefields with an engine breakdown and had to put about. He did not go to Dieppe but played his part in the aero-naval battle in the Channel, and took in tow S.G.B.5, seriously damaged off Berneval in the mêlée we have already described. Thus only

---

They took to their heels and in their shorts, this mad gallop ended on the beach where Dubuc was lucky enough to find his wounded Colonel. After apologizing for his unmilitary garb he carried him to one of the L.C.A.s which had appeared for the evacuation from behind a smoke-screen.

After all, truth is often stranger than fiction. Colonel Stacey merely wrote that Dubuc's small group penetrated some distance, was captured, but managed to overcome the guard and to return to the beach.

six chasseurs, Nos. 14, 43, 13, 41, 10 and 5, assembled off Dieppe, awaiting orders to try and force an entrance to the harbour.

At 0645 hrs. Captain Hughes-Hallett sent for Ryder. The affair appeared to him more than adventurous. He had no knowledge as yet of the disaster at Puys, and aboard H.M.S. *Calpe* it was still believed the Royals had not yet landed. In any case the coup had failed at Blue beach and the Neuville cliff remained firmly in the hands of the enemy, dominating the fairway of the outer harbour at point-blank range. Ryder agreed that the attempt must be abandoned, particularly, as he told his chief, since *Locust* herself was gravely handicapped by a direct hit received on her bridge.

General Roberts, who was of the same opinion, suddenly suggested that since the Royal Marines were idle, why should they not be sent to White beach as reinforcements, as the Canadian Fusiliers had just been sent to Red beach. Ryder approved and Hughes-Hallett gave his consent.

I am bold enough to suggest – although this is only a personal opinion – that the two British naval officers could not bear the idea of being thought more sparing with the lives of British Marines than this Canadian general was towards his own compatriots. A new holocaust was in preparation.

All the L.C.F.s available – it turned out to be only one, the L.C.F.2 already mentioned – and all the chasseurs received orders to concentrate their fire to support the landing of the Marines, who in the meantime had been trans-shipped to the L.C.A.s.

Here, seen from the bridge of Chasseur 43, Ensign Boju, F.F.N.F., is what has been described by a British eyewitness as a repetition of the famous Light Brigade.

0615 – Five miles from Ailly lighthouse in sector 50. A large number of aircraft overhead.

0620 – A Spitfire crashed into the water 20 yards on our starboard bow.

0627 – Engines stopped. Received orders to trans-ship the Commandos to landing-craft B.L.9.

0705 – Received the order to accompany and give cover to the

Commandos as far as the landing beach. Took up my position behind Chasseur 14.

0710 – Violent firing from the shore batteries, which got our range several times. Smoke-screens on land made it impossible to spot the German batteries.

0718 – Stopped to wait for the landing-craft, which we had slightly outsailed.

0720 – Under way again. The firing from the shore batteries doubled in intensity and now concentrated on the landing-craft. Lit a smoke flare to mask them from the shore.

0733 – Spotted a barge emerging from the smoke which appeared to be in difficulties. Drew alongside to starboard of this barge to offer assistance, but it was refused.

0804 – Took up my position again to stern of Chasseur 14. Course 165.

0815 – Lost sight of Chasseur 14 which disappeared into a thick cloud of smoke. Changed course to 40° to approach land and to lay a new smoke-screen between the beach and the landing-craft.

0820 – Returned to my course on the port entrance. Intense fire from the shore batteries which 'framed' us. Spotting of these batteries very difficult on account of the smoke-screen. Spotted a battery of 77s near the West Jetty of the port. Opened fire with our 75 at 3,900 yards. At the third salvo, which seemed very near the mark, the target disappeared in the smoke.

Similar incidents will be found in all the other naval reports. And this continued until at about 1330 hrs., Chasseur 43, escorting the last convoy of survivors, set its course for the shores of England.

But we must not anticipate. With what in retrospect seemed to be a complete misappreciation of the facts, General Roberts had briefed Colonel Phillips to make good the setback of the Royals at Puys 'by skirting the town to the west and south, so as to attack from the south the batteries placed on the cliff above the town'.

In fact, a mere walk of two to two and a half miles along the rue de Sygogne, where no one had yet advanced more than 20 yards, the rue Chanzy, the Arques road, the inner harbour and the heights of Neuville! It is not difficult to understand that, when quoting these orders, the official historian of the Canadian army speaks of 'an over-optimistic plan'.

Needless to say, this plan was never put into execution. Greeted in the manner we have just described, Lt.-Colonel Phillips lost three or four of his L.C.A.s the moment he beached. He was quick to realize the position. Putting on a pair of white gloves so that his gestures might be more visible, he leapt on the deck of his landing-craft, making broad signs to tell the others to withdraw behind the smoke-screen. Mortally wounded a few seconds later, we hope that he had had time to realize before he died that his heroic gesture had been understood.[1]

This time it was the end. Moreover there was no one else to put ashore. On the contrary, it was now necessary to try and evacuate those who were not already dead.

At 0935 hrs., according to the report from the O.C. Chasseurs describing the desperate situation reigning on White and Red beaches, Hughes-Hallett gave orders to prepare for the evacuation.

[1] Thanks to the sacrifice of Lt.-Colonel Phillips, the Royal Marine Commando lost only 66 dead and prisoners, whereas the Mont Royal Fusiliers lost 459 out of complements which were 370 and 584 respectively.

CHAPTER TWENTY

THE ENEMY DEPLOYS HIS RESERVES

It has been correctly assessed that if a defensive battle is the most powerful form of combat on the tactical plane, that if to attack at one point it is necessary to concentrate at least three times more forces than the enemy can align for his defence, this concentration is, on the contrary, far easier for the assailant than for the defender, since it is he who takes the initiative and chooses the sector of attack. One cannot pretend to be strong everywhere for fear of being strong nowhere, and this is why it is impossible, merely with local forces, to pretend to ensure the integrity of a continuous front such as that represented by the Channel coast. It is necessary to have to the rear sufficient mobile reserves ready to be directed to the weak spot, and to restore a situation that the effect of surprise might have compromised at the outset.

But on all these beaches where the blood flowed so generously, in all these death traps where death waited these young Canadian soldiers, who were so impatient to fight, nature had so lavishly favoured the defence that the battle had already been won by the Germans before they had any need to call upon their reserves. This of course was not evident at the outset, and the German command could not fail to keep at its disposal a sufficiently important force to repel any British attempt.

As we have already seen, it was not until 0458 hrs. that the staff of the 302nd Division sent from Envermeu a report on the engagement of the Boulogne convoy. No one as yet envisaged a landing, and there was a certain surprise at the Hq. of the 81st Corps at Canteleu when, a quarter of an hour later, Colonel Sartorius, G.S.O.1 (Ia.) of the 302nd Infantry Division, reported that landings had taken place at Pourville and Quiberville, and that Dieppe had just been heavily bombed. To the left of the 302nd Infantry Division, in the Fécamp–Le Havre sector, the 332nd and the 811th on the lower Seine had nothing abnormal to report. To the right, in the sector of the 321st on the Somme, everything was equally quiet. As a preliminary precaution General Kunsten alerted all the Army Corps Reserves – i.e. the I/676 Battalion at Doudeville and the III/376 and the staff of the regiment at Yvetot, the III/570 at Bacqueville, the Gollé Regiment, etc. At 0550 he alerted Jafu 3 (3rd Fighter Group) and the 13th Flak Division. At 0645 hrs. the III/570 was dispatched to Ouville-la-Riviere on the orders of the 302nd Infantry Division, while the 676th Infantry Regiment was dispatched from Yvetot to Bacqueville, reinforced by Panzerkompanie 81.

We have already seen that at his level, General Haase had taken all the necessary precautions, and we know their effect. Now the great decisions fell upon the High Command, in other words the Oberkomando des Heeres, O.K.H., kept informed by the 15th Army.

In high places the first impressions remained rather vague. Was it an attempted invasion ? Admittedly it was the first time the enemy had shown himself on a 12 mile front. This was a considerable stretch for a single raid, but too narrow to be a bridgehead. But perhaps something was being prepared elsewhere ? Taking no chances, orders were given to the 10th Panzer Division and the S.S. Adolf Hitler Armoured Brigade[1] to hold itself in readiness for all eventualities. 'Things were still somewhat obscure, but the order for the alert could arrive at any minute.' And this actually happened. At 0625 hrs. the 10th Panzers and at 0628 hrs. the S.S. Adolf Hitler Brigade received the Alarmstufe II (No. 2 alert).

The alert was received at 0630 hrs. at Amiens at the Hq. of

[1] We have already mentioned that the 10th Panzers had been at rest in the Amiens region since the 10th April. Like it, the S.S. Adolf Hitler Brigade had fought throughout the Russian campaign. It defended the Mins front in the Donetz basin until the 2nd July, 1942, and was then brought back to France. It had just arrived in the Vernon region.

The S.S. Adolf Hitler motorized regiment commanded by the famous Sepp Dietrich had fought brilliantly in Poland and France. It became an armoured brigade at the time of the opening of the Russian campaign, and was eventually to develop into a division. Dietrich commanded this formation practically throughout the war, and proved to be an excellent commander of armour.

General Wolfgang Fischer, commanding the 10th Panzers. At 0640 hrs. the Ia. was awakened; as chief of operations it was his duty to set all the wheels in motion. But this G.S.O.1 could not be found. Had he slept away from home? It was a mystery. In any case his telephone line was dead. Another regrettable detail, of which account was taken on this occasion – no arrangements had been made in advance for radio contact between the 10th Panzers and the 81st Army Corps in the sector in which they were to operate. Moreover, the 10th Panzers had no map of the Dieppe region. Their depot was at Lille. A truck had to be sent 70 miles one way and perhaps double this distance for the return journey, if the division had moved in the meantime.

In any case, no one appeared to expect an immediate intervention by the 10th Panzers. Alerted at 0630 hrs., it only received orders from the 81st Corps to clarify the situation at Dieppe by a telephone call from O.K.H. received at Tourcoing at 0847 hrs., by the 15th Army, at 0845 at Canteleu, by the Army Corps and five minutes later at Amiens by the division itself. The orders were that the advance guard was to set out at 1000 hrs. and the main body an hour later.

As we know, by 1000 hrs. all danger had been averted. It was already some time since General Roberts and Captain Hughes-Hallett had agreed to cut their losses, and to prepare for the evacuation.

Manifestly the German High Command was not disturbed. Otherwise how to account for these delays? And it was better thus, for with the 10th Panzers things followed a slow and reasonable course. It needed five minutes to make contact with the 7th Tank Regiment which formed part of the advance guard with a flak battalion of the 90th Panzer Artillery Regiment, designed to guard the bridges over the Somme, the Second Battalion of the 86th Panzergrenadiere Regiment, the motor cyclist battalion No. 10 and a brigade of Panzer Grenadiers.

The leading columns set out at 0940 hrs., on the route Doullens, Abbeville, Blangy, Neufchatel, Torcy-le-Grand. The main body prepared to move off at 1000 hrs. via Amiens, Poix, Formerie, Forges-les-Eaux. General Kunzen had given orders to the 10th Panzers to send a reinforced battalion to wait at Torcy-le-Petit and to keep the rest in readiness in the Neufchatel–Londinières sector. General Fischer was expected at midday at Envermeu, General Haase's Hq., to discuss the employment of his division.

We shall see later what happened to the 10th Panzers, which actually reached the sea but were never in action. As for the S.S. Adolf Hitler Brigade, it spent the day on the alert, but did not leave its quarters.

While the military operations progressed very favourably for the defence, air reconnaissance at sea brought the German command a new cause for perplexity. As early as 0640 hrs., the Admiral Kanalküste had reported to Marinegruppe West, i.e. to the Naval C.-in-C. for the whole theatre of operations, situated to the west of Denmark, that he was out of telephonic communication with the Dieppe commander, but that he was in perfect contact by radio with the reconnaissance post at Ailly Point. It was this post which had been the first to report the tank landing, and this piece of information caused the High Command to wonder whether the enemy's intention was not definitely to create a bridgehead at Dieppe. Now during the course of the morning O.K.H. received a report from a Luft-waffe reconnaissance of various concentrations in the Channel – six big transports, some 25 miles west of Dieppe, three others 37 miles away, and finally near Selsey Bill, hugging the coast, some 26 vessels of 6,000 tons each 'stuffed with troops', and escorted by three destroyers.

Let us state straight away that the two first of these three groups were the L.S.I.s which had been sent back to England after the trans-shipment of their troops to the L.C.T.s of Groups 10, 11 and 12, which had not approached the beach. As for the 26 big transports 'stuffed with troops', they formed a convoy of small coasters – Convoy C.W.116 – which had just crossed the Pas de Calais from east to west, from the mouth of the Thames, making for St. Helens, Isle of Wight. An ordinary routine convoy which the British Admiralty had not considered it necessary to cancel on account of the raid, and which in any case the German radar stations had kept under observation from the French coast, as was subsequently learned.

At the moment, however, this innocent coastal convoy posed

some serious problems. Who was to know whether the British were not foxing their enemies at Dieppe with a diversionary attack, whereas a far more important operation was being planned elsewhere – in Brittany for example ? On the same line of reasoning, were not the vessels sighted near Dieppe carrying floating reserves which must be prevented from landing ?

From O.K.W., General Jodl requested the navy to send submarines into the Channel. Admiral Doenitz agreed to divert three submarines, which were under orders to reach their fields of operation in the battle of the Atlantic, to the western Channel approaches. But this order was cancelled as soon as B.d.U.[1] knew the real position.

In any event it was necessary to put everyone on their guard, not only in the sector of the 15th Army, but also its neighbours on either flank, as far as Holland and Brittany. At 1030 hrs., Field Marshal von Rundstedt ordered Alert No. 2 for the 7th Army (lower Normandy and Brittany), for all the reserves of D Army Group, i.e. the 7th Infantry Division, the 6th Panzers, the 337th Infantry Division and the Herman Goering Brigade.

Matters had reached this point when the aviation reported that the famous Selsey Bill convoy had set its course north-west and appeared to be making for Portsmouth. This at least proved that the enemy was loth to engage it in the Dieppe sector even if it had been the original intention. But this did not prove that he had definitely given up the idea.

As the morning advanced, the local reports became more and more satisfactory. It was soon obvious that the enemy was abandoning the fight and cutting his losses. It was now or never to make a double effort to try and cut off his retreat, or at least to make him pay for his coup as dearly as possible. All the messages intercepted confirmed this difficult situation: 'Several tanks destroyed, situation at Dieppe very critical.' Moreover, one of the British commanders, who was unidentified, demanded a smoke-screen to protect his re-embarkation. Towards midday C.-in-C. West was able to send the following message to the 15th Army, the LXXXIst Corps, Marine-gruppe West and the 3rd Luftflotte:

[1] Befehlshaber der Unterseeboote, C.-in-C. U-boats.

'The enemy forces which landed at Dieppe are retiring. It is essential to destroy as many of these forces as possible. To this end powerful detachments of the 10th Panzers (tanks and artillery) will advance immediately. All guns and weapons must be engaged. All the points where the adversary had set foot must be mopped up without delay.'

C.-in-C. West.
Signed: von Rundstedt.
Generalfeldmarschall.

The 10th Panzers were at this moment advancing without undue haste. It had been agreed that they should operate west of the River Bethune, south of Dieppe, while the 302nd Infantry Division would ensure the defence of Dieppe itself. At 1355 hrs. the left column of the armoured division reached Longueville in the valley of the Scie, ready to advance in the direction of Pourville, which the local commander considered the most threatened sector. Then, since the intelligence officer of the 302nd Infantry Division announced that, in accordance with the position at 1400 hrs., everything was well in hand at Dieppe and at Pourville, it received orders not to advance north of the line Arquès-la-Bataille–Tourville-sur-Arques and to keep itself in reserve of the Army Corps in the region Tourville–Londinières–Neufchatel–Saint-Saëns. Cyclist Battalion No. 10 alone advanced as far as the coast where it arrived at 1600 hrs. to comb the woods and gardens between Pourville and Quiberville. Its efforts were fruitless. The comb did not produce a single Tommy.[1]

In the meantime, the official reserves of the LXXXIst Army Corps received similar orders. The Gollé Regiment was ordered to remain in the Tôtes–Yvetot sector, the Sandkühler column was to send forward one company to Tôtes and one to Yvetot.

By 1800 hrs. the scare was over. All that remained was to mop up Varengeville Wood where it was believed that a few British commandos were still in hiding; to count the prisoners and the material captured. On the 20th at 0800 hrs. Alert No. 2 was cancelled. The 676th Infantry Regiment resumed its

[1] Report of the LXXXIst Army Corps.

place in Army Corps reserve, and the 10th Panzers were with-drawn from the orders of the LXXXIst Corps.

It had not been under fire, but this alert was later considered an extremely instructive exercise. Everything which had gone amiss was carefully recorded – the circumstances of the diffu-sion of the alert, the organization of the convoys, the orders for routing, not to mention the ridiculous affair of the maps which had not been on the spot. To sum up, the cynics who con-sidered these pinprick raids to be as profitable to the enemy as to those who organized them, were not far wrong. We shall in fact have occasion to see that the Dieppe raid was as informa-tive to the Germans as to the British.

CHAPTER TWENTY-ONE

THE WITHDRAWAL

DURING the major part of Operation *Jubilee*, according to Captain Hughes-Hallett's report, one might think that H.M.S. *Calpe* was taking part in a regatta, so great was the activity of small landing-craft around her. It was a rare occurrence to see less than a dozen at a time, one bringing a cargo of wounded, another an urgent report, and a third a messenger to get instructions or a group leader summoned by his superior officer. . . . It was no easy task to manoeuvre in the midst of this confusion, to take avoiding action from the enemy's fire. Imperturbable, Lt.-Commander Wallace weaved his ship amongst the shell bursts and barges, doing his best to avoid both. It was difficult to see what was happening on land, because of the smoke-screen which the wind bore slowly towards the coast, and it was only by seeing the landing craft, repulsed from the beach by enemy fire, return, that it was realized in the flagship that things were not progressing according to plan.

At 0900 hrs. Hughes-Hallett decided to send back to England H.M.S. *Garth*, whose ammunition was almost exhausted, and H.M.S. *Alresford*, hampered by a damaged L.C.T. which she had taken in tow, and the L.C.T.s of Group 10 and 11, from which the idea of landing the tanks had been abandoned. A little later he also sent back those of Group 12, transformed into hospital ships, because the L.C.T.s which were to come alongside at the moment of evacuation had been unable to adhere to the plan since there was no longer any chance of their approaching the beach without immediately being destroyed. He was to regret this later in the operation.

Now he had to try and save the whole of the landed forces. Hughes-Hallett informed General Roberts that in his view this attempt must be considered as an urgency, and that it was out of the question to try and think of salvaging any material.

1030 hrs. was agreed upon. This delay was necessary to warn the aviation and to give orders to the landing craft.

After the landing, all the assault craft had been formed into a kind of 'pool', a mass manoeuvre directed by Commander McClintock, commanding the L.C.P.s of Group No. 6. Hughes-Hallett ordered him to take the L.C.T.s to within a mile of the beach and to organize a shuttle service of L.C.A.s and L.C.M.s to take off the troops from the various beaches upon which they had landed.

McClintock went aboard M.L.187 to distribute his orders. In the meantime the destroyers had to form up on a north-east–south-east line, parallel approximately to the shore at a distance of four to six cables (from 800 to 1,100 yards). All the ships in a position to do so were to lay a maximum smoke-screen to mask the re-embarkation.[1] This was a double-edged weapon, for with the wind blowing towards the shore, it was impossible to spot the enemy guns which it would have been desirable to neutralize. On the other hand it was the only possible solution, if an attempt were to be made to save some of the troops.

It was decided that during these operations, H.M.S. *Calpe*, whose guns were not to be used for fear of disturbing the radio apparatus aboard, should cruise off Green beach (Pourville) where it was thought she would have no need of support from her guns. This was correct while the cliff below the town was still in the hands of the South Saskatchewans, but when the Germans reoccupied these positions, *Calpe* was a target for their heavy machine guns. She ceased to bother about her delicate instruments and let rip with all her 102 mm. guns. In actual fact nothing happened, and despite the shocks, the radio functioned no better or worse than before. The same applied to H.M.S. *Fernie* for which the same fears had been entertained, and which was now also forced to fire against the shore batteries.

We already know how the re-embarkation progressed at Pourville. At Puys, there was no hope left. It only remains now to follow the progress of the operations off Dieppe.

[1] In addition to the smoke bombs which are simply fired from the deck of the ship, the destroyers were also able to emit black smoke by opening their smoke stack ventilators.

The time of this re-embarkation coincided with increased activity on the part of the Luftwaffe, whose bombers now appeared in the sky escorted by Messerschmidt 109s and Focke-Wulf 190s. The fire from the German aircraft combined with that of the shore batteries, heavy machine-guns and snipers was positively murderous. Of the eight L.C.A.s from the *Prince Charles*'s Flotilla which Lt. Phillips led to Red beach, six were destroyed. At White beach four L.C.A.s from the *Princess Astrid*, led by Lt. Howitt, were received by a hellish fire but managed to approach the shore and were immediately rushed by the Canadian soldiers. One of them overturned and sank. The three others each brought back 70 men, double their normal capacity. Only two emerged unscathed. The third, on the point of sinking, managed to reach an L.C.T. just at the moment when the latter, having received several direct hits, was itself beginning to sink.

At about 1100 hrs., when Lt. Corke reached the same White beach with the *Glengyle*'s L.C.A.s, it was almost entirely occupied by the enemy, who had seized some abandoned tanks and turned their guns against a sort of redoubt which the Royal Hamiltons had constructed behind a derelict L.C.T. Corke was able to embark the whole group, but three of his craft were sunk as they withdrew. The remainder conveyed their passengers – for the most part wounded men – aboard H.M.S. *Calpe*, where the jam now began to be appalling.

Protected by M.L.343, which laid a heavy smoke-screen ahead of it, L.C.T.166 collected from Red beach the passengers of several L.C.A.s. To get them off safe and sound it had to avoid the concentrated fire from all the enemy guns.

These heroic, though fatally improvised and sometimes disorderly efforts continued until 1230 hrs. It is virtually impossible to describe an operation which bore no resemblance to the original plans and relied entirely on skill and individual initiative. On paper an orderly retreat had been envisaged, in the course of which the L.C.T.s were to have taken off from the beach the tanks and the infantry, with the L.C.F.s acting as rear-guards to evacuate. In practice, as we can read in a British report, everyone did what he could, as best he could, across those two or three hundred yards of naked beach – the tide was now right out – to reach the landing craft with the water sometimes up to the shoulders when they were not forced to swim.

The battle continued in the air where the Luftwaffe became more and more aggressive. The R.A.F. had to produce a great effort to ensure air cover to the end, while the destroyers continued to fire against the shore batteries.

Not without grave difficulties! At 1130 hrs., H.M.S. *Brocklesby* which had sailed to within 500 yards of the shore for better observation of the gun emplacements from which the firing came, was now the target for weapons of all calibres. She received several direct hits from 77 mm. shells in her engines, which were put out of action, and began to sink by the stern.

Fortunately her engineers managed to get the engines going within a few minutes, which allowed her to get out of this more than critical situation without damage. When she left, at about 1215 hrs., the enemy, who had reoccupied the Casino, fired with all his guns against a group of 100 to 150 soldiers, sheltering behind three L.C.T.s, which had been left completely high and dry by the ebbing tide.

A quarter of an hour later it was H.M.S. *Fernie* whose gunnery control was put out of action as she approached Red beach to lay a smoke-screen. Closer inshore, Chasseur 13, with engines stopped and drifting, asked for assistance, which the destroyer was not in a position to give her. Chasseur 13 had to extricate herself as best she could.

The few messages still received from the land announced the end of resistance. The last received by Roberts' chief of staff aboard H.M.S. *Fernie* broke off abruptly: 'Good-bye, pass on this message to . . .'

Two hours earlier, at the moment arrangements were made for the evacuation, Brigadier-General Mann turned to his American colleague, General Truscott, who had sailed in H.M.S. *Fernie* as an observer, and said: 'General, I am afraid that this operation will go down in history as one of the greatest disasters.' Events were proving him right. The sight of these destroyers crammed with wounded men was sufficient evidence. According to Truscott, the deck of H.M.S. *Fernie* was covered with wounded. Some of them were breathing heavily, a sign of approaching coma, others lay there calmly under the effects of the opium which had been administered to them. 'Many pairs of eyes, however, watched me intently, in silence. Without paying much attention to what I was doing, I brought out my tobacco, rolled and lit a cigarette. "Have you got one to spare?" cried someone. I gave him my cigarette and then rolled and lit cigarettes for the others until my pouch was empty. The only sound to be heard was the screams of the seriously wounded, and the warm thanks of those to whom I had been able to give a cigarette.'

No warship is less suited to serve as a hospital ship than a destroyer. The sick bay occupies a very small space, and there is a minimum of medical supplies. It is possible, in case of emergency to tend the members of the crew, but when wounded men are picked up in scores, the task of the M.O. becomes almost impossible. This is why the plans, carefully studied by the chief M.O. of the expedition, included the adaptation of four L.C.T.s from Group No. 12 into hospital ships, with two doctors each, and special installations in each of the L.C.F.s, which also carried a doctor. Had things turned out as planned, all the wounded could have been picked up on the beach in the most satisfactory conditions, instead of which these unfortunate fellows had to be content with very precarious improvisations.

*   *   *

Accompanied by two L.C.A.s on either side of its hull, H.M.S. *Calpe* approached Red beach for a last tour of inspection. She was heavily peppered and replied with all her armament as she continued her exploration. There were no more troops in sight. Emerging from the smoke-screen, *Calpe* joined *Locust* which had just finished emptying her ammunition lockers against the Le Pollet cliff. Hughes-Hallett hailed her, in order to obtain Ryder's opinion.

At the same moment Roberts received the last message from Brigadier-General Southam: 'Our men here have surrendered.' There was nothing to do but retire. A carrier pigeon was dispatched with the following melancholy report addressed to the G.Hq. of the 1st Canadian Corps: 'Very heavy losses in men and ships. Have done everything possible to extricate our troops, but in order to be able to save some, it was necessary to take the hard decision to abandon the others, a decision entirely agreed upon by the two commanding officers. It is obvious that the element of surprise failed us completely.'

At 1240 hrs. the order was given to the fleet to assemble four miles off shore in quadrant 330, off Dieppe. At 1330 hrs. the last convoy set its course for England.

*   *   *

This was the third time in 500 years that an important British naval force had attacked Dieppe. The first went back to the end of the Hundred Years War. In the summer of 1442 the famous Talbot, crossing the Caux country by the valley of the Scie, had established himself at the spot on which today stand the suburbs of Le Pollet. Marking time the whole winter he was waiting for the fine weather to return and the support of a powerful squadron commanded by the Duke of Somerset, when he was forestalled by the army of the Dauphin, the future Louis XI, who made his solemn entry into Dieppe on the 14th August, 1443. Ejected from the citadel, Talbot had to raise the siege and Somerset left as he had come.

Two and a half centuries later, Admiral Berkeley reduced Dieppe to ashes on the 22nd July, 1694. Anchored a few cables from the town, his galiots set fire to 3,000 houses with fire bombs. Dieppe was erased from the map and Berkeley withdrew in triumph.

History is full of strange coincidences. From the whole naval force commanded by Hughes-Hallett – apart from the amphibian craft – a single sea-going ship was lost – the destroyer H.M.S. *Berkeley*.

The tragedy took place a little before 1300 hrs., at the moment the commanding officer had given the orders for a general retreat. *Berkeley* was busy, on the model of her illustrious forerunner, bombing the houses on the sea front off White beach, when the Luftwaffe pressed its attack home and three big Dorniers bore down on her threateningly. One of them involved with British fighters suddenly jettisoned its bombs when taking avoiding action. By chance two of these bombs hit

H.M.S. *Berkeley* to starboard, ahead of the bridge. The ship broke in two.

Lt. Griffiths, who was close by in S.G.B.8, immediately went to the rescue of the sinking destroyer and picked up the whole crew. A few moments later a torpedo from H.M.S. *Albrighton* sent the hulk to the bottom.

No account of Dieppe fails to mention the heroic behaviour of the American Lt.-Colonel Hillsinger, who sailed in the *Berkeley* as an observer and who was wounded in the engagement. Hillsinger, relates Truscott, was wearing that day a magnificent pair of new boots, of which he was extremely proud. A bomb burst cut off one of his feet. He himself made a tourniquet with his tie; then catching sight of his new boot which seemed to taunt him, floating alongside with his foot inside, he tore off his second boot with an air of disgust, and sent it to rejoin the first. Picked up by S.G.B.8 he refused to be tended before all the other wounded men had been dressed. Lying on the deck of the small gunboat, he was one of the most attentive in reporting the approach of enemy aircraft to the gunners.

The return journey was sinister. After a calm and beautiful sunny morning, the weather turned sour. A sou'wester began to blow, making things very uncomfortable for the small damaged landing-craft. The Luftwaffe pursued the retreat. It almost dealt the same fate to H.M.S. *Calpe* as had overtaken H.M.S. *Berkeley*. Her bridge was damaged and Air Commodore Cole was seriously wounded. A little later, when rescuing a British pilot who had fallen into the sea, *Calpe* had to leave the rest of the formation, where the ships protected each other mutually with their ack-ack fire. The isolated destroyer was the object of several attacks, two of which inflicted serious damage on her: relief came when she rejoined the rest of the convoy at the entrance to the minefield. They were now approaching the English shore, and the protective umbrella of the R.A.F. became more dense. Admiral James had sent destroyers from Portsmouth to reinforce the escort.

One after the other the survivors of this hard day arrived off Newhaven, where the jam was so great that Captain Hughes-Hallett preferred to sail on to Portsmouth with the destroyers. A hospital train was waiting for the wounded at Newhaven, but for some reason it took the passengers to Birmingham, 200 miles away! This did not help the state of those who needed immediate attention. At Portsmouth Admiral James had requisitioned a whole fleet of ambulances, but as no selection had been organized the lightly wounded were the first to be taken off. All the beds at Haslar naval hospital were soon occupied and no one knew where to put the seriously wounded.

It was past midnight when H.M.S. *Calpe* and *Locust* tied up, the last ships to arrive, bringing more than 200 wounded men. It was long after dawn when the last mutilated man was finally settled and dressed in his hospital bed.

CHAPTER TWENTY-TWO

THE AIR BATTLE

'*Tommies tous repartis.* This evening all planes German, this morning all English.'

Nothing could sum up better the air battle of Dieppe than this phrase uttered by a German soldier who, on the 19th August, at the end of the day tried to get into conversation with one of the inhabitants. In actual fact, from the moment the Spitfires began to machine gun Ailly lighthouse at 0445 hrs., until a relatively late hour in the afternoon, the sky over Dieppe had belonged to the British.

It must be said that they paid the price with a double purpose in view:

Firstly, of course, to give maximum support to the amphibian forces which were to land.

Secondly, because the R.A.F. wanted to provoke the Luftwaffe into what was to be – and what was in fact – the greatest air battle since the Battle of Britain.

Air Vice-Marshal Leigh-Mallory had under his command for the occasion:

– 34 fighter squadrons of the R.A.F., six Canadian, one New Zealand, one Free French Air Forces, one Belgian, five Polish, two Norwegian, two Czech and three American, in all 55 squadrons of land fighters to which must be added three provided by the Fleet Air Arm (squadrons from the aircraft carrier H.M.S. *Eagle*), making a total of 58 fighter squadrons;

– 2 squadrons of bombers;
– 4 squadrons for ground support, and
– 3 squadrons for laying smoke-screens (Smoke Force).

In addition to this, the American bomber force, which had recently taken over bases in the United Kingdom, was to carry out a very useful diversion at 1030 hrs. at the moment the evacuation started, by bombing the Abbeville–Drucart airfield which was put out of action for two hours for the German fighters.

As we already know, the first sortie of the Flying Fortresses of No. 97 American bomber group had led them on the previous night to the sky over Rouen.

On the 19th, 24 B.17s were sent to Abbeville. Twenty-two attacked to good purpose and, according to Leigh-Mallory, disorganized the German fighters at one of the most critical moments of Operation *Jubilee*.[1]

*   *   *

Normally the Dieppe sector came within the zone of action of Jafu 2 (*Jagdfliegerführung* 2) commanded by Colonel Huth. The early morning mist prevented his planes from taking off, but the airfields of Jafu 3 were clear, and at 0530 hrs. Colonel Igel was able to send a first reconnaissance to the north-west of Dieppe.[2] The Jafu 2 planes were airborne half an hour later, since visibility had improved at their bases. This does not alter the fact that for three-quarters of an hour the R.A.F. met with no opposition in the sky apart from flak. Doubtless the operations of Lovat at Varengeville and of Young at Berneval were greatly facilitated by this. This is what also permitted the perfect synchronization of the first air attack on Dieppe at the time of the main landing.

At 0700 hrs. there were still only about 30 F.W. 190s in the air, and Leigh-Mallory began to have doubts whether the great air battle, which for him was one of the main objectives of the day, would ever take place.

[1] Furthermore, reconnaissance carried out by the R.A.F. the following day indicated serious material damage, the accuracy of which was not confirmed later. *Army Air Forces*, Vol. II, p. 226.

[2] The only accurate figures I have been able to discover on the activity of the German fighters on the 19th August, are given by Josef Priller in *Geschichte eines Jagdgeschwaders*. He mentions in the case of the Schlageter Squadron, J.G.26, 36 missions, representing 377 sorties of Focke-Wulf 109As, between 0618 and 2121 hrs. (presumably German time).

At the cost of six pilots killed, J.G.26 claimed 38 victories and 11 probables.

In addition the fighter bombers of No. 10 Jabo/J.G.26, equipped with specially adapted F.W.190As claimed, without giving figures, a certain number of hits registered on British ships.

We must mention on this score, that although the British have always defended themselves by making *Jubilee* out to be a diversion in favour of the Russians – at least as far as naval and land operations were concerned – they willingly agree that by their air operations they reckoned to bring a certain relief to the Soviet aviation on the East Front. It seemed to them obvious that if hard blows were to be given to the German air forces in the west the repercussions would undoubtedly be felt in the Russian sky. The German High Command could not agree to surrender western air supremacy to the enemy without a fight. It was therefore an indirect method of aid to Russia, a method which had already been set in motion, although on a more modest scale, by extending the operations of Fighter Command to northern France.

But as Alanbrooke reveals with a certain bitterness, these tactics had already cost the R.A.F., with little apparent result, a thousand aircraft and pilots. Once more it was to lose a good hundred, at least twice as many as the Luftwaffe, but this bloody affair at least had the merit of putting an end to these practices.[1]

Leaving aside these strategic considerations, there was something even more immediately regrettable on the tactical plane. This air bombardment turned out to be no more effective than the naval bombardment. None of the shore batteries, which the infantry managed to reach – the Rommel, Goering and Hitler Batteries – had been seriously handicapped by the British air force. It suffices to study the German reports to realize that they fired regularly throughout the battle – on an average 300 shells per gun – exactly as if there had been no British plane in the air. 220 400 lb. and 250 90 lb. bombs, in all less than 70 tons was not enough. The only possible success registered by the British planes on the German coastal batteries, according to German reports, was the destruction of the ammunition dump of the Varengeville battery. I doubt whether the veterans of No. 4 Commando would agree to give the credit to their R.A.F. comrades of a destruction which they claimed for their own.

Similarly, the attack prepared against the headquarters of the 110 Infantry Division at Arques-la-Bataille failed because

[1] Arthur Bryant, *The Turn of the Tide*, I. 488.

four out of the six Hurricanes entrusted with this mission crashed, and the remaining two did not find the target. This was of little importance, in any case, except for the unfortunate crews and the eight civilians who were killed: there was no divisional headquarters at Arques-la-Bataille and no 110th Infantry Division in the sector.

*   *   *

It was not until 1000 hrs. that the Luftwaffe appeared in full force. From now onwards there were constantly a hundred German fighters in the sky. Next to appear were the fighter bombers and finally the heavy bombers with their own escort which, ignoring the troops on the ground, devoted their attention to the boats with little success. With the exception of the bombs jettisoned which hit H.M.S. *Berkeley*, the Luftwaffe scored no victories against the British naval force, apart from a few cases of damage. The vigorous fire from the ships accounted for this. The French crews did not lag behind in this respect. Chasseurs 41 and 43 shot down one, if not two Messerschmitts.

At the moment of the evacuation, the R.A.F. Bostons returned to attack the batteries round Dieppe, while the Smoke Force laid new smoke screens. The fighter cover was reinforced and numerous air battles developed during the retreat.

In the last analysis, although the R.A.F., and the Allied pilots who fought with it played their part to the advantage of the landing forces, the price of the encounter was very high. The losses amounted to eight bombers or smoke-launchers, 10 reconnaissance or support aircraft, 88 fighters – all in all, 106 machines. As regards personnel: 113 killed and 40 wounded in a total of 2,617 sorties.[1]

The fast launches of the Air-Sea Rescue sailing in close to the French coast, rescued 13 unharmed pilots and one wounded observer.

The first British estimates gave some hope that the losses of the Luftwaffe compensated largely for these sacrifices. On the 28th August, the claims were:

[1] In this list of losses, the Canadian Air Force figures to the extent of 13 aircraft and 10 pilots.

	Certain Victories	Probables
Junkers 88	11	4
Dornier 215	—	2
Dornier 217	30	4
Heinkel 111	5	—
Messerschmitt 109	3	—
Focke-Wulf 190	47	29

In other words, a total of 96 victories and 39 probables, to which had to be added 143 aircraft damaged.

Unfortunately these brilliant results were not confirmed. In reality the Luftwaffe lost only 48 machines with 24 damaged, in 945 sorties. Its losses in personnel amounted to 104 dead or missing and 58 wounded. These figures included the personnel of units attached to the Luftwaffe – flak, radar, Luftnachrichten Regiment. . . .

Thus the object of the operation was far from having been achieved. It is rather surprising that one can read in a work published in Great Britain, at a period when these figures were perfectly well known, that with 170 aircraft destroyed, the Luftwaffe had lost between a quarter and a half of its fighting force in the western theatre of war. Neither in the air nor on land did Operation *Jubilee* bring the slightest relief to the pressure being exerted on the Russian Front. The Germans transferred no squadrons from the East any more than they brought back any divisions to the West.

*   *   *

Although it was not possible to enter into details of these operations, which in one way or another involved hundreds of aircraft (2,617 British sorties and 945 German), I have borrowed a few details from the book by Lt.-Colonel Dupérier,[1] commanding the Ile de France group of the F.F.A.F. stationed at Hornchurch, and from the diaries of René Mouchotte, his second in command.

The Ile de France pilots – No. 340 Squadron of the R.A.F. – were familiar with the coast of the lower Seine, above which they had already carried out many missions. They were a

[1] *La vielle équipe*, Berger-Lerrault, 1946.

mixed crowd. Mouchotte had left a North African airfield, just as Sub-Lt. Claude had taken off one fine morning during an inspection. Lieutenant Scitivaux had distinguished himself with the fighter arm at Dunkirk in 1940, and had been wounded. Leaving France in epic circumstances, he had arrived in England via Gibraltar. Halna du Fretay had managed to leave Brittany aboard a small private aircraft under the nose of the owner. Fayolle was the son of the director of Naval Artillery at Vichy and grandson of the Marshal of France. He had just left No. 340 Squadron to take command of a British squadron, the 174th. Gibert had strafed the Panzers on the French roads, and then operated in Italy.

On the 18th August, at 1730 hrs., all the Ile de France pilots learned to their delight that a Canadian division was to land the following morning at Dieppe . . . to re-embark at 1100 hrs., which poured cold water on this enthusiasm. Never mind.

Fayolle's squadron of Hurricanes formed part of the Bostons' escort, for the first attack on the coastal defences. Dupérier's Spitfires acted as cover. They took the air at 0545 hrs. and, before the end of their mission, ran into the first Focke-Wulfs of Jafu 3 to appear in the air above Dieppe. One plane did not return, that of Kerlan, hit by a F.W. 190 before the eyes of Lt. Gibert, and picked up in the sea within five minutes. To offset this Cadet Boudier seriously damaged a German fighter; it was seen to go down in a spin and would in all probability never reach its base.

At 0916 hrs. No. 340 Squadron took off on its second mission. 'Arrived over Dieppe without incident,' reported Dupérier, 'but on the ground things do not seem to be going too well.' Dogfight with Dornier 217s, two certain victories and one probable. . . . Delayed by his undercarriage which refused to retract correctly and forced to land, Mouchotte did not take off again until 1000 hrs. . . . this time alone. On arriving over the French coast he spotted an important formation of bombers apparently coming from the north. This was immaterial. Nothing proved that the Germans had not made a detour to surprise the British ships, by attacking them from the flank where they were not expected. Mouchotte approached them. They were Flying Fortresses, and he escorted them part of the way to Abbeville before flying on to Dieppe, delighted to witness an excellent demonstration of bombing.

Third mission at 1200 hrs. At Dieppe the retreat was in full swing. The group claimed a Dornier. 'An inglorious victory,' writes Dupérier modestly, describing the engagement as 'an extraordinary kill where everyone fired badly, being in too much of a hurry, in the hope of being the one to bring down the enemy, among the bullets of his fellow pilots.'

Fourth mission at 1810 hrs. to protect the last convoys on their way home.

In all the Ile de France was credited with two D.O. 217s shot down, five damaged and one F.W. damaged, against two machines lost and one pilot missing (Darbins). But No. 174 Squadron on its first morning sortie lost three French pilots serving with it: Fayolle, du Fretay and van Mersch.

For his gallantry, a few days later in addition to his D.F.C., Mouchotte was given command of a British squadron at Gravesend.

CHAPTER TWENTY-THREE

THOSE WHO WERE NOT CONSULTED

ANXIOUS to avoid a repetition of the incidents which occurred at Saint-Nazaire, the British High Command did its best to discourage the French population from taking part in the fighting at Dieppe: 'This is a raid and not the invasion,' announced the leaflet which we reproduce here, and of which thousands of copies were dropped on the town and its environs. 'We beg the population of all the sectors concerned,' broadcast the B.B.C., 'to refrain from all action which might compromise its safety. When the day comes for us to ask the French people for their active collaboration, we shall tell you. . . . Today we say to you, do nothing. Do not expose yourself to German reprisals. France and her Allies will need you on the day of liberation.'

These appeals for calm, carried out to the letter, were to earn the people of Dieppe a very appreciable testimony of satisfaction, awarded not by those who had launched them but by the enemy.

To be quite truthful, the population acquired no great merit for keeping quiet, because with a few exceptions it was unaware of what was happening until everything was over, until bleeding and half naked Canadians passed through the streets, only escaping the perils of water and bullets to find themselves facing the bayonets of their conquerors. For many people the 19th August had been a mere air display, rather tougher and more prolonged than those to which they had been accustomed. No one realized immediately what was taking place on the beach and its environs. In practice, only the sub-prefect, the mayor, the firemen and the police were allowed to move about the town, let alone observe what was going on on the beach.

M. Michel Sassier, sub-prefect of Dieppe, was woken at 0558 hrs. German time[1] by the first aircraft. Shortly after this

[1] We shall continue to use this time during the present chapter.

FRANÇAIS!

Ceci est un coup de main et non pas l'invasion.

Nous vous prions instamment de n'y prendre part en aucune façon et de ne faire quoi que ce soit qui puisse entraîner des représailles de la part de l'ennemi.

Nous faisons appel à votre sang-froid et à votre bon sens.

Lorsque l'heure sonnera, nous vous avertirons. C'est alors que nous agirons côte-à-côte pour notre victoire commune et pour votre liberté!

he learned that the German Security Services had requested the French population to take cover and at 0615 hrs., when he made a tour of inspection of the town, complete calm reigned. The telephone was cut at 0635 hrs., but M. Sassier, from the Central Commisariat on the Quai Duquesne, was able to communicate with the town hall and with the Biomarine shelter, hollowed out under the chalky cliff dominating the suburb of La Barre.[1] The fire brigade brought out their ambulances, and groups of police spread out in all directions to organize the points to which those in need of first-aid had to be directed. The wounded could be picked up and taken either to the Biomarine or to one of the surgical clinics of the town. Dr. Maillard, head of the medical services of the passive defence, whose house in the rue de Sygogne had collapsed, reached his post as best he could. The milk supplies for the children was normally delivered at nine o'clock in the morning.

At 0930 hrs. M. Sassier was informed that the British had penetrated the town, and an hour later that there were tanks on the beach. The firemen, who were trying to cordon the fires, found themselves caught between the bullets of the defenders and those of the assailants. The Germans ordered them to withdraw.

Finding it impossible to telephone to the provincial capital and anxious not to be overwhelmed if the number of casualties assumed greater proportions, the sub-prefect decided to send Inspector Kemp to Rouen and to inform M. Bouffet, the regional prefect, and to ask for additional ambulances. At this

[1] The Biomarine laboratories figures in the orders of Operation *Jubilee* as a target to be destroyed, together with the gas works, the power station and the port installations. They were situated against the cliff, hollowed out in the caves where in peacetime a whole population of troglodytes lived. The Biomarine caves under the cliff below the town and of Le Pollet under the cliff above the town, formed excellent shelters against bombing from the air, thanks to the protection afforded by a layer of chalk, many feet thick. These shelters were considerably improved later. In 1944, the Biomarine possessed a small underground hospital, where some of the patients spent whole weeks without ever seeing the sun. Thousands of civilians went there every night – practically half the population which had remained in Dieppe during the weeks prior to the liberation.

moment, however, the situation appeared very critical for the wounded. The power had been cut. In the Biomarine caves, operations were carried out by the light of candles and electric torches. The trucks which could have been used to evacuate the wounded remained imprisoned in their blazing garages.

At the beginning of the afternoon, when the battle was over and the people of Dieppe could leave their houses, the first columns of prisoners filed along the streets of the town coming from Pourville through the suburb of La Barre, or from the Dieppe beach along the quai Duquesne, to assemble in the courtyard of the hospital. For many of the inhabitants, this was their first knowledge of the landing.

The roar of aircraft continued until late into the afternoon. The British tricolour cockades had disappeared, but machines sporting Iron Crosses continued to plough the sky at lower and lower altitudes, with a deafening roar. At 1600 hrs., Kommandantur officials appeared for the first time in the sub-prefecture, to say that the streets were now free, the shops could be opened and supplies organized.

Access to the beach was still forbidden. A few people, however, were able to discover what had happened – M. Caseau, the engineer of the municipal services, whose aid the Germans solicited for collecting and burying the dead; M. Le Bastard, as interpreter to the Kriegsmarine was allowed to spend the day in his house on the boulevard Verdun. The picture which presented itself outside his windows when he returned in the afternoon was terrifying. An almost intact tank stood in front of his house – everywhere corpses, rubble, weapons – a classical picture of a battlefield after the fighting. A naval shell had landed in his drawing-room without exploding, but apart from the many scratches on the façade caused by machine-gun bullets and aircraft cannon, the house seemed undamaged. Not far away the tobacco factory continued to blaze.

The dead were counted. The first civilian casualty figures gave 36 dead – 24 from Dieppe, three from Neuvilles-les-Dieppe and eight from Arques-la-Bataille. At Pourville a boy of 17 was killed on the beach trying to re-embark with the Canadians. There were about 60 wounded. By 1900 hrs. they were all evacuated, either to Rouen hospitals or to the main hospital at Lintot-les-Bois. But, as is often the case, the final balance sheet was to prove far heavier, finally reaching the figure of 48 dead and 100 wounded.

By and large the material damage was confined to the sea front sector – the Grand Hôtel, the Hôtel Régance, the Hôtel Royal, the tobacco factory[1] and the town hall. . . . Considerable damage in the town, but on the whole only of a minor nature. The suburb of Janval on the heights, dominating the town and the River Scie, suffered in particular. Thirty houses were rendered uninhabitable. At Arques-la-Bataille, the working-class city of Viscosa was sorely tried. Some damage was reported at Braquemont and Berneval. At Varengeville the bombs from an aircraft which fell near the little chapel of ease exploded a little later, and the chapel was destroyed. At Pourville, despite the tough fighting which had accompanied the re-embarkation, the houses were more scratched than seriously damaged. Towards the end of the day the departmental authorities, the regional prefect, the police commissioner, and the director of supplies, arrived. From Vichy Marshal Pétain sent his congratulations to the town of Dieppe on the worthy behaviour of its population, and his condolences for the victims.

There is no doubt that the Dieppe population, applying to the letter the orders distributed by radio and the R.A.F. leaflets, had shown complete calm. No doubt, too, that no temptation had been offered for it to intervene in a battle which had taken place almost exclusively within the confines of the beach and the sea front to which it had no access. Apart from the services of the passive defence – doctors, firemen and first-aid men – who had given of their best, the most sensible thing the inhabitants of Dieppe could have done that day was to take shelter – which is precisely what they did, for their own good and to the great satisfaction of both adversaries, who managed to agree on this point.

Two days after the battle, M. Levasseur, the mayor of

---

[1] The manufacture of tobacco in Dieppe dates from the eighteenth-century. Suppressed at the Revolution and transferred to Le Havre, it was subsequently re-established. In 1939 it came once more under review for suppression. It has never been rebuilt.

Dieppe was summoned to the sub-prefecture. In the office of M. Sassier were Colonel Bartelt, commanding the 571st Infantry Regiment and the Chief of the Kreiskommandantur.

'M. le Maire,' declared the latter, 'you have suffered casualties and damage. I have been ordered to hand you the sum of 10 million francs to be distributed among the inhabitants of the town of Dieppe.'

Standing by the door, M. Levasseur remained silent.

The German officer insisted. 'Aren't you satisfied?'

'Oh, as regards the money . . . it's obviously something . . . but . . .'

'But what?'

'The prisoners!'

The Kreiskommandant gave a slight start, and reflected for a moment.

'How many?'

M. Levasseur hesitated in turn.

'About a thousand.'

At this juncture, Colonel Bartelt intervened.

'I support the Mayor's request.'

'I won't say no,' replied his colleague after a short silence. 'I'll make inquiries.'

The request could not have come at a better time. In the flush of their victory, the Germans were prepared to make a gesture. Hitler gave his consent on the 25th August, and Dieppe was notified next day by telegram. The news was officially announced at the end of the official communique of the German High Command of the 29th, and published in France on the 31st. It read:

'The behaviour of the French population has been more than correct. Despite the losses suffered, they aided the German troops in their combat, rendering services of all kinds. They put out fires, tended the wounded and provided the combatants with food and drink. In recognition of this behaviour, the French prisoners of war domiciled in the localities of the Dieppe sector of combat will be liberated.'[1]

---

[1] *Journal de Rouen,* édition de Dieppe and de Neufchâtel, Monday August 1942.

This appreciation must be regarded in its true aspect. It was only too tempting for the propaganda services of the German High Command to attribute – not without a certain ponderousness – a germanophile behaviour to the whole of the Dieppe population.

I was lucky enough to find the monthly report on the morale and behaviour of the population in the sector of the 302nd Division, completed on the 24th August by the 2nd Bureau (Ic.) of the division. It is infinitely more equivocal!

Admittedly General Haase's staff has not failed to pinpoint cases where the aid given by the population exceeded the demands of simple humanity. We cannot blame him for this. That there were civilians prepared to give refreshment to German soldiers was nothing extraordinary. This does not in any case show any indication of sympathy. We quote from the diary of Madame Mirabeau, one of the many incidents which may have happened:

The battle was just over and to recover from the shock she had sat down with her housekeeper Suzanne, to a 'rich coffee' and a slice of bread and butter, when tin helmets suddenly appeared at the window. Were they German or English? We had no time to reflect because the green uniforms appeared on the threshold. 'No Tommies here?' 'No Tommies.' Suzanne gesticulated and said in her best German. 'Nix Tommies, du peux nachschausen.' Two sweating exhausted soldiers searched the house and reassured, began to look enviously at our repast. 'Oh please, we are thirsty and hungry.' There were soon a dozen of them. Suzanne rapidly brought out glasses after carefully removing the bread and butter. One of the soldiers, casting an eye on our cups, said: 'No French coffee?' 'No, only water from the tap.' As soon as she saw the soldiers leaving by the kitchen garden, eating potatoes and raw carrots, she flew into a rage. 'You are thieves, not correct.' A young soldier, blackened with dust and sweat, looking completely exhausted, smiled his apologies 'Potatoes lying there, we are so hungry.'

Naturally Suzanne gave food and drink to the enemy.

And she was not the only one. There was also the good woman whom the Mayor of Varengeville saw run up with a bottle of brandy to comfort a poor 'Englishman' who had just

landed by parachute, having lost his two boots, which were
incontestibly made in Germany.

Who would be surprised that the peasants delivered carrier
pigeons to the Kommandantur, when one knows the appalling
consequences meted out to members of the occupied population who picked up these messengers.[1]

But what will be found in this report, which I have given in
full in the appendix, are long reflections on the manifestations
of sympathy and respect given to the Canadian prisoners and
their dead, and on the trends and hopes expressed in Anglophile circles.

In short, the head of the 2nd Bureau of the 302nd Infantry
Division carried out his duty correctly, by reporting all the
trends, and we can congratulate ourselves that his superiors up
to and including Adolf Hitler retained only those which they
deemed most favourable to their cause. It is certain that had
this account only contained reports of sabotage and ambushes,
the Kriegsgefangenenläger would not have opened their gates
to free the Dieppe prisoners, but the concentration camps
would have closed their gates on their compatriots.

To sum up, it was decided that the prisoners who were
natives of Dieppe, Neuville, Arques-la-Bataille and Hautot-
sur-Mer should be released. This was not what had been
promised, for the German High Command communiqué
mentioned all the localities affected by the fighting of the 19th
August, and as I have already remarked, neither Varengeville,

[1] The R.A.F. had dropped by parachute small cages containing
carrier pigeons and a questionnaire, which the finders were asked to
fill in before releasing the bird. These questionnaires covered the
following points:

  1. Information on the raid of the 19th August:
     – Military objectives destroyed or damaged,
     – Enemy losses in men, arms and equipment,
     – Preventive destructions carried out by the German troops
       (bridges for example),
     – The bringing up of reinforcements,
     – The moral effect of the operation.
  2. Have the B.B.C. broadcasts had any success among the
    population?
  3. Are there any signs of German operations planned against
    England?

Berneval, Belleville-sur-Mer nor Sainte-Marguerite benefited by this measure.

It is easy to imagine the disappointment felt by the prisoners from these small localities and their families. On the other hand the folk of Arques-la-Bataille could congratulate themselves, for no fighting had taken place there, except in the air. It is true that they had suffered the consequences.

The condition for release required that the prisoner was to have been domiciled in the locality mentioned on the 1st September, 1939, according to his mobilization papers. The town hall worked all night at full blast and at dawn on the 28th, a clerk went by train to deliver to the office of M. Scapini, the prisoners' spokesman, a list of 1,200 names. A supplementary list was sent on the 2nd September, via the Feldkommandantur at Rouen.

The first contingent was liberated remarkably quickly, since on the 12th September, the special train was solemnly received at Serqueux Station, before continuing on its route to Dieppe, where the German authorities had banned any official welcome.[1] The second contingent raised more difficulties, but after some lengthy pourparlers it was released during the second half of October.

What nearly ruined things was that according to the statement of the German police, the liberated men of the first contingent had been caught in the port cafés abusing Germany and the Führer. The sub-prefect put matters right with the Germans by saying that these good folk had been victims of agents provocateurs. Incidentally, the report on the morale of the population, compiled on the 23rd September by the 302nd

[1] By a curious coincidence, an event was to occur on that same 12th September, 1942, which was to bring about the release of a certain number of French prisoners. That day in the South Atlantic U-boat 156 torpedoed the British steamer *Laconia*, carrying 1,800 Italian prisoners of war. A great number of these prisoners after countless mishaps were picked up by French warships from Dakar, and as a reward to the crews of these ships, the Germans offered to release one member of their families, corresponding to the number of prisoners saved – 414 in all. But in this case things did not go so smoothly. There were interminable discussions to obtain the release of these prisoners, who finally returned home on the 23rd July, 1944.

Infantry Division, was quite disposed to this view, since it ended with the words: 'They (the freed prisoners) speak of the Führer with particular esteem.'

The compiler of this report could have had few illusions as to the sincerity of this behaviour, for next month he wrote that the goodwill of the people was largely the result of hopes of seeing its behaviour rewarded by further releases of prisoners or by some other advantages.[2]

It will come as no surprise when I reveal that more than one of the liberated prisoners had never inhabited either Dieppe, Arques-la-Bataille or Le Hautot. M. Levasseur told me a very amusing story on this subject. The scene took place at the Compiegne centre, which he visited at the beginning of March 1943, together with the sub-prefect to meet about 50 prisoners, who were still missing from the second convoy, and whom he had finally traced, thanks to his tenacity.

'Where do you come from?' M. Sassier asked a young soldier who was awaiting his turn for the last formalities.

'From Marseilles.'

'Ah, you're from Le Pollet. Perfect,' replied the sub-prefect very loudly, casting a glance at the German N.C.O. who had not raised his head from the list.

Two days later, however, the Gestapo asked the Mayor of Dieppe a very embarrassing question. Had not 50 men been released at Compiegne, the previous day? How did it happen that only six of them had arrived in Dieppe?

The Mayor had his reply ready. The occupying authorities were aware that the population of Dieppe had been 75 per cent evacuated. The absentees had obviously joined their families in the places to which they had been sent.

Alas, if a few false Dieppois were able to profit by the occasion, the Germans would admit no exception in the case of the people of Berneval and Varengeville. A few passed through the mesh, because they had land at Hautot or a fictitious employer at Dieppe; the others were ruthlessly eliminated. In Paul

---

[1] *Auch von Führer wird mit besonderer Hochachtung gesprochen.* (*Monatsbericht für September 1942.*) *Stimmung und Verhalten der Bevölkerung der besetzten Gebiete.*
[2] Ibid. October 1942.

Voisin's convoy there was a farmer from Varengeville. At Trier, after three days' journey, he was sent back. I know another who never recovered from his disappointment, and died in captivity the following year.

*   *   *

Three years almost to the day after these events, the Dieppe raid was to have an unforeseen reverberation in France. In the indictment of Marshal Pétain by the High Court on the 15th August, 1945, it was stated that the latter had sent his congratulations to Hitler for 'the clearance of our soil after an abortive attempt at a British landing at Dieppe.'

In fact, on 24th August, 1942, the whole press of the occupied zone had published the following communiqué:

'Marshal Pétain and M. Pierre Laval, head of the government, have requested M. de Brinon to convey to the German High Command in France their congratulations on the success achieved by the German troops who, by their defence, achieved a rapid clearing of French soil.'

M. Louis Noguères, at the time President of the High Court and hardly likely to favour the Marshal and the members of his government, justifies this accusation in his book.[1] The message had been sent on the orders of the Marshal. No one has discovered any intervention on his part in the publishing or the signature of this telegram. On this subject, Noguères mentions the following feature:

Received by the Marshal a few days after the publication of this communiqué, the Dieppe sub-prefect had been unable to disguise the amazement he had felt on reading it. 'M. Le Maréchal,' said Sassier, 'what am I to think of this telegram?'

To which the Marshal, full of indignation, blurted out:

'This is another of that swine de Brinon's mistakes.'

*   *   *

To end on a more pleasant note, let us record that the ten million francs, to which the Mayor of Dieppe had preferred his prisoners, was paid all the same by the German government.

[1] Noguères, Le véritable procès du maréchal Pétain, Fayard, 1955, p. 560.

The municipality of Rouen, however, who had got wind of the affair, remarked that its town had also suffered from the bombardment of the 17th August, and that this bombing must logically be considered as a preparation for the attack on Dieppe.

Whether justified or not, the argument bore fruit, and Dieppe had to share with Rouen this sum of money, which had obviously been earmarked as part of the indemnity of the occupation, in other words, money to be paid by the French taxpayers.

CHAPTER TWENTY-FOUR

CHAINS AND WOODEN CROSSES

WHEN the last British ship had disappeared over the horizon, harassed by a pack of German planes, the defenders of Dieppe were finally able to realize what had happened and to compile a balance sheet which the German High Command awaited with the greatest impatience.

They were soon fully aware of the enemy's intentions. The assailants had scattered their marked maps all over the ground. Better still, an almost complete copy of operational orders which had actually only been entrusted to two brigade staffs, was found on a dead officer. The whole time-table was recorded. There were even certain orders applicable to eventual prisoners, which were to provoke serious incidents.

On the German side, the High Command communiqué announced the overall figure of losses as 591. Subsequent analysis gives very similar results: the 302nd Division reported 121 dead including five officers, 201 wounded and 11 missing; the coastal artillery 28 dead and 33 wounded; the Kriegsmarine 78 killed or missing and 27 wounded:[1] the Todt organization three killed and seven wounded; the Luftwaffe 105 killed or missing and 58 wounded. In all 345 killed or missing and 268 wounded, making a total of 613. Among the missing were about 30 prisoners – four brought back by No. 4 Commando, and the survivors of UJ.1404 picked up by H.M.S. *Brocklesby*.

As regards material, the losses were relatively small. Apart from the six guns of the Varengeville battery, the army lost only four 37 mm. anti-tank guns, while the Navy lost the UJ.1404 and the *Franz*, and the Luftwaffe 48 aircraft shot down.

[1] Including 30 killed or missing among the land personnel, including Lt. Goebel who had taken command of a combat group of the Kriegsmarine.

By comparison the booty left behind by the attackers reached a very important figure.

Twenty-eight tanks,[1] six self-propelled guns, one command car, 1,242 rifles, 165 sub-machine-guns or Bren guns, 22 heavy mortars, 58 light mortars, 60 anti-tank rifles, 50 machine-guns, ammunition, three L.C.T.s, one of which was refloated and taken to the port of Dieppe on the 21st August, and a certain number of L.C.A.s, some of which were salvaged in the port the same day.

All this war material was of the greatest interest to the Wehrmacht, particularly the tanks, which the 302nd Division received orders to preserve with the greatest care, in order to avoid any additional damage. At the same time the Amphibian Army Training Centre at Flushing wired that it was particularly interested in the L.C.T.s, and sent an officer to Dieppe to examine them (Oberleutnant Bechlin).

But before compiling a list of this booty and counting the prisoners, there were the dead to bury. Their number continued to increase. A figure of 475 was given for 23rd August, but the sea continued for some time to wash up further corpses.

On the evening of the 19th, the town engineer M. Caseau was summoned by the German command. An officer took him on a tour of the battlefield to make the necessary arrangements. In view of the urgency, it was decided to dig a long trench at Janval cemetery in which the Canadians were placed side by side.

But a few days later an officer from the Graves Commission arrived at Rouen. The German Army, he insisted, considered that these enemy soldiers had not been buried in sufficiently honourable conditions. It was decided to give them a more decent burial.

It was recalled that the British, at the time when Dieppe had been a hospital base during the 1939–40 campaign, had

[1] Belonging to three different types:

I. 28 ton tanks armed with a 47, one 4 cm. mortar and one machine-gun.

II. 30 ton tanks arms with a 57, one 4 cm. mortar and two machine-guns.

III. 32 ton tanks armed with a 75, one 4 cm. mortar and two machine-guns.

acquired a piece of ground for their wounded and the sick who eventually died. This piece of ground situated above the valley of the Scie near Vertus wood in the commune of Hautot-sur-Mer was ideal. The Wehrmacht sent coffins. 500 men were conscripted and for days on end the bodies were exhumed, placed in the coffins, and carried to Vertus Cemetery with full military honours.

The entire British press reported this gesture, which was certainly much appreciated.

Remarkably appointed and tended, the 'Canadian cemetery' as it is called locally is one of the most moving that I know.

*   *   *

Less honourable, and certainly far less appreciated, was the treatment meted out to the Dieppe prisoners on the discovery, in circumstances I have already mentioned, of an order clumsily inserted in the British operational orders which ran:

'Whenever possible the hands of the prisoners will be tied to prevent them destroying the documents they are carrying.'

General Roberts had not concealed his disgust before the Chief of Combined Operations. He did not win his point. In any case, it was highly irresponsible to insert such an order in a document which might fall into the hands of an enemy with whom they were to leave so many of their own men. The German reaction was not long delayed. The High Command alluded to this unfortunate business in its communiqué of the 30th August. On the 2nd September, stating that the British Government had made no decision on this point, it was decreed that all the British officers taken prisoner on the 19th August should be chained from the 3rd September at 1400 hrs., and that this justified measure would not be cancelled until the British Government made an official statement on the incriminating orders.

'Any recourse to similar methods, worthy of the Far West,' continued the German note, 'constitutes a shameful and ignominious treatment of brave soldiers and calls for the most serious reprisals.'[1]

That evening the Reuter agency published the terms

[1] *Journal de Rouen*, September 1942.

demanded by the German High Command. 'It is energetically denied,' replied the British communiqué, 'that the German prisoners had their hands tied. Had such an order been given it would have been reported.'

It is true, in fact, that this order was never carried out. Apart from the German sailors picked out of the water, the only prisoners taken were those of the Varengeville battery, whom Lord Lovat had considered more judicious to use as stretcher-bearers than to carry off with their hands tied.

Satisfied with this denial, the Germans cancelled their order and the incident was considered closed.

Unfortunately a month later, on the night of the 3rd/4th October, 1942, C.O. Hq. dispatched to Sark, one of the Channel Islands, a small commando under a certain Major Appleyard who was to win a certain fame at a later date. Appleyard and his men landed on the island without much difficulty; they surprised five German soldiers in their billets, and proceeded to take them back to England. The prisoners, observing the weakness of the group which had captured them, gave them the slip. They did this so efficiently that they were able to alert a German patrol which hurried to the scene at all speed.

The British had no choice left. They ran to the beach and managed to re-embark with one of their prisoners, abandoning four others, who were discovered by their comrades in their shirts and with their hands tied.

This news aroused the anger of the German Government which, by way of reprisals, announced that the 1,376 Dieppe prisoners would be manacled.

The British Government was very embarrassed. It retorted by ordering the fettering of a similar number of German prisoners in Canada, but this did not solve matters. While *The Times* indulged in more or less fortuitous denials, the Minister of War remarked more ably that there was a slight difference between tying up a prisoner to see that he did not escape during an action and that of retaining his fetters after having taken him into custody.[1] But the German propaganda did not yield, and in one way or another the unfortunate prisoners continued to have their hands tied.

[1] Alan and Mary Wood, *Islands in Danger*, p. 140 et seq.

The British were the first to tire and ordered the bonds of the German prisoners to be removed on the 12th December, in the hope that the Germans would do the same. But the order was not definitely revoked in Germany until the 22nd November, 1943. According to the statement of an officer who was a victim of this measure, it had soon become purely symbolical. The prisoners appeared at roll call in handcuffs, but immediately afterwards were given the freedom of their four limbs.[1]

*   *   *

The following is the total figure of the Anglo-Canadian losses:

British Army:	14 killed and 128 missing or prisoners, among whom many were killed.
Royal Marines:	31 killed, 69 prisoners.
Royal Navy:	75 killed, 269 missing.
R.A.F. (including the Allies):	69 killed.
Canadian Army:	907 killed and 1,874 prisoners.

These figures, which I have borrowed from the work of Stacey, include those who died in captivity. The figures quoted by other authors vary considerably. One cannot expect too much accuracy in this type of statistics. The main thing is to have some yardstick, and from this point of view it is particularly interesting to note that of the 4,963 Canadians who actually left on the raid, only 2,210 returned to Great Britain on the evening of the operation, among whom 586 were wounded.

[1] Stacey, op. cit., p. 397.

CHAPTER TWENTY-FIVE

PROPAGANDA AND REFLECTIONS

IT goes without saying that Operation *Jubilee* gave the German Command great cause for satisfaction.

At 1650 hrs. on the 19th August, the O.C. LXXXIst Corps expressed his satisfaction to the 302nd Infantry Division in the form of the following telegram:

> '*Gut gemacht 302 I.D., insonderheit Besatzung in Dieppe !*'
> *Gez. Küntzen,*
> *General der Panzertruppe.*[1]

It was short and to the point – and well designed to please the men. But General Küntzen could not stop at this. The telegram was reinforced by an order of the day expressing thanks to the coastal artillery, the navy, the Luftwaffe and the Todt organization. The 10th Panzers were not forgotten. Nor was the health service whose chief, Colonel Dr. Richter and his staff were given a special mention.

The congratulations of the 15th Army ended with an exhortation to vigilance by General Kurt Haase:

> '*Augen und ohren auf !*' (Keep your eyes and ears open).

Then followed the personal thanks of Field-Marshal von Rundstedt, and finally those of the Führer conveyed on the 21st August in a telegram from the German High Command which read:

> 'The Führer and the Supreme Command have sent me the following message: Thanks to the careful foresight of the command and of the troops, a strong attempt at a British landing was crushed with the shortest possible delay. You are requested, Herr Feldmarschall, to convey my thanks and my gratitude to the three arms of the Wehrmacht. I know that I

[1] 'Well played the 302nd and particularly the Dieppe garrison!'

53

Fernschreibstelle *Gen. Kdo. LXXXI. A.K.*

HEAXD Nr. 1361
Fernschreibname Laufende Nummer

Angenommen:
Aufgenommen:

Datum: *19.8.* 19*42*
um: *1718*
von: *Ia*
durch: *Ofw. Wagner*

Befördert:
Datum: *19.8.42*
um: *1745*
an: *302. I.D.*
durch: *Ofw. Wagner*
Rolle: *27*

L.D.N. - LXXXI. A.K.
19 AUG. 1942
1745

Vermerke

Fernschreiben:
Postfernschreiben: von Gen.Kdo. röm. 81.A.K. röm. 1.a
Fernspruch:

19.8.1942 | *(1718)* | Fn *302. I.D.*
Abgangstag   Abgangszeit

Vermerke für Beförderung (vom Abf. auszufüllen)

Bestimmungsort

Gut gemacht 302. I.D.: insonderheit Besatzung

in Dieppe!

gez. *Günther*

General der Panzertruppe

vol.
Wagner 7

Knochel
Unterschrift des Aufgebers

Fernsprech-Anschluß des Aufgebers

J.A.2.38

can rely in future on the command and the soldiers of the Wehrmacht. Adolf Hitler.'

> C.-in-C. West, commanding Army Group D.
> Signed: von Rundstedt Generalfeldmarschall.
> 2130/21/8.

In view of what was known at that time, the Wehrmacht communiqué of the evening of 19th August was reasonably objective:

Great Headquarters of the Führer, 19th August, 1942.

'The German High Command announces:

'An important landing carried out by British, American, Canadian and Gaullist troops, the first wave of which corresponded approximately to a division, took place on the French coast near Dieppe.

'In the early morning hours, protected by powerful naval and air formations and supported by a tank landing, this attempt crumbled in the face of the reaction by German forces ensuring the protection of the coast.

'The enemy's losses in men were extremely heavy. From 1600 hrs. onwards, no enemy soldier remained on the Continent. This great success was obtained without it being necessary to call upon any part of the reserves available to the High Command. According to reports received from our units and from interrogation of prisoners, these landing operations evolved in the following manner:

'The first wave of landing troops was trans-shipped in the early hours at sea on to 300–400 landing-craft, reaching the coast at 0605 hrs., under the protection of 13 to 15 cruisers and destroyers, in addition to powerful formations of chasseurs.

'In the second line at sea, was a reserve of six transports and three cargo vessels, and a little farther north a group of transport ships, presumably constituting the main landing force. These troops were to be engaged as soon as the first landed group had succeeded in obtaining a bridgehead round the port of Dieppe. They were unsuccessful. The troops landed were dispersed everywhere in hand-to-hand fighting and flung back into the sea.

'So far we have counted 28 assault tanks destroyed among

those which were landed. All our strongpoints were firmly held by our valiant coastal garrisons.

'More than 1,500 prisoners have fallen into our hands. Among them 60 Canadian officers. The enemy losses in men are extremely high. Our artillery sunk three destroyers, two chasseurs and two transports. The Luftwaffe shot down 83 British planes, and sunk two special transports and a M.L. Five cruisers or large destroyers and two transports were damaged by heavy bombs.

'In the course of this attempted invasion, carried out in opposition to all good military sense, and which served only political ends, the enemy suffered a crushing defeat. The German army guarding the West has given the necessary reply to this amateur undertaking. It will await with resolution any new attempt at landing with the calm and power of an army which, in the course of a hundred battles, has known how to win victories for its flags.'

No exaggeration in the number of prisoners, which is lower than that finally established, or in the number of tanks captured in battle. False interpretations of the British intentions, and exaggerated estimates of the successes achieved by the Luftwaffe and the coastal artillery. But that is quite normal. It can be stated, moreover, that although the figure of British ships announced as destroyed far exceeded the truth, that of the aircraft shot down is below the actual total (83 instead of 106).

*   *   *

But the propaganda machine now went into action. The press and the radio exulted. The *Berliner Börsen Zeitung* on the day after the raid bore the headlines: 'Catastrophic Defeat.' 'A setback to an invasion,' wrote the Hamburger *Fremdenblatt*. The *Münchener Neueste Nachrichten* of 21st August showed how the invasion was broken on the German rampart, but the most perfidious comment was from the *Völkischer Beobachter* in which we can read: 'What does Stalin say about this disaster to Churchill's invasion?'

By and large, these different commentaries stressed the speed of the setback to this attempt, which had only lasted some ten hours; the fact that, despite British affirmations, it was an attempted invasion, that this attempt had been carried out under pressure from Moscow, and finally that all the profit was for Germany who had found proof of the perfection of its defensive organizations.

In the *Münchener Neueste Nachrichten* we can read: 'Dieppe has enriched us by much precious experience. Firstly, the world now knows that the military situation of Soviet Russia demands an attempt at rescue at all costs and cannot bear a moment's delay. Furthermore, it has been proved that in Great Britain political considerations are paramount in military enterprises, even when from a military point of view success is impossible. Possibly the British military authorities did not yet consider preparations for invasion as complete, but they had to bow to the disastrous policies of Churchill, who had pledged himself to Stalin, with the shortest possible delay. . . . Dieppe has shown that the German rampart on the Atlantic coast is up to all tests. We are sincerely grateful to the British for having given us this precious experience, but they must recognize that in future they have nothing to seek on the Continent.'

'Dieppe, of course, was an attempt at invasion,' wrote the *Deutsche Allgemeine Zeitung*. 'The British pretend not to have taken the affair seriously, but the whole progress of this action denounces this lie, just like the echo aroused in America at the beginning of this adventure. . . . In the United States Churchill could not make a single boot-black believe that a division with tanks landed at the point on the Atlantic coast nearest to Paris, with a floating reserve closely behind the first wave, was simply an exercise. After the Dieppe enterprise, the only results show the complete failure of the attack, bitter disappointment on the part of the Soviets, disappointed hopes in the United States, and Great Britain covered with shame.'

For the *National Zeitung*, 'there is no doubt at all that this unfortunate raid constituted a personal defeat for Churchill.'

We could continue with these quotations ad infinitum. Despite their exaggerated tone, these comments were not entirely devoid of sense. The main error, however, was to insist in presenting the raid as a real attempt at invasion, based on erroneous information. That they were able to think for a moment that the convoy spotted on the English coast was waiting to be directed to Dieppe is plausible. But from the moment it turned out that it consisted merely of coasters, ensuring as a matter of routine the traffic on the south coast of Great Britain, it would actually have been far more intelligent not to stick by this obviously inaccurate interpretation. The most skilful propaganda relies on facts which are materially beyond dispute. There are plenty of facts in the Dieppe raid, without having to look for something else.

*　　*　　*

In London it was more a question of embarrassment.

The affair had been announced at 0600 hrs. by a communiqué from C.O. Hq. stating that the French population had been notified that it was merely a raid. The communiqué published at 1300 hrs. must be recognized as a model of its type. There was not a single lie, and yet no one could have foreseen the disaster it entailed.

'The troops engaged in the raid on Dieppe have been landed at selected points. Strong opposition was encountered in some places. On the left flank a landing group, initially repulsed, managed to reform and take the beach by assault.

'On the right wing the troops, having reached their target, which consisted in the complete destruction of a battery of six guns and an ammunition dump, have been re-embarked.

'In the centre tanks were landed and a violent battle is in progress.

'The land forces consist in the main of Canadian troops. Also taking part in the raid are British troops of the Special Service, a detachment from a battalion of American Rangers and a small contingent of the Free French Fighting Forces.

'This force was transported and escorted by units of the Royal Navy. Air support and ample cover have been assured by the bombers and fighters of the R.A.F. in the face of considerable enemy opposition.

'A later communiqué will follow.'

Delayed by the censor, this communiqué was not published in Great Britain until after that of the German High Command. Experience has shown that it is always fatal, after suffering a defeat which it is impossible to disguise, to allow the enemy to be the first to announce the fact.

The censorship felt the draught, and finally decided to release the 1300 hrs. communiqué (No. 2) for the morning newspapers (20th August), followed by No. 3 which was just as able as it predecessor.

'Despite the perfectly clear declarations made in our first communiqué of this morning, and in the radio information transmitted to France at 0615 hrs. on the Dieppe raid, the German propaganda, incapable of drawing any more important conclusions from the turn taken by the operation, insists in trying to present this raid as an attempted invasion repulsed.

'In actual fact, the re-embarkment of the main force began six minutes after the prescribed hour, and was completed as foreseen nine hours after the first landing.

'A few tanks were lost in the fighting ashore. Reports show that the battle was very violent and it is probable that the losses have been heavy on both sides. A definite report cannot be given until the return of our forces to Great Britain.'

Then no more news until the evening! No one to reply to the blast from the German radio. . . .

The 4th communiqué published on the 20th at 2250 hrs. stressed rather clumsily that all the objectives had been reached. Here for the first time is mentioned the term (devised by Churchill) 'reconnaissance in force'. The importance of the losses was mentioned in these terms:

'As a result of the violent fighting which took place during the operation, our losses are high, but not excessive, considering the object of the raid.'

The British press and public opinion had, at the outset, shown the most admirable goodwill in accepting as gospel truth the communiqués issued to them. They seemed satisfied, if we are to believe the Governmental spokesmen, that 'the raid, despite its limited objectives, must have had an appreciable psychological effect on the enemy'. But this goodwill could not last. 'Neither the dress rehearsal of Dieppe nor the air offensive directed against the nerve centres of German industry,' wrote The Times of the 27th August, 'can dispel the impression that the British war effort is inadequate at a moment when Russia is facing her gravest crisis.'

Some explanation was needed. Churchill gave it on the 8th September in the House of Commons with his customary skill and as briefly as possible. His speech fills 16 columns of the 'parliamentary debates'. The passage devoted to Dieppe does not fill one. We therefore quote it in full.

'It is a mistake to speak or write of the attack upon Dieppe as a "commando raid", although some commando troops distinguished themselves remarkably in it. The military credit for this most gallant affair goes to the Canadian troops, who formed five-sixths of the assaulting force, and to the Royal Navy, which carried them all there and which carried most of them back. The raid must be considered as a reconnaissance in force. It was a hard, savage clash such as are likely to become increasingly numerous as the war deepens. We had to get all the information necessary before launching operations on a much larger scale. This raid, apart from its reconnaissance value, brought about an extremely satisfactory air battle in the West which Fighter Command wish they could repeat every week. It inflicted perhaps as much loss upon the enemy in killed and wounded as we suffered ourselves. I, personally, regarded the Dieppe assault, to which I gave my sanction, as an indispensable preliminary to full-scale operations. I do not intend to give any information about these operations, and I have only said as much as I have because the enemy can see, by his daily reconnaissances of our ports, many signs of movements that we are unable to conceal from his photography.'[1]

I have one point to make. I do not know to what extent Fighter Command would have been so happy to repeat every week a battle in which it lost two machines for one, but it is certain that no M.P. questioned Churchill on this point. The cold douche came from Canada a week later when the Minister for Defence at Ottawa declared that, of the 5,000 Canadians engaged, the casualties amounted to 3,350 of which 2,717 were killed or missing (i.e. prisoners). On 30th September an M.P., Mr. Henderson Stewart, asked the Prime Minister whether he would explain how the House should reconcile the announcement made on 8th September that most of the Dieppe invading force came back with the official statement of the Canadian Minister of National Defence that, of 5,000 Canadian troops involved in the raid, casualties totalled 3,350, of whom 2,717 were killed or missing? The Prime Minister replied: 'In my statement of 8th September, I was referring to the assaulting force as a whole, the greater part of whom were brought back by the Royal Navy. There is no inconsistency with the statement of the Canadian Minister of National Defence, who was referring only to casualties among the Canadian troops who took part.'[1] Obviously if the 7,750 sailors and 1,179 airmen were counted, and all proportions retained had been far weaker, it could be considered that the major part of the forces had returned.

Nevertheless the Canadian losses exceeded 65 per cent. As Vagts remarks, this gave some food for thought about the cost of combined operations.[2]

It was a shock for public opinion. Not only in Canada but in all the other Dominions, particularly in Australia and New Zealand where the precedent of the Dardanelles was not yet forgotten. In Great Britain itself Admiral Keyes, who always spoke his mind, did not hesitate to declare that the whole affair 'badly conceived and ill starred, constituted in the last analysis a very costly experiment'.

In addition to this the expression 'reconnaissance in force' used by Churchill exposed him to controversy. It seemed to be a contradiction in terms. By definition a reconnaissance is not a battle. It is carried out with the idea of obtaining information without engagement, or at least, of not becoming engaged except when absolutely necessary. The moment that it is admitted *a priori* that there is a need for fighting, it is no longer a reconnaissance.

To sum up, on the propaganda plane, we had given Hitler a weapon to which there was no reply, when he boasted that the European fortress was impregnable. For the Russians we had killed the hope of seeing a Second Front opened in Europe in

[1] Ibid., column 769.
[2] Vagts, op. cit., p. 711.

the near future – and all this to train soldiers more than half of whom did not return to profit by the experience they had gained.

Let us mention, on a more general plane, the comment of the German naval staff, which was even more objective since it was certainly not destined for publication.

'Things being as they are, the mere fact that the landing was repulsed will no doubt have serious and very unpleasant political consequences for the enemy. Even if this undertaking was in fact only a "mosquito" raid of limited military dimensions, it was clumsy merely from the political point of view, because it was to involve heavy losses without bringing any tangible success. The most able propaganda will convince no one that it is a paying proposition to undertake an operation of this nature simply to destroy a port like Dieppe, together with a few batteries or radar stations placed in the neighbourhood. Nor that such excessive losses are too great a price to pay for the experience acquired.

'It is impossible to separate the Dieppe raid from the context of the continued discussions which have been taking place for weeks on the establishment of a Second Front in Europe. We are faced, therefore, with a political fiasco which is even more regrettable since it has been combined with a military setback. It is not surprising, therefore, that the nation most interested in an invasion, in other words, Russia, should receive the news with extreme coldness. . . .'

And in a further paragraph:

'From the purely military point of view an operation of this nature appears even less comprehensible than from the political standpoint. At best, the occupation of Dieppe for a few hours would have afforded the enemy a possibility for landing swiftly a few additional regiments with heavy armed tanks or guns. Even if the enemy had managed to establish a bridgehead in the Dieppe sector and to land between 1,500 and 2,000 men, this operation would only have had a significance when combined with a successful attempt to pin down our reserves, by simultaneous landings carried out at other points on the western seaboard, and more particularly by important landings of paratroops carried out behind our lines. From the moment that no plan of this type appears to have existed – at least we have no indication of this – the operation of 19th August was fated to end in a setback for which no military justification can be found. . . .'

Quite naturally the benefit of experience acquired was reaped by the combatants who survived, that is to say, the German soldiers. Dieppe in fact taught them a great deal by showing up all the defects in their coastal defences, transmissions, bringing up of reserves, etc. With the attention to detail for which the Germans are renowned, they immediately set about remedying all these defects. It is particularly edifying on this score to read the report of the 302nd Infantry Division in conjunction with the comments of the LXXXIst Corps, the 15th Army and finally the German High Command. Nothing seems to have been neglected.

In future they would be prepared for anything, even for a landing in full daylight, since breaking with the custom of commandos of operating in complete darkness, the British landed at dawn. They would have to be trained to fight in a smoke-screen, and the German chemists were encouraged to improve their own smoke layers. They were also forced to provide their reserves with adequate artillery instead of massing all their guns in the front line. The coastal batteries were reviewed as well as the stocks of ammunition. The artillery had to learn not to open fire at too long range, and not to waste ammunition. These examples could be multiplied indefinitely. The remarkable precision of the information provided by the British air reconnaissance – recall the maps left on the battlefield – gave Marshal von Rundstedt the idea of constructing dummy gun emplacements and wooden batteries, which often deceived the enemy beyond his wildest hopes.[1]

All this experience acquired at the cost of six guns lost, two patrol boats sunk and material damage less than was to be expected from an average air raid, the greatest being the

[1] The most remarkable example of this was the Titan battery on the eastern point of Levant Island. Duly spotted by the allied reconnaissance aircraft, this battery seemed to command the beach of Cavalaire so dangerously that during the landing in Provence, the Americans would not agree to use it until they had staged a foray against Levant Island, where they captured, apparently without difficulty, four fine wooden guns!

destruction of the tobacco factory from which only the French suffered. The losses in personnel did not reach an eighth of the enemy losses. One is inclined to agree with General Dittmar who, broadcasting on the 20th August, declared:

'We can feel happy that the first landings succeeded, for had this not been the case, the British defeat would not have been so complete.'

But for the German command, the experience of Dieppe led to conclusions, the effects of which were to be felt later in the solutions brought to the problem of defence against landings. Confirmed, by the example of 19th August, in the view that the actual moment of landing is the time when the enemy is the most vulnerable, Hitler and certain of his advisers became more and more convinced of the categorical necessity for flinging the enemy back into the sea as soon as he set foot ashore. 'At Dieppe,' declared Hitler, 'it needed only a regiment engaged at the right time, to repel a raid which a few hours later might have involved three divisions. In no case must we allow the landing to last more than a few days – if not a few hours. The example of Dieppe must serve as a model.'[1]

By and large it is the well known story of the fire which can be extinguished in the first few seconds by a glass of water, half a minute later by a pail, and which beyond that cannot be got under control.

Reasoning which is true in itself but false in practice, from the moment one has 1,800 miles of coast to defend, for it is obvious that one cannot be strong everywhere and that if the reserves are withdrawn too far from the coast, it will be impossible to direct them at the given moment to the sensitive spot.

There has been much discussion of the conflict which existed at the moment of the Normandy landing between Rommel in command of Army Group B, who wanted to defend himself at all costs on the coast, and his superior Marshal von Rundstedt, who preferred to concentrate his fluid troops inland, to be able to intervene at the opportune moment. In this observers have seen one of the causes of the collapse of the defence of the Atlantic Wall.

[1] Speech to the commanders in chief of the three armed forces on the West Front, 20th March, 1944.

In actual practice it was not this divergency of opinion which paralysed the German defeat, but the fact that the armoured divisions – incidentally concentrated too far from the coast – were not under the orders of Rommel, because the Führer himself reserved the right to dispose of them. With a few battalions of tanks in hand, the commander of Group B would perhaps have transformed the serious difficulties encountered on the Omaha beach by the American troops into a debacle. And, finally, it must not be forgotten that masses of troops concentrated too far from the battlefield would never have been able to intervene in time, because the Allied air force, which enjoyed complete supremacy, would have pinned them to the spot.

Before leaving the German camp, let us say a word about the repercussions of Operation *Jubilee* on the distribution of forces between the East and West Fronts. It has been proved that, in the month following the Dieppe raid, the number of German divisions in the western theatre of war increased from 26 to 33. From this, to deduce that the raid had brought about a troop movement advantageous to the Russian defence is only one step. In actual fact troop movements from east to west were frequent even before 19th August, for France was considered an ideal rest centre for reforming divisions which had been sorely tested in the Russian fighting. This for example was the case with the 10th Panzers. These troop movements continued as before. The only ones which could have been in direct relation to Operation *Jubilee* consist in the withdrawal of two divisions engaged on the Don front. At the end of August, Hitler gave orders to dispatch to France the motorized division *Grossdeutschland* and the *S.S. Leibstandarte* division. Only the latter actually left the Eastern Front. The former was recalled to fight in the centre of the front, where it was needed to repel a Russian counter-attack.[1]

There ended the reliefs. All the other formations which reinforced the western defences were chosen from those stationed in Germany.

*   *   *

[1] Cf. Buchheit, *Hitler, War Leader*.

If I have dwelt at some length on the debit side of Operation *Jubilee* it is because this has too often been neglected, whereas the history books are full of fruitful information drawn by the Allies from this first experience.

But after acting as the devil's advocate, I cannot remain silent on the positive elements of the raid. Let us recall that the British considered the price sufficiently costly never to repeat it – at least on the same scale. Probably this was also the opinion of the Canadians, for the 19th August raid ruined the career of General Roberts, who seemed to have a brilliant future ahead since, from Lt.-Colonel in June 1940, he had become a Major-General in 1942. Replaced on 12th April, 1943, at the head of the 2nd Canadian Division by General Simmonds, his name never appeared again among the generals who led the Canadian soldiers on the battlefields of Sicily, Italy and France. According to Vagts, he had to retire.

Mountbatten himself was to leave C.O. Hq. at the moment when the great operations for which this organization had been created were being prepared. He was not to participate in Operation *Overlord* planned for August 1943, and, on the concerted decisions of Roosevelt and Churchill, took over command of the South-East Asia war.

Hughes-Hallett alone continued to the end preparing the great landings. With the exception of a short spell on the staff of the Supreme Command of the Allied forces, from May to August 1943, he remained until the eve of the Normandy landing in command of a special assault group, Contingent J (J for *Jubilee*), designed with several others to train selected troops for the landing on 6th June, 1944. It is he who was to determine with the British Navy and C.O. Hq. and ultimately with the C.O.S.S.A.C.,[1] the lessons to be drawn from the Dieppe raid.

For there were definite lessons to be learned. That they were too dearly paid for, as Montgomery admits today, I will let the reader judge for himself, but that is only one side of the question. In military history there have been many bloody operations, the usefulness of which appear more than doubtful. Had there only been the psychological factor, and all the proofs

[1] Chiefs of Staff to the Supreme Allied Commander.

show that Operation *Jubilee* was very badly conceived, it would still be very risky to try and condemn it. After all, war is a dangerous business and if one is not prepared to take a risk, one might as well capitulate immediately.

For a start Dieppe taught the Allies as much as it taught the Germans! For there is no doubt that the British, in common with their adversary, did not fail to study all the reports of the affray. The field of observation was not the same, and the naval part took on a greater importance, but all in all, on the tactical plane, the information was of great value. I shall not discuss this in detail and shall be content to quote the points which appear to me the most relevant:

Above all, the need for a formidable aero-naval preparation. By and large the invasion of an enemy coast posed the same problems as a frontal attack in 1914–18. It deserved the same barrages and the same intensity of fire. On the pretext that it was merely a miniature invasion, Operation *Jubilee* had been given an extremely weak artillery preparation. Only 16 5·9 inch guns! This was doubtless one of the first causes of the fiasco. The error was not to be repeated. 'The most important lesson,' written in capital letters in the C.O. Hq. report of October, 1942, 'is the need for very powerful fire support, particularly at close range during the initial stages of the landing.' This support was to be ensured by: 'A naval bombardment with guns of heavy and medium calibre, by the Air Force, by special engines of war designed to operate close to the land, and by the utilization of the fire from the assault forces while they were still afloat.'

Thus, after Dieppe, were born the L.C.G. (landing-craft gun) and the L.C.T. (R.), rocket firing launches. The idea was also accepted, contrary to the dislike the British Admiralty had always evinced in this respect, of using cruisers and even battleships in the Channel as well as heavy bombers against the enemy coastal defences.

Secondly, the difficulty of attacking a port frontally. This must have, or should have been known as the official historian of the Canadian army recognizes, but Dieppe brought the fact into the limelight. Hughes-Hallett is credited with the statement 'that since the capture of a port by direct attack turns out to be impossible it only remains to tow one from England'. It would be nevertheless a mistake to think that the idea of artificial ports derived from Operation *Jubilee*. It had already been mentioned in the spring, witness a note from Churchill to Mountbatten dated 30th May, 1942, but the question was certainly studied more intensively after the raid.

Thirdly, the need for ensuring protection for the troops engaged in the destruction of obstacles. This engendered the A.V.R.E. (Assault Vehicle Royal Engineers) thanks to which the appalling losses inflicted on the sappers at Dieppe were never repeated. . . .

I could easily elaborate this list. It is better to refer the reader to works devoted to the story of the Normandy landings. The memory of Dieppe is evoked on every page. It also suffices to make a comparison between the operational plans conceived before Dieppe (Operation *Sledgehammer* for example) and those which were prepared subsequently. From whatever angle it is studied, and will no doubt be studied in future, the Dieppe raid will be one of the most controversial subjects in the history of the Second World War, and more particularly of amphibian operation. The reason that it costs so dear, as Colonel Stacey writes, is probably because 'the importance of the geographical conditions and the strength of the German defences had been under-estimated'.[1] On the other hand, he goes on, 'the blood shed at Dieppe represents part of the price which had to be paid to obtain the knowledge, thanks to which the gigantic undertaking of 1944 was carried out with infinitely less loss than had been feared'.

These two phrases sum up the debit and credit sides of the balance sheet of Operation *Jubilee*, considered solely from the military point of view.

[1] It seems impossible to avoid the conclusion that from the beginning the planners underestimated the influence of topography and of the enemy's strong defences in the Dieppe area. Op. cit., p. 398.

To the best of my knowledge, Stacey is the only one to have drawn attention to these geographical conditions as being one of the causes of the setback to Operation *Jubilee*. It may be considered that, two years later, comparable geographical conditions would largely account for the difficulties encountered by the first American division at Omaha beach, whereas the landings took place favourably at other places.

When one considers the situation in which the Allies found themselves at the moment when this raid was decided upon, one still wonders what part purely military considerations played in this decision, among the manifold strategic, political and psychological considerations we have reviewed in the first part of this book.

THE CANADIANS AT DIEPPE 1ST SEPTEMBER, 1944

'I am sure that the 2nd Canadian Division will attend to
Dieppe satisfactorily.'
Field-Marshal Montgomery's Order of
the Day, dated 20th August, 1944.

Two years had passed since the raid of 19th August. To the
injuries suffered from the invasion, and from the Canadian
landings, new ones had been added. Bombed intermittently
without any apparent reason for these attacks, Dieppe's list of
dead mounted as did the map of the destructions which, by the
day of liberation, had reached 43 per cent. The population was
now sparse. The school children had long since been evacuated
and only a few thousand inhabitants remained in the town.
Most of them left at nightfall for the open country or spent the
night in the caves of the Biomarine or Le Pollet. There was
some talk of total evacuation.

From December 1943, the Allied operations, directly or in-
directly connected with the preparations for invasion, increased. They had begun with Operation *Crossbow* – the
systematic bombing of the V.1. sites under construction – and
heaven knows there were enough of these round Dieppe. The
neighbouring villages were not spared by the airmen, who were
not always very skilful or very well briefed. Bures-en-Bray,
Foucarmont and many other villages in the neighbourhood
had a disastrous experience of this.

It must be mentioned that these 'softening-up measures'
were a serious headache to the Allies. The V.1. offensive was
not launched by Hitler until 13th June, 1944, a week after the
landings. But the Allied command had known for some time
that something was being prepared. Intelligence agents had
sent valuable information, but air reconnaissance had shown
indisputably that the ramps were orientated on their targets –
London for the emplacements from Dieppe to the Pas de

Calais, and Bristol for the sites in the Cotentin Peninsula.

The matter was taken very seriously. Powerful bomber formations dropped thousands of tons of bombs on these ramps, causing the damage I have mentioned. At the beginning of February 1944 there was some talk of repeating the Dieppe raid by organizing an armed reconnaissance on one of them. The plan was abandoned because the American air force chiefs thought that the problem could be solved by improving the bombing technique. We know that it was impossible to halt this offensive. For weeks on end the people of Dieppe saw these 'flying bombs', with their small wings and a flower-pot spitting fire in the tail, pass overhead with their very characteristic roar. They were nicknamed 'casseroles'. Sometimes they turned round and crashed in the countryside.

Then there were mass attacks on the whole Channel coast against the German radar stations. One of them cost the little town of Saint-Valery-en-Caux, which had already been sorely tried in 1940, very dear. Next, for a change, diversionary attacks were made on the Atlantic Wall. I have mentioned in an earlier chapter how Berneval-le-Grand was practically wiped off the map on 3rd June, 1944.

Since Operation *Jubilee* the Atlantic Wall had been considerably reinforced. As early as 29th September, 1942, i.e. 40 days after the Dieppe raid, Hitler had a conference with Marshal Goering, Albert Speer – at that time head of the Todt organization before becoming Minister for the Armament of the Reich – Marshal von Rundstedt, the supreme army commander and his chief of staff, General Blumentritt, General Jakob, the C.-in-C. Sappers at Great Headquarters and Lt.-General Rudolf Schmetzer, inspector of fortifications.

'A successful large-scale landing on the West Front would put us in a bad position,' Hitler declared. 'The British are bound to do something. They cannot help themselves. I want 15,000 pillboxes on this coast defended by 300,000 men.'

I have not bothered to find out whether these 15,000 pillboxes were ever built, but I know that at Dieppe, in a single square formed by the River Scie, the coast, the roads to Quatre Vents and Le Havre – a square of less than a mile – they numbered no less than 229 in 1944.

The Germans were apparently still convinced that Dieppe would be once more one of the points chosen for the landing, which explains why the Todt organization brought an army of slave labourers from all the occupied countries to build really formidable defences round the town and its port.

On the sea front from Berneval to Pourville the coast literally bristled with guns: Battery 2/770 of Berneval which we have already met, at Caesar's Camp; a new battery of eight 155 mm. guns on platforms in the ancient Roman camp Puys-est; a 105 mm. gun next to the pillbox whose machine-gun had been so devastatingly effective on 19th August. From Puys-ouest to Le Pollet, the cliff was a single chain of emplacements along a strip 1,000 yards long and 50 in depth. This strip was defended to the east by a battery of six 88's in turrets, two 77s, pillboxes, subterranean galleries, etc., and to the west by a battery of four 77s and one 105 mm.

At the foot of Le Pollet cliff, two 47 mm. guns enfiladed the narrows in which were sunk 18 large mines, which could be fired electrically from a distance.

But this was nothing compared with the powerful fortified zone on the cliff below the town, from the castle esplanade to the golf course at Pourville. In this entrenched camp, almost two acres in size, which afforded shelter to thousands of troops, there were 12 77s and 88s capable of firing at aircraft and at ships. Three large radar stations (apparently one Freya and two Würzburg's) with their own perimeter defences, 47 mm. guns in pillboxes, etc. At the edge of the cliff the Caudecote emplacements, covering 875 yards, and complementing the fortified strip I have already described between Puys and Le Pollet.

It is pointless to prolong this catalogue of details, which can be shown to better advantage on a map. Let us say that the defence of Dieppe was equally well assured from the land side with a zone of barbed wire and anti-tank traps running from the golf course to Neuville-lès-Dieppe, via the racecourse, and supported by a score of guns of a calibre of 77 mm. or more, interspersed with countless pillboxes. The air defences had not been forgotten.

Let us add in conclusion that, dissatisfied with the work of

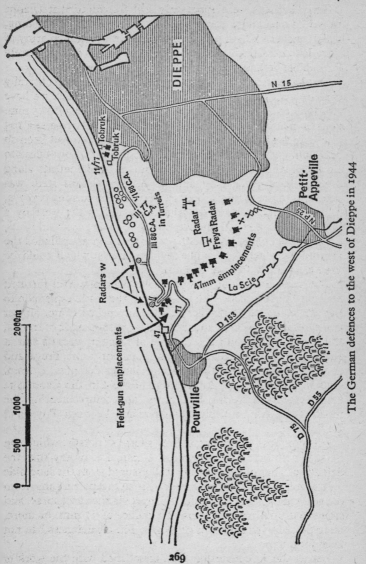

DIEPPE

N 15

Tobruk
Tobruk

II 77

III 88 C.A.

II 88 C.A.
II 77 C.A. in Turrets

Radar
Freya Radar

Radars w

47mm émplacements

La Scie

77

47

Field-gun emplacements

Pourville

Petit-Appeville

N 25

D 153

D 55

D 75

2000m
1000
500
0

The German defences to the west of Dieppe in 1944

the Todt organization, which was too often carried out without its users being consulted, Field-Marshal Rommel, in the course of an inspection of the Atlantic Wall made at the end of 1943 and the beginning of 1944, had introduced a certain number of improvements – Rommel 'asparagus' – a complex of minefields (land and sea mines), foxholes to shelter snipers, flooding of the estuaries, etc.

At Dieppe all this was to serve no purpose.

Since 1942 the German battle order on the West Front had been profoundly reorganized. Marshal von Rundstedt remained C.-in-C. West, but Army Group D, which he had commanded directly in 1942, disappeared at the end of 1943 in favour of Army Groups B (Rommel) and G (Blaskowitz). The sector of Group B extended from the Low Countries to the Loire, with the LXXXVIIIth Corps in Holland, the 15th Army in Flanders and the Pas de Calais, the 7th Army in Normandy and Brittany. The sector of Army Group G covered the coast from the Gulf of Gascony to the south of the Loire, with the 1st Army, and that of the south coast of France with the 19th.

The 302nd Infantry Division left the Dieppe sector at the end of 1942 for the Eastern Front. It was heavily engaged on the Don and the Dneiper, where it was encircled and destroyed in August 1944. At the time of the Normandy landings, the LXXXIst Corps still responsible for the defence of the Caux country consisted of the 711th Infantry Division between the Orne and the Seine, the 245th in the Fécamp–Dieppe sector, and the 348th between Dieppe and Le Touquet.

Since the end of January 1944, Dieppe had been declared a fortress. The occupying authorities introduced an exceptional regime, and no one could remain in doubt that the battle would be very tough, from whichever direction the place was attacked – from the sea or the land.

There was great activity during the first few days of May. The air raids were continuous. On the 26th, as a result of a fight which broke out between German units in the course of which shots were fired, the mayor was arrested by the *Feldgendarmerie* and taken to the commandant's headquarters in a shelter hollowed out of the esplanade of the old castle. The

German colonel had orders to shoot his prisoner, but waited for the result of the trial. M. Levasseur was released with the encouraging proviso 'that he was to consider himself in future a hostage whose head would fall at the first attempt made against the occupying troops!'

Paradoxically, the unleashing of operations on the 6th June brought a certain relief to Dieppe. The air raids grew less frequent and were not repeated until the eve of the day the Allied forces approached the town.

The Allied plans entrusted Field Marshal Montgomery's 21st Army Group with the operations on the coast of the western Channel. This 21st Group comprised on the left wing the 1st Canadian Army, General Crerar, on the right, the 2nd British Army (Dempsey). Dieppe was one of the targets of the 2nd Canadian Corps (Lt.-General Simmonds).

It was the 3rd Canadian Division, commanded by Major-General Keller, which had been chosen to form the first wave. Landing on the 6th June at Courseulles-sur-Mer, it was in action at Caen. At the end of the first week of July, the 2nd Infantry Division, commanded by Major-General Foulkes, disembarked in turn, together with the rudiments of the 2nd Canadian Corps.

This corps was to play a major part in the battle of Caen where the 2nd Infantry Division, debouching on the 7th and 8th August, together with the 51st British Division – the Saint-Valery division reformed – advanced on Falaise, to participate in the memorable encirclement where the 7th German Army was to meet its fate. As soon as this battle of extermination was ended, the 1st Canadian Army, finally constituted after the landing of the 4th Armoured Division, took up its positions on the Seine to undertake the conquest of the Channel coast.[1] On the left wing the 1st British Army Corps attached to

[1] A truly international force, the 1st Canadian Army at the time of the capture of Dieppe consisted of:
– the 1st British Corps (Crocker), with the 49th and 51st Infantry Divisions; the 6th Airborne Division and a Dutch brigade.
– The 2nd Canadian Corps (Simmonds) with the 2nd and 3rd Infantry Divisions.
– The 4th Canadian Brigade, 1st Polish Brigade and a Czech armoured brigade.

Crerar's army crossed the river at Caudebec (49th British Division) and at Duclair (51st Highland Division). In the centre the 2nd Canadian Army Corps dispatched its 2nd Infantry Division against Rouen and its 3rd against Elbeuf-Tourville–Boos, with the 4th Brigade on its right wing. Attentive to historical detail, Field-Marshal Montgomery did not forget that the 51st Highland Division had to wipe out the insult of Saint-Valery, and that the 2nd Canadian Division had to make good the setback suffered at Dieppe. On the eve of crossing the Seine, he did not fail to remind General Crerar in his orders of the day dated 20th August, 1944:

'The whole of Scotland will rejoice if the commanding officer of the Canadian Army could see fit that the taking of Saint-Valery is accomplished by the Highland Division. I am sure that the 2nd Canadian Division will attend to Dieppe satisfactorily.'

His orders were carried out.

While the 3rd Canadian Division on the 27th August thrust its first units north of the Seine, between Pont-de-L'Arche and Elbeuf, the 2nd after three days of heavy fighting in the Forest of Londe, entered Rouen on the 30th August. The 1st British Army Corps encountered some difficulties below the town, but on the 1st September it had established itself north of the estuary.

Above Rouen the entire 4th Brigade had been on the right bank of the Seine since the 29th.

It was not only in memory of *Jubilee* that Field-Marshal Montgomery attached importance to a speedy liberation of Dieppe. He saw in this an essential condition for the attack which the 1st British Corps was to make without delay against Le Havre, whose swift capture was to be desired, for it would, it was hoped, bring great relief to the problems of supply.

At Le Havre, as at Dieppe, fierce resistance was expected. The example of St. Malo and of Brest showed that the enemy had fully understood the embarrassment he was causing his adversary by clinging on desperately to the ports. This was the case at Le Havre, but to the general amazement Dieppe was not defended.

Thrusting forward from Rouen to Dieppe, the 2nd Canadian

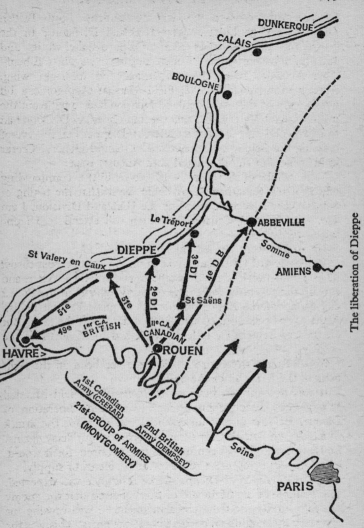

The liberation of Dieppe

Division had a burning desire to avenge their comrades who had fallen on the 19th August, 1942. It was probably greatly disappointed to find not a single German. Everything had been prepared to give them what was called 'the full treatment'. A powerful naval force consisting of two battleships and a monitor were to bombard from the sea. R.A.F. Bomber Command was to stage one of its most formidable 'shows'. After which the South Saskatchewans, the Cameron Highlanders, in fact all the units of the 4th and 6th Brigades which had taken part in the 1942 raid, were to go into the assault . . . but this time from inland. This was operation *Fusillade*.

On the morning of 1st September, indications of the German evacuation had already reached the headquarters of the 1st Army, established near Brionne, but at Crerar's Hq. there was still some hesitation in cancelling the raid by Bomber Command scheduled for the afternoon. The decision was delayed until the moment the advance guards reached the perimeter defences of Dieppe.

The 8th Reconnaissance Regiment (14th Canadian Hussars) had the previous evening taken Tôtes, 19 miles from Dieppe on Route Nationale 27. At 1000 hrs. on 1st September, its advance units were cautiously approaching Dieppe, skirting the minefields and the barbed wire. The German guns remained silent. Two motor cyclists risked showing their noses in the rue Gambetta. The whole of Dieppe was awaiting them in the street. The Canadians met with no further obstacles except a delirious population which surrounded the tanks, jeeps and command cars, shouting, weeping and throwing flowers . . . 'and many other articles which it would take too long to list.'[1]

The object of this triumphant welcome, Colonel Allway, in command of the advance guard, declared with a broad smile:

'We once tried to enter by the main gate, we did not succeed. Today we are returning by the back door.'

But there was better to come. With the exception of Nantes blocked by the pockets of Saint-Nazaire and of Bordeaux by those of the Gironde, no port was to fall intact into the hands of the Allies. Dieppe had suffered considerable destruction, but the two great basins, the Canada and Paris basins, were

[1] Stacey, *Canada's Battle in Normandy*.

both usable. Not even the entrance had been obstructed. A few days later the Royal Navy entered with its first transports, and traffic soon rose to 6,000 tons a day. For the month of October it exceeded 300,000 tons. This was a marvellous trump card at the moment when the bad weather was to cause the closing of the artificial port of Arramanches. 'The reason why the Germans decided to abandon this port without defending it,' remarks Colonel Stacey, 'still remains a mystery.'[1]

The Canadian historian is not the only one to be dumbfounded by this abandon without a struggle. At Dieppe where everyone congratulated themselves on what might be called a 'manifestation of divine providence', there were whispers that there had been some treachery in the German camp.

On the basis of this idea, there is the romantic story of a pretty young woman of the region for whom the commander of the 245th German Infantry Division harboured the most tender feelings. According him with her favours, this young woman kept up relations with the agents of an intelligence network, working for the C.B.I.A.[2] The few initiated could but encourage this idyll which, in addition to providing military information, they expected to exert discreet psychological effect on the mind of the German general.

To all the officials whose circumstances obliged them to have dealings with this general, he gave the impression of being a cultivated, intelligent man and an opponent of all fanaticism. It is possible that he considered at this period the defence of Dieppe to be a hopeless undertaking which, without doing anything to better the lot of his country, would merely produce a few more ruins and a few more corpses. From there to conclude that he deliberately agreed to betray the mission with which he had been entrusted is something I should not venture to suggest, particularly since circumstances allowed me at the period to follow this matter at close quarters. In any case, this

[1] Colonel Stacey, *The Canadian Army*.
[2] The Central Bureau of Intelligence and Action, an organization in London which collated the information from the network of the French resistance.

is a plausible explanation for an episode upon which light has never been thrown.

On the other hand, one cannot close this file without recalling some elements which might divert the inquiry on to a different line.

To begin with, there was the confusion in which the attempt on Hitler's life on 20th July, 1944, had plunged the German command on the West Front. We must not forget that General Karl Heinrich von Stülpnagel, military commander in France, implicated in the conspiracy, after an abortive attempt at suicide, was brought before a People's Court and barbarously executed; that Marshal Erwin Rommel, commanding Army Group B, although he was out of action on the 20th July, having been the victim of an attack by an Allied fighter during a visit to the front line, was given the alternative on 14th October of committing suicide or of facing a similar tribunal; that Marshal Gunter von Kluge, Rundstedt's successor since 4th July, had been axed in turn a few days before the liberation of Dieppe, and had considered it preferable to take his own life rather than risk the prosecution which awaited him in Germany; that General Hans Speidel, Chief of Staff of Group B, was to be arrested a little later and would only escape by a miracle the sad fate meted out to all his peers who were compromised in the 20th July attempt . . . that, in this more than chaotic atmosphere, a divisional general, apart from all other considerations, including the sentimental, should hesitate as to what attitude to adopt, would not have been very surprising.

M. Pierre Mouquet, former president of the Dieppe Chamber of Commerce, was kind enough to communicate to me the report of an interview he had been granted on the 24th August, 1944, by the commander of the 245th Infantry Division. In the course of this interview, the German general, who was apparently still unaware of the dismissal and suicide of von Kluge, was very understanding when his interlocutor insisted very forcibly upon the gravity of the responsibility which he would incure by ordering destructions in this port, for which there was no justification.

But there is more. There is nothing definite to prove that the commander of the 245th Infantry Division contravened his orders by evacuating Dieppe without a fight. Dieppe was not actually mentioned in the Führer's directive of the 17th August, 1944, prescribing the defence to the last man of the coastal fortresses of western and southern France. On 28th August, a few days after taking over command, Field-Marshal Model, Kluge's successor, ordered for midday of the 31st a line of resistance to be organized on the line Compiègne–Beauvais–Neufchâtel-en-Bray, in other words, above Dieppe. In any case, General von Zangen, who had taken over command of the 15th Army, received orders to maintain garrisons in the coastal fortresses which were to fight to the last man. This applied to Dunkirk, Calais, Boulogne and Le Havre, but not to Dieppe and Le Tréport in the sector of the 245th Infantry Division, nor for Fécamp in the sector of the 348th. The two latter ports, although powerfully fortified, had too little traffic to be of any great help to the Allies. This reservation did not apply to Dieppe which everyone quite logically expected to put up a stout defence.[1]

The evacuation began on the 30th August. On the evening of the 31st, there were no troops in the port except a few teams of saboteurs busy blowing up their stocks of mines. Once more the able intervention of the French port authority, M. Quesnel, managed to prevent the demolition squad from obstructing the entrance to the basins and of blowing up the swivel bridge, uniting Dieppe with the suburb of Le Pollet, as had been their intention. Quesnel had studied his facts for some time. He managed to convince the German sailors that it was imprudent to leave this bridge open to circulation, for if it were hit by bombs it risked subsiding into the channel and blocking the small flotilla vessels moored in the basins. On 31st August the air raid siren had wailed practically without interruption. When the demolition squad tried to swivel the bridge to blow it up into the water, by a great piece of good fortune – Quesnel was always lucky – the machinery did not function. The bridge

[1] The 245th Infantry Division, escaping the encirclement caused by the arrival of the British at Antwerp, managed to cross the Walcheren estuary of the River Escaux and to reach subsequently Holland, where it played an important part in the Arnhem action on September 17th.

was destroyed on the quayside in a position where its debris could not interfere with shipping movements.

This intelligent and effective resistance invoked the admiration of the representatives of British Naval Intelligence. A few months later, for his success, Quesnel was awarded a well-deserved Legion of Honour. I should like to be able to state that the tireless devotion of the mayor of Dieppe to his town was equally rewarded. Alas, this would have been too much to expect in the atmosphere reigning just after the liberation. He did not even have the satisfaction of welcoming officially the 1st Canadian officers. A few days later, the sub-prefect was thanked in his place. . . .

*　　　*　　　*

The plans for Operation *Fusillade* had been worked out on the 26th August by the staff of the naval C.-in-C. Allied expeditionary forces, Admiral Sir Bertram Ramsay, whose maximum collaboration had been requested by the army against Dieppe on 1st September, and against Le Havre immediately afterwards. On the 29th August, Admiral Ramsay announced that a bombarding force – Force 130 – would assemble under the orders of Rear-Admiral Tennant. It consisted in the main of the battleships H.M.S. *Warspite* and *Malaya* (carrying 15 inch guns), the monitor H.M.S. *Erebus* (15 inch) and the cruisers H.M.S. *Mauritius* (8 inch) and *Bellona* (6 inch). The weakest armed of these ships had a fire power nearly equivalent to that of the four destroyers, which on the 19th August, 1942, had constituted the bombarding force of Hughes-Hallett.

God be praised that neither this naval force nor the squadrons of Bomber Command had to intervene at Dieppe. On the other hand, Force 130 engaged some of its units against Le Havre a few days later, and the inhabitants suffered heavily from the effects. It will be remembered that the 51st Highland Division had been sent to Saint-Valery-en-Caux, which it captured on 22nd September. Its commanding officer, General Rennie, assembled his men at Cailleville, where his unfortunate predecessor General Fortune had established his headquarters in 1940, to tell them in a few words of the sacrifice of the veterans. Then after a period of rest, the division moved in the

direction of Le Havre, upon which the 49th British Division
was already advancing.

Le Havre was defended to seawards by redoubtable fortifications. On the landward side the defence was more mediocre,
less so apparently than at Dieppe. Recalled from Italy a few
days earlier, Colonel Eberhard Wildermuth found himself in
command of the garrison of 12,000 men who had recently
arrived from Denmark. One wonders to what extent he had
been chosen for a distant theatre of operation to replace a
leader whom the convulsions of 20th July might have unsettled.
It is remarkable in any case that the O.C. Calais defences was
also demoted in similar circumstances.

In short, Wildermuth rejected out of hand the ultimatum
which was delivered to him on the 4th September. On the other
hand, he asked for a truce for the purpose of evacuating the
civil population, which was refused. The air preparation began
immediately and reached an exceptional intensity.

On the 5th September the Allied bombers dropped 18 tons
of H.E. and 60 tons of incendiary bombs. On the 6th, 1,468 and
25 tons respectively. On the 7th the bombing was confined to
the neighbouring communes of Montivilliers and Feville. On
the 8th the monitor H.M.S. *Erebus* appeared and started
systematically to bombard the square with its 15 inch guns. On
the 9th came a hail of phosphorus bombs. On the 10th, in an
apocalyptic setting, 4,993 tons of bombs exploded, while to the
firing of *Erebus*, which lasted for 15 hours, was added that of
the battleship H.M.S. *Warspite*, the glorious veteran of Jut-
land, Narvik, Matapan and Salerno – also firing with 15 inch
guns.

At 1745 hrs. the Scots of the 5th Infantry Division went over
to the attack and captured Fréville. But the Germans, refusing
to accept defeat, concentrated their entire artillery fire on this
locality. It needed another 870 tons of bombs on the 11th to
convince Colonel Wildermuth, who capitulated at midday of
the 12th.

In all 11,000 tons of bombs and 300 salvoes of 15 inch
shells. . . .

Remarkably entrenched in its shelters, the German garrison
suffered insignificant losses. The Scots had 28 killed.

Unfortunately there were the people of Le Havre. The figure of identified dead amounted to 2,053, but this represents a small part of the victims of this siege, for whole families disappeared together with the shelters in which they had taken refuge. When the British entered Le Havre there were no flags left to deck the corpses. They had been burnt with the rest.[1]

There is nothing to prove that comparable losses would have been suffered at Dieppe as a result of Operation *Fusillade*. On the 31st August, 1944, there were only 2,000 inhabitants left to kill. It was fortunate, however, that there was no necessity for this, and Notre-Dame-de-Bon-Secours, by whatever mysterious ways she worked to show her protection, did not cheat the pilgrimage of thanks which had been solemnly promised to Her, some time before, by all the devout of the country.

Varengeville-sur-Mer,
Paris, 16th October, 1961.

[1] J. Guilmart, *L'Enfer du Havre*.
I owe the above figure to the courtesy of the mayor of Le Havre. This town suffered 5,176 casualties from enemy action throughout the hostilities, of which 2,053 were officially confirmed during the siege, from the 2nd to the 12th September, 1944. 12,500 buildings were totally destroyed, and 4,500 partially destroyed.

APPENDIX

*Report from the 302nd Infantry Division on the
behaviour of the Civilian Population*

SECRET

31st Infantry Division.   Hq. 24th August, 1942.

Department: Ic 713/42g.(1)
Subject: Monthly report for August 1942
Ref.:   Order No. 66/42 g I.c XXXIInd Army Corps
                (2)
Enclosures: 1
Addressee: The officer commanding LXXXIst Army
                Corps

1. *The state of mind and behaviour of the population in the
divisional sector.*

The civilian population in the divisional sector manifested
complete indifference at the scene of the British raid of August
19th, 1942. The great victories won by our troops in the east
and in North Africa combined with our successes at sea – the
annihilation of a convoy in the Western Mediterranean – dealt
a fatal blow to the pretentions expressed by the British propaganda, that a Second Front was shortly to be opened. Except in
a few isolated circles no one believed in the establishment of
this Second Front in the West. They hoped for an attack at
harvest time, as a prelude to an invasion. In certain places there
was a rumour that the British would arrive on the night of the
20th/21st August, 1942.

Operation *Jubilee* carried out by the British on the 19th
August, 1942, on Dieppe and the adjacent fortified positions of
Berneval, Puys, Pourville and Quiberville is the sole topic
of conversation among the French civil population. On the
actual scenes of the combat the population was given complete
liberty. There have been no records of sabotage. It has, however, been reported that the population did not disguise its

satisfaction at the rapid conclusion of the conflict. Many people displayed some bitterness in noting that the British had carefully spared their own troops, at the expense of non-British forces.

It has been learnt in certain cases that the French were specially well-disposed to the German soldiers engaged in the battle, thus an ambulance reported to be French, carrying two French nuns immediately went to the aid of German wounded soldiers and drove them to the main first aid post. They were at pains to give first aid to the German soldiers. A few of the French, despite the enemy fire, gave information about the enemy. In the fighting sectors, the troops in the line received refreshments and cigarettes from the inhabitants. One unit reports that reinforcements en route were offered bicycles and motor cycles to reach their destination more rapidly. The Dieppe fire brigade, despite the cannon and machine-gun fire from aircraft, unremittingly fought the fires.

The outcome of the combat – the crushing defeat of the enemy – has filled the German troops with confidence and considerably reinforced our defences. During the day of the battle and during the following days the civil population did not conceal its admiration by its behaviour and by its friendly gestures. The anglophile section of the population, although the prospects of a British attack in force are evidently finished, and despite all outward reservations, has expressed its satisfaction at this event. The sympathizers assembled in small groups to await the liberators.

The German victory has been accepted unwillingly by these implacable anglophiles. They insist that if the British had not been restrained by their anxiety (!) to spare the civilian population and the town of Dieppe, the latter would rapidly have fallen into their hands.

The purely peasant section of the population remained quiet and absolutely indifferent, solely preoccupied with getting in the harvest. The only emotion shown was at places where their wains were requisitioned.

Three civilians, two men and a woman, were arrested at Envermeu, for openly expressing their sympathy for the British prisoners and for giving them presents and shoes. At

Saint-Nicolas the bodies of two British fighter-pilots, shot down at dawn of 18th August, were covered with flowers. By this behaviour and by the distribution of clothing, refreshments and provisions to the prisoners at the assembly camp of Saint-Nicolas, these civilians wanted to express their sympathy for the British. It needed energetic action on the part of the guards to control the civilians who flooded the camp to stop these manifestations.

After the battle, the civilian population helped to pick up and bury the fallen British, after having been invited to do so by the military authorities.

In two places, French peasants brought in carrier pigeons which had been dropped in cages by parachute. These passenger pigeons carried questionnaires apparently designed to be filled in by civilians before the birds were released. The division has been ordered by the competent authorities to reward these civilians. It is also reported that at Varengeville, near the battery, some civilians revealed the presence of a British soldier carrying a special apparatus. The *Feldgendarmerie* is checking this information.

2. *Relations with the Military Administration:* No difficulties.

3. *Relations with the French services of all kinds:* Further complaints that the system of ration cards for the workers is far too cumbersome and causes hardships. (Cf. report Ic. of the 27.4.42.)

4. *Absences without leave:* 1.

5. *Cases of suicide:* (a) Attempts, nil.
       (b) Successful, nil.

For the Divisional Commander
G.S.O.1.

BIBLIOGRAPHY

Army Air Forces (World War II). Office of Air Force History (7 vols.). Cambridge University Press, London, 1948–58.

BEKKER (Cajus). – *Radar*. France-Empire, Paris, 1961.

BLORE (Lieutenant-commander Trevor – R.N.V.R.), *Commissioned Bargees. The Story of the Landing-Craft*. Hutchinson, London, 1946.

BONIN (von). *Wir waren dabei. Der Invasionversuch von Dieppe* in Die Wehrmacht, t. 3. 1942.

BOUDIER. – *Dieppe et la region à travers les ages*. Edition nouvelle, Paris, 1952.

BRYANT (Sir Arthur). – *The Turn of the Tide, 1939–1943*. Collins, London, 1957.

BUCHHEIT (Gert). – *Hitler chef de guerre*, Arthaud, 1961.

BUCHNER (Alex). – *Dieppe, das erste Invasionsunternehmen*, in Deutsche Soldatenzeitung, 8th November, 1957.

BUCKLEY (Christopher). – *Norway, the Commandos, Dieppe*. H.M. Stationery Office, London, 1951.

CHURCHILL. – *The Second World War* (6 vols.). Cassell and Co., London, 1948–54.

Dieppe, Die Bewährung des Küstenwestwalles. Berlin, 1943.

DURNFORD-SLATER (Brigadier John). – *Commando*. William Kimber, London, 1953.

FERGUSSON (Brigadier Bernard). – *The Watery Maze. The Story of Combined Operations*. Collins, London, 1961.

GUIBON (Georges). – *A Dieppe*.

HARRISON (Colonel). – *Cross-Channel attack*. Office of the Chief of Military History, Washington, 1951.

HIGGINS (Trumbull). *Winston Churchill and the Second Front*. Oxford University Press.

HOFFMANN (Oberstleutnant Karl Otto). – *Das Unternehmen Jubilee*. Unpublished documents of the Luftnachrichtengruppe Münster, Westphalia.

HUGHES-HALLETT (Captain J. – R.N.). – *The Dieppe Raid*, Supplement to the London Gazette, nr 380–45, 14th August, 1947.

HUGHES-HALLETT (Rear-Admiral – R.N.). – *The mounting of Raids*, in Journal of the United Service Institution, November 1950.

HULL (Cordell). – *The Memoirs of Cordell Hull*. Hodder and Stoughton, London, 1948.

JAMES (Admiral Sir William). – *The Portsmouth letters*. Macmillan, London, 1946.

LEPOTIER (Contre-amiral). – *Raiders from the Sea*. William Kimber, 1954.

LIDDELL HART (B. H.). – *The other side of the hill*. Cassell, London, 1951.

MAUND (Rear-Admiral L. E. H. – R.N.). – *Assault from the sea.* Methuen and Co., London, 1949.

MCNEILL (William Hardy). – *America, Britain and Russia, Survey of International Affairs, 1939–1946.* Oxford University Press, 1953.

MONTGOMERY (Field Marshal the Viscount – of Alamein). – *Normandy to the Baltic.* Hutchinson and Co., London, 1947.

MONTGOMERY (Field-Marshal the Viscount – of Alamein). – *The Memoirs of Field-Marshal Montgomery of Alamein.* Collins, London, 1958.

MORISON (Rear-Admiral Samuel E. – U.S.N.R.). – *Strategy and compromises.* Little Brown and Co., Boston, 1957.

NOGUÈRES (Louis). – *Le véritable procès du maréchal Pétain.* Fayard, Paris, 1955.

RICHARDS (Denis) and SAUNDERS (Hilary St. George). – *Royal Air Force 1939–1945.* H.M. Stationery Office, London, 1953 et seq. (3 vols.).

ROMMEL (Marechal Erwin). – *The Rommel Papers.* Ed. B. H. Liddell Hart. Collins, London, 1953.

ROSKILL (Captain S. W. – R.N.). – *The War at sea*, Vol. II. H.M. Stationery Office, London, 1956.

RUGE (Vice-Admiral Friedrich). – *Sea Warfare, 1939–1945.* Cassell and Co., London, 1957.

SALMOND (J. B.). – *The History of the 51st Highland Division.* W. Blackwood and Sons Ltd., Edinburgh, London, 1953.

SAUNDERS (Hilary St. George). – *The green Beret.* Michael Joseph, London, 1949.

SCOTT (Lieutenant-Commander Peter – R.N.V.R.). – *The Battle of the Narrow Seas.* Country Life, London, 1945.

SHERWOOD (Robert E.). – *The White House Papers of Harry L. Hopkins.* (2 vols.) Eyre and Spottiswoode, London, 1948–49.

SPEIDEL (General Hans). – *We defended Normandy.* Herbert Jenkins, London, 1951.

STACEY (Colonel C. P.). – *Six years of war.* Official story of the Canadian Army in the Second World War. Vol. I. Ottawa, 1955.

STACEY (Colonel C. P.). – *L'armée canadienne, histoire résumée.*

STACEY (Colonel C. P.). – *Canada's Battle in Normandy.* King's Printer, Ottawa, 1946.

THOMPSON (R. W.). – *Dieppe at dawn.* Hutchinson, 1956.

THOMPSON (R. W.). – *The Price of Victory.* Constable, London, 1960.

TRUSCOTT (Lieutenant general L. K., Jr. – U.S.A.). – *Command missions. A personal story.* Dutton, New York, 1954.

TURNER (John Frayn). – *Histoire du Débarquement*, Juin 1944. Arthaud, 1960.

VAGTS (Alfred). – *Landing Operations.* Military Service Publishing Company, Washington, 1946.

VITET (Louis). – *Histoire de Dieppe.* Librairie Charles Gosselin, Paris, 1844.

WILMOT (Chester). – *The struggle for Europe*. Collins, London, 1952.
WOOD (Alan and Mary). – *Islands in danger*. Evans Brothers Ltd., London, 1955.